Capitalism's Transcendent
Time Machine

Capitalism's Transcendental Time Machine

—— Anna Greenspan ——

Edited by Peter Heft

Foreword by Wassim Z. Alsindi,
Max Hampshire, and Paul Seidler

Miskatonic Virtual University Press
Arkham • London

Originally published by University of Warwick, 2000
University of Warwick Publications service & WRAP
University of Warwick Library
Gibbet Hill Road
Coventry, UK CV4 7AL
wrap.warwick.ac.uk

Republished by Miskatonic Virtual University Press, 2023
Arkham, Massachusetts and London, Ontario
mvupress.net

ISBN: 978-1-7781549-0-4

Cover design by @CritDrip
Interior design by Peter Heft

First printing, 2023

Contents

Acknowledgements

I would like to thank my supervisor Andrew Benjamin for his support. This thesis has been written with the help of Louis Greenspan, Michelle Murphy, and the CCRU. It is dedicated to my family.

Editor's Introduction

Editing, proofreading, and formatting *Capitalism's Transcendental Time Machine* proved to be much more difficult than I had originally anticipated. Given that—and insofar as I've spent hundreds of hours with the text—a few editorial notes seem warranted.

First, I have tried to limit my editorial interventions into the text, except in places where absolutely necessary. I have, by and large, kept Greenspan's original wording and stylistic choices. What a reader will thus notice is that the text you hold in your hands is by no means one which would go to a 'proper' publisher. Laced as it is with Greenspan's lexical eccentricates, the text is, first and foremost, a doctoral dissertation and, as such, reads like one. Indeed, over the course of the text, one will find lines such as, "this thesis seeks to…," "as we will see…," "as we have seen…," etc. I have made no attempt to alter or remove such phrases except in places where they proved redundant and got in the way of the flow of the text. Further, it ought to be noted that as a doctoral dissertation, *Capitalism's Transcendental Time Machine*, full as it is with novel—and indeed, brilliant—insights, is still, in large part, exegetical. While there are incredibly unique and powerful moves within the text, a reader not already familiar with the milieu from whence the text comes ought to be aware that as a doctoral dissertation, the text necessarily had to serve as proof that its author knew what she was talking about. I have made no effort to excise the exegeses—indeed, they themselves are powerful readings. Thus, I hope that any reader from outside the 'Weird Theory' milieu will forgive any repetition within the text.

Second, the editorial interventions I have made have primarily been small punctuation changes to assist with the flow of the text, as well as a few small rewordings to clarify points that were otherwise somewhat opaque. While I certainly take full responsibility for any egregious lexical errors—errors I do hope will be pointed out and fixed in subsequent editions—I beg forgiveness from a reader for any argumentative missteps and/or points of confusion. I did not intervene in the argument of the text itself, not only to preserve Greenspan's unique perspective, but also because any outside intervention on that level would be the height of hubris.

Flipping through the book, one will notice a slightly unorthodox mixture of footnotes *and* endnotes, an editorial choice I ought to explain. At the behest of the University of Warwick, UK, Greenspan's original dissertation made extensive use of in-text citations with abbreviations. For example, when citing Kant's *Critique of Pure Reason*, "(CPR, page number)" would follow the quotation. In-text citations offend my moral and aesthetic sensibilities and thus, with Greenspan's approval, I opted to change them to endnotes (in Roman Numerals) located at the end of a quoted passage or sentence with a quotation in it. The endnotes themselves—the numeration of which restarts every section—however, are only partial and of the form [Author][Title][Page], with the full citation being given in the bibliography. For example, when looking at the notes, one might find a citation that says, "Deleuze, 'Kant: Synthesis and Time,' 35." One should thus look to the bibliography and find the relevant entry under "Deleuze, Gilles," should one want to pursue the source further.

I have made every effort to double check the location of all quotations, but since there have been many reprintings of the various sources Greenspan cites, I cannot be entirely confident that the pagination will be consistent across editions. That being said, for works with unified systems of pagination—*e.g.*, Plato, Aristotle, and Kant—I have incorporated the requisite systems. With Plato, I have included the Stephanus pagination in hard brackets following the page number in the specific edition cited. Aristotle sees Bekker pagination similarly, and all references to the *Critique of Pure Reason* have the [A] and [B] edition page numbers as well.

While I have tried to verify the integrity of the quotations, in some places I was simply unable to locate the original quotation in the cited source and either found it elsewhere, or not at all. All such cases are indexed by a † next to the quotation with its probable or certain location cited (if known). Additionally, some of the books Greenspan used were published by obscure and/or small publishing houses in the UK and, as such, are not readily available anymore (*e.g.*, Unwin Hyman's edition of Weber's *The Protestant Ethic and the Spirit of Capitalism* and a specific edition of Notre Dame's publication of Descartes' *Meditations*, among others). Given that, I have, in order to promote accessibility, opted to find the quotations in more commonly available editions. While I have striven to maintain the integrity of the original text, some of the quotations vary slightly from the dissertation's original version, and thus the quotations Greenspan uses are retained *unless* I found the quotation to be slightly different. For example, an epigraph to the *original* section 1.2 sees Rimbaud saying, "It is false to say: I think. One should say: one thinks me...I is another." This version of the Rimbaud quotation was not readily available and thus has been changed following a more accessible version of the *Complete Works* which renders the same line as, "It's wrong to say: I think. Better to say: I am thought. Pardon the pun. *I* is an *other*."

What's more, Greenspan makes extensive use of commentarial footnotes (in Hindu-Arab Numerals) to add extra context, cite additional sources, etc. I have preserved these in their entirety (even when I deemed some to be redundant) and the footnotes are located at the bottom of the page upon which they appear.[1] Their numeration, contrary to the numeration of the endnotes, is running throughout the entirety of the text. Additionally, there are several places where the footnotes and endnotes overlap. After much consternation and stress, I decided the simplest thing to do is provide both notes superscripted of the form footnote/endnote. For example, one might find"10/ii".

Additionally, the original bibliography only contained material quoted *in the text proper*—references within footnotes were, generally speaking, left out of the bibliography. For the sake of completeness, I have included all texts referenced anywhere within *Capitalism's Transcendental Time Machine* in the bibliography. While this does bloat the bibliography, I felt it was nevertheless important. Furthermore, as this text was originally a doctoral dissertation, there was no need for an index. As the text is being reprinted as a book—a book that theorists will hopefully use—an index seemed necessary. I went back-and-forth on how best to write one, but I settled on, admittedly, a slightly larger dual index of names and subjects. There are, no doubt, many other ways to index this text—indeed, there are likely many different keywords than I have chosen—but I feel as if the index I have created is sufficient. The only other change to Greenspan's text itself is the in-line incorporation of two figures that were appended to the original dissertation: the Kantian Axes and the Table of Categories.

One more note is relevant: In Alsindi, Hampshire, and Seidler's foreword, I have again opted for a perhaps unorthodox approach to citations. The three not only cite external sources in their essay, but they also quote from the book you hold in your hand. Given that, I figured it would be simplest to retain the Roman Numeral endnote schema used throughout the text for all external sources, while incorporating parenthetical pagination for all quotations from *Capitalism's Transcendental Time Machine* itself.

Ultimately, I feel that it's only fitting to end the arduous, multi-year journey of preparing this text with several notes of appreciation. I

1: There is a single exception to this. Footnote 41 (number 3 in section 1.2 in the original PDF of the dissertation) misattributed a quotation on Cartesian doubt to Deleuze. The quotation actually comes from an essay by Nick Land, and has been edited to reflect that.

would like to extend my deepest thanks to Anna Greenspan herself for not only authorizing the re-printing of this brilliant work, but also for taking the time to dig through an old hard drive and find the word document written in 1999–2000. Without such a file, producing this book would have taken significantly longer as PDF→word conversions are notoriously terrible. I would also like to thank Wassim Z. Alsindi, Max Hampshire, and Paul Seidler for donating their time to write a wonderful foreword to the text, Amy Ireland and Matt Colquhoun for checking over the foreword and offering valuable insights, @CritDrip for the cover design, and the continued enthusiasm of the denizens of 'Weird Theory Twitter.' Additionally, I express my thanks to all the above for putting up with my incessant emails, Twitter DMs, etc. If this book makes Greenspan's work more accessible to future thinkers, then my job here has been successful.

Peter Heft
London, Ontario
2022

Foreword: Twenty-Two Years of Transcendental Time Machines

I t has been 22 years since Anna Greenspan published *Capitalism's Transcendental Time Machine* as her doctoral dissertation at the University of Warwick, UK. Amongst Greenspan's acknowledgements, she mentions the Cybernetic Culture Research Unit (CCRU), and indeed, it is difficult at first to completely separate Greenspan's investigations from the theory-production of the notorious collective. Points of departure, connection, and convergence: Kant and Deleuze and Guattari, alongside Schopenhauer, Spinoza, and Nietzsche, run through the varied CCRU outputs that emanated alongside—and prior to—*Capitalism's Transcendental Time Machine*.

Greenspan's style of writing in *Capitalism's Transcendental Time Machine* is concise, measured, and didactic in tone—a sharp contrast to the wilder nature of the CCRU corpus. Having said that, both the thematic content of Greenspan's work and her methodological approach are no less prescient or evocative; they are arguably more so. Greenspan's materialist analysis of the concept of time is mediated through thinkers as diverse as Plato, Marx, and Foucault. As a result, the text incorporates philosophical positions from ancient to modern eras, in parallel with associated conditions of social and material production. Despite the breadth of the work under discussion, Greenspan's clarity of thought allows a reader to approach *Capitalism's Transcendental Time Machine* without any prior knowledge of either contemporary philosophy, or the adjacent CCRU body of work. Indeed, Greenspan's discussion of transcendental materialism, planes of immanence, and machinic autonomy with reference to the temporal drives of capital increases the legibility of other CCRU texts and concepts.

The notion of time is, inarguably, one of the most crucial pillars of the CCRU theoretical fabric, later referred to as 'accelerationism.' This isomorphic relation is best described by Amy Ireland when she Tweeted:

> Accelerationism is a theory of time. The end.[i]

For Greenspan, as well as for Ireland, the development of conceptions of time can only ever be thought of in relation to emerging techno-capitalist apparatuses—which *themselves generate time*—and it is the distribution, ordering, and arbitration of time that these apparatuses control.

Capitalist time is ultimately born of strict equivalence with capital. In essence, 'Time = Money.'

Kantian Chronosis

A lthough radically different in scope and historical focus, both *Capitalism's Transcendental Time Machine* and Greenspan's subsequent work have, at their core, an engagement with Kant's framing of time as a transcendental structure, delimiting the conditions under which experience occurs. It is this temporal conception that Greenspan rearchitects for the time of machinic capitalism. Her twist on the Kantian subsumption of space into time arises from differing perspectives as to where the conditions of experience are produced.

> With Kant, then, the certainty of self-consciousness dissolves into questions about the relation of time to itself (28).

Within his *Critique of Pure Reason*, Kant finds two basic requirements for the cognitive faculty of the human subject: sensory perception and understanding. A theory of perception, which is inherently bound to the pure forms of appearance—time and space—is given by Kant in the chapter on the 'Transcendental Aesthetic.' In his terminology, space is defined as an 'outer' sense, and time as an 'inner' sense. Time becomes the necessary precondition for any potential experience, inverting the dependency-relation of pre-modern thought that follows on from the Platonic tradition wherein space is the necessary precondition for subjective experience. The crux of this claim: there is no experience and, subsequently, no synthetic understanding of experience, that can be constructed without this *a priori* spatio-temporality. For Kant, time is abstract in that it undergirds the potential for experience to even be understood.

Greenspan's reading of Kant might horrify the secular humanist. Reason is not evaluated as an ordering principle, but rather as a misguided by-product of a process that *originates* within the realm of the transcendental. The Cartesian notion of the ego as an intentional, legislative force is washed away by the autogenerative alterity of time, with the ultimate determination of human interiority arising from the outside. Given that the interiority of the subject is defined by *'what happens in Time,'* the exterior is the *a priori* productive force of time itself. As a consequence, the human no longer appears to be an enlightened subject guided by reason and free will, but instead resembles a puppet unable to grasp what is pulling its strings.[ii]

Through her readings of Kant and Deleuze and Guattari, Greenspan puts forward a rectification of the Platonic concept of time which begins with a dualism between time as perceived by the subject, and a realm of transcendent, infinite 'eternity.' In the Kantian paradigm, this latter category is structurally immanentized and absorbed into the synthetic *a priori*. Consequently, exterior time is not only anchored *in* the subject, but synthetically *determines* all experience. For Kant, however, time does not only have a generative impact on perception, it also serves as its precondition. To overcome the gap between mind and perception—that is, to explain how the mind subsumes raw sensory material under a concept—Kant needs a joint that is both rational and sensually anchored. This joint—which Kant describes as a *schema*—allows the application of a conceptuality to a sensual non-conceptuality (experience). The mediating factor is time because it is rooted in appearances and also in concepts, whilst being produced by a different faculty: the productive imagination.

Time thus becomes an abstract diagram in Kant's transcendental philosophy, without which cognition and epistemology would be impossible:

> The schema is neither an image nor a concept, but a diagram. Like all true diagrams, it is not a static representation, but a functional machinic component [...] With the chapter on 'The Schematism' then, Kant frees time from being locked into any particular determination—either on the side of the image or on the side of the concept—and makes of it instead the abstract plane of connectivity on which his whole system depends (39–40).

Even if Kant's discovery of the transcendental has freed time from empirical movements and located it in an immanent outside, according to Greenspan, the true horror is only beginning.

> Thus, abandoning both the interiority of the subject and the transcendent, eternal idea, the *Critique of Pure Reason* subordinates thought to the abstract production of time (36).

Neither a materialist analysis of history—*via* Karl Marx—nor a Kantian transcendental critique can alone shed light on the conditions of this abstract production. At this point, Greenspan turns to concrete and material practices of timekeeping to establish a connection between the abstract concepts of transcendental philosophy, and the technologies of time measurement.

These technologies simultaneously shape, and are shaped by, the production-logics of capitalism. The clock, which for the first time enabled a truly autonomous mode of timekeeping, was first essential to ensure the synchronization of industrial production and transport systems, while also being an instrument and symbol of hierarchical power.

The introduction of global temporal standards such as Greenwich Mean Time (GMT), time-zones, daylight saving time, and network-mediated machinic temporalities all served to imbue timekeeping practices with greater precision and universality. This was motivated by the desire to better serve capital flows, enforce authority, and to cement the production logic of 'Time = Money' as a universal and commensurable epistemological infrastructure.

> [T]he production of capitalist time converges with the Kantian system inaugurating a revolution—not in time but of time— which substitutes a transformation in time-marking conventions for a much more fundamental shift in the nature of time itself (57).

Plateaunic Thinking

> Aeonic occurrences break down the distinction between the constant structure of time, and the changes which occur inside it [...] Aeonic events do not occur in time not because they belong to a transcendent outside, but because they are flat with the single plane of immanence which collapses the distinction between time and that which populates it (104).

For Deleuze and Guattari, transcendental critique has to be progressed *vis-à-vis* Kant in a non-epistemological manner. Firstly, the synthetic *a priori* is freed from the interior of the individual subject *via* the recognition of the unconscious mind. Deleuze and Guattari use the third injury to humanity—Freud's discovery of the unconscious and its immediate Oedipalization by normative psychoanalysis—for a detailed, generative critique in which the political conditions of production are approached in holistic and material terms. Kant's binary distinction between essence and appearance is then flattened through a Spinozistic, monist interpretation of materialism.

Spinoza's concept of the plane of consistency is read by Deleuze and Guattari as an abstract machine of production, which is by no means to be understood as a metaphor. The bodies on it, bodies which can be described mainly by temporal properties—slow, fast, at rest, and so on—are real phenomena. While on this plane of production, effects are expressed by speed and affect, juxtaposed with a plane of "forms, substances, and subjects."[iii] One plane is assigned to linear time-production, which subjectivizes, while the other is "simultaneous[ly] too -late and too-early," as this plane itself *produces* time.[iv]

Through her reading of Deleuze and Guattari, Greenspan invokes two conceptions of time, both defined by Deleuze in *The Logic of Sense:* Chronos and Aeon. Chronos is characterized as linear, successive, metrical time, which corresponds with the empirical ego's experience of corporeality and causality. In contrast, Aeon is an empty time of intensive quantities and multiplicities, in which affects emerge through interactions of '*Thisness.*' At this point, it might dawn upon the reader as to why Greenspan mentions the focus on "*the occulted nature of time*" (12) at the beginning of her thesis: *Thisness*, or Deleuze and Guattari's '*haecceity,*' is a de-subjectified mode of individuation—that is, an effect or mode with individuality but without subjectivity. Without explaining the exact derivation of the term *via* Medieval scholars (and Deleuze's inversion of it), it can be stated that haecceity denotes an individualization without a subject—an event which temporally precedes any subjective individualization process. Haecceities present a conceptual tool to decompose the Indifference of Identity through affects of preindividual events. In *A Thousand Plateaus*, the reader finds several examples of such presubjective processes: a certain hour of a day, the wind, the atmosphere, etc. In Greenspan, as in Deleuze and Guattari, haecceities appear as networked and temporal entities; it is solely the interplay and networking of different presubjective processes which give rise to an emergence of affects.

> [I]t is not in the same time, in the same temporality. *Aeon*: the indefinite time of the event, the floating line that knows only speeds and continually divides that which transpires into an already-there that is at the same time not-yet-here, a simultaneous too-late and too-early, a something that is both going to happen and just happened. *Chronos*: the time of measure that situates things and persons, develops a form, and determines a subject. Boulez distinguishes tempo and nontempo in music: the "pulsed time" of a formal and functional music based on values versus the "nonpulsed time" of a floating music, both floating *and* machinic, which has nothing but speeds or differences in dynamic. In short, the difference is not at all between the ephemeral and the durable, nor even between the regular and the irregular, but between two modes of individuation, two modes of temporality.[v]

This inversion of the Platonic division of lived time and static infinity reanimates an immanent eternity as the proper locus of experiential production. However, in this plane of Aeon, neither static forms nor transcendent ideas manifest themselves as images in the world. Instead, the effects of interaction of non-uniform singularities manifest in Aeonic events that virtually haunt the sphere of Chronos.

Instead of claiming that these conditions are created in the *"mind of the knowing subject,"* (131) Greenspan draws upon Deleuze and Guattari, claiming that these conditions of experience are in fact *"produced by techno modernity."*[vi] The place of production is always the outside: the market and the technological-capitalist machinery.

Let Them Eat Y2Cake

> An act of calendric insurgency, Y2K threatened the authority of the Gregorian calendar by replacing it with cyberspace's own cyclical count. Operating in this manner, it constructed itself as a time-bomb that permeated the distributed network of contemporary technology by directly targeting the pre-existing unity of capitalist time (120–121).

As a literal and figurative representation of the limitations of digital timekeeping and machinic mnemotechnics, Y2K was an *atimely* exemplar of an Aeonic occurrence. Much of the work that went into producing *Capitalism's Transcendental Time Machine* was undertaken with the prophesied chaos of the year 2000 looming on the horizon, foretold but not yet actualized. Y2K heralded the dawn of the new millennium in the Gregorian calendar, dovetailing eschatological premonitions of apocalypse with concerns regarding the widespread and synchronized failure of critical, technical infrastructure worldwide.

Towards the end of the twentieth century, concerns began to mount that many antiquated computer systems would experience issues at the end of 1999 due to the way that they recorded time. Many mainframe and punch-card computing systems that were built in the 1960s and 1970s were still in use decades later, their useful lifetimes extended far further into the future than their creators would have imagined. As a result, the year count in their primitive digital timekeeping systems only extended to two digits—*e.g.*, '1984' would be represented as '84')—in order to minimise the use of then-precious memory and storage space. The cost of storing information was prohibitively high in the early days of digital computing (as high as $1/bit in the 1960s). A century—or millennium—change would thus potentially cause unpredictable effects to the systems reliant on these machines, as '99' (1999) rolled over to '00' (2000).

At the root of this issue was a divergence between human and machine time. Instead of staying in sync with the human (with '00' referring to the year 2000), computers disrupted the linear accumulation of numerical time by rolling back to 1900 when '99' reverted to '00,' spiraling back to the start of the century as the number buffer 'overflowed' and began the two-digit loop anew.

The increasingly networked and interdependent paradigm of computation only exacerbated this problem. The 1990s saw a transformation of the Internet from the domain of a niche cadre of computer technicians, to a mass-usage medium, as captured by the notion of 'eternal September' in 1993. While this drive towards the distribution and networkization of computation led to paradigm-shifting affordances in the scale and dispersal of computing resources, it had the side effect of creating new fragilities and contingencies, some of which may not have been immediately apparent. The encroachment of Y2K brought these frailties to the forefront of mass consciousness. All that having been said, it is remarkable to look back at the turn of the millennium and see that, ostensibly, *nothing happened*. At the stroke of midnight, the mouth of the looming time-spiral simply dispersed.

> Y2K occupies the whole of time, to a greater or lesser degree. Y2K will never be anything other than a virtual catastrophe. Though it has had enormous effects inside empirical history, it impacted Chronos only as a pure potentiality; as an immanent machinic accident, Y2K is intensive rather than actual. As such, it must be considered not as a moment extended or unfolded in Chronos, but rather as a plateau or, in other words, a virtual occurrence composed on the immanent and intensive plane which constitutes the exteriority of Aeon (113).

A key concern within Greenspan's thesis is, 'in what ways did this catastrophe manifest?' For the first time in the machine age, it became impossible to address the question with any degree of clarity or confidence. In the logic of Greenspan, Y2K could be said to have happened in Aeonic (transcendental/virtual) time but not in Chronic (empirical/actual) time. Perhaps the most pertinent consequence of Y2K itself—the fact that this question could even be *asked* by Greenspan, regardless of the event's 'actual' occurrence—was a resurgent Millennialism pre-Y2K that made evident the conceptual cracks in an established global, temporal hegemony that began with the imposition of GMT. These ruptures became evident not only to those working directly with computational time-systems—at the time, a vanishingly small percentage of the global population—but to a broad social milieu of radicals across the religious and political spectrum, all of whom began to prepare for the 'Approaching End' with renewed energies.

> Technologies are shot through with myths that frame the story of time, myths of utopia and cataclysm alike. So it should not be surprising that many of the stories circulating about the "information revolution" feed off the patterns of eschatological thought, nor that technological images of salvation and doom keep hitting the screens of the social imagination.[vii]

Y2K—we argue—heralded the now-evident Balkanization of machinic and networked temporalities, manifest through the overflow of the incessant accumulation of Chronic time though the finite nature of digital address space. Temporal scarcity realigning Time and Money as necessarily *strict equivalents* in the emerging techno-capitalist hegemony—in order to support its globe-spanning apparatus of time-production—was shown to have been built on shaky techno-material foundations. The temporality of Y2K, according to Greenspan, was the time of cyberspace. With its counting and representation, its standardization beyond space—except for limitations of optical and electronic signal transmission—once again enacted the Kantian paradigm. An absolutely universalised temporal schema was produced which was necessary to connect spatially separated network participants using a synchronous distributed computer system such as the Internet.

> Cyberspace, as the technological system of global capitalism in its contemporary phase, supplements—and in part even replaces—the previous dependence on physical trade routes and transportation networks with a virtual web in which geographical boundaries have become redundant. Dependent on instantaneous communications irrespective of place, this virtual web makes the demand for a standardized time that accompanied previous technological grids even more urgent. Cyberspace, like the capitalist system itself, is a distributed network which can only be united by a precisely synchronized and globalized time (116).

By cementing the primacy of machinic time in cyberspace over the time of the clock and/or calendar, Y2K signaled the dawn of a new Millennialism which willed on the ongoing collapse of time *into* money as virtual spatio-temporalities allowed for most of the physical and corporeal limitations to information processing and transfer to be mediated away.

> The virtual nature of Y2K—a nature which allowed it to be entirely affective (as a potentiality) and yet never empirically manifest—suggests that it cannot be understood through the successive temporality of Chronos. Rather, Y2K is a sign—which operates as both a name and a date—for an event composed on the intensive plane of Aeon. It is as an Aeonic event that Y2K makes the connection between the transcendental philosophy of time and the socio-economics of capitalist timekeeping practices [...] it dissolves the distinction between time and the materiality of timekeeping systems (133).

The groundwork laid by European colonization of much of the world, centering zero-time in London's Greenwich, was rapidly overlaid by the signal cables of pre-millennium globalization. This was the beginning of the world running on Unix Time, the first digital timekeeping metric, distributed according to Network Time Protocol (NTP).

Mnemotechnics: An Aside on the Production of Digital Timekeeping

At this juncture in the journey—positioned at the precipice of the millennium of machine time—we largely phase out of the specifics that Greenspan laid forth in *Capitalism's Transcendental Time Machine*. Immediately following the temporal rupture and virtual catastrophe of Y2K, Greenspan's account reached its own *"teleological termination point"* (109) with the publication of her thesis by the University of Warwick. With the benefit of hindsight—arguably a transcendental time machine of its own—here follows a speculative continuation of the trajectories extant within *Capitalism's Transcendental Time Machine*.

Our goal is to situate and further develop Greenspan's theories in the context of the present day (2022). Within the moment of Y2K, there was present an understanding that the machinery of networks and digital computation facilitates new potentials for universalities and totalities. The remainder of this accompanying text serves to propose an extrapolation from Y2K to the present, through a historical examination of different modes of networked time, culminating in Bitcoin's decentralized clock.

All of the techno-economic affordances of virtual capital flows through cyberspace are rendered achievable through the proliferation of chronometers for cyberspace, in the ascendance since Y2K. Digital timekeeping at scale began in earnest at the dawn of the 1970s, with the creation, *ex nihilo*, of Unix Time.

Unix Time is a 32-bit integer counting system, representing the number of seconds that have occurred since the Unix Epoch—00:00:00 UTC on January 1st, 1970. It takes its name from the early multiuser operating systems derived from the original Unix project, which began development at AT&T in 1969. The start date was decided upon by programmers ostensibly out of convenience as the beginning of this novel, and ultimately hybrid, time with one foot in the digital, was still being rooted in the calendric. Unix Time is the first instance of a purely digital time, and is distributed to other computers *via* NTP, a 'time-sharing protocol.' The architecture of NTP relies on different strata of *timeservers*, all of which themselves receive time from a master atomic clock. This master clock regulates Chronic time through the stochastic measurement of the radioactive decay of elementary matter *via* a quasi-digital binary process.

> With common computers, we take timekeeping for granted. However, there is a rigorous mechanism that works behind the scenes. The Network Time Protocol (NTP), for instance, addresses the timekeeping issue using a hierarchy of servers distributed globally. This includes up to 15 Stratums the routing paths of which are developed to synchronize in the most optimized manner. This is also enabled by the construction of a Bellman-Ford shortest-path spanning tree that decreases both latency and transmission time inconsistencies.[viii]

> NTP must take into account the locations of both the timeserver and the client, given variables such as network latency and the physical constraint of the speed of light. Unix Time is not trivially spatialised, but relies on organized networks of strictly hierarchical nodes providing an intermediation between the speed of light and spatial distribution of nodes. This is undertaken in order to facilitate the homogenous and globalized temporality of post-Y2K capitalism handed down from the temporal authority of atomic clocks to all clients in the network.[ix]

With Y2K now decades in the past, another Aeonic *Epochalypse* is looming. In 2038, the integer representation of Unix Time will bloat above the limitations of a 32-bit string, and the procession of techno-time is set to again panic, overflow, or simply freeze in place. Although Y2K38 is ostensibly bound to similarly remain virtual(ized), its appearance on the horizon renders explicit the tradeoffs required to maintain control of the unilateral, downward flow of temporal authority. Starting from stochastic clocks, cascading through time server networks, and from there to individual laptops, PCs, and phones; from the network's eye view, we humans exist as hapless subjects between virtual cataclysms brought about by techno-capital.

Chronaissance: The Rise of Networked Temporal Regimes

Having passed through the Aeonic Rubicon of Y2K and into the age of ascendant cyber-spatio-temporality, the focus of this text now shifts to the structure and composition of these nascent, virtualized, temporal regimes. For Greenspan, the development of conceptions of time can only ever be thought of in relation to a techno-capitalist apparatus, which itself generates time: *the* time.

> [T]here are mechanisms through which the machinery of techno -capitalism has the capacity to create the form of time itself, rather than just operate within time. And that's its most abstract power [...] if you have the capacity [...] to create a form of time at this abstract level, then there's a realm of experience or appearance or manifestation that happens inside that. That's the ultimate abstract power of techno-modernity.[x]

But *the* time is only one possible instantiation of a *temporal regime,* even one mediated by a digital networking apparatus such as the post-2000s Internet. Temporal regimes—mechanisms for the distribution of temporal authority—can be imagined with a variety of different structural cues, which can be considered within the rubric of two architectural ethea.

First, there are *centralized* 'command-and-control' structures for the authoritarian dictation and imposition of universalized, temporal constructions. Such structures are common in history, seen in the imposition of Western temporalities in colonized lands—such as Railway Time in India—and GMT as canonized by a coalition of Imperial-friendly states in the late nineteenth-century. This is the architecture of post-Y2K time: ever-more-precise measurements of sub-seconds cascading downwards through layers of authority *via* NTP. Contemporary examples of these methods include digital and Internet standardizations such as Google's Spanner, as well as 'spatialized network clocks' such as the USA's Global Positioning System (GPS) satellite array. The power centralization in all of these approaches remains tightly concentrated within institutions of material science, policy production, and militarism.

The continuing efficacy of these institutions is, however, in crisis. Post-Y2K capitalist time is fragmenting as the cracks appear in a previously hegemonic temporal regime. The decidedly non-virtual crisis of capital in 2008 led to a fundamentally different approach to digital time production, with *decentralization* and peer consensus being the foundational elements informing the nascent architectural designs. This is the second form of temporal regimentation, and a multitude of novel timekeeping systems adopting the logic of decentralization are being built around protocols governing the creation of a canonical ordering of networked events, recorded in a distributed but shared and verifiable timeline.

The invention of a peer-to-peer consensus algorithm in applied computer science points to a problem of industrialization that Greenspan also discusses: how can clocks, and the production processes associated with them, be synchronized? In post-Fordian capitalism, this question shifts again, as capital itself becomes the very means of production: how can information technology systems determine an order of events (for instance, transactions of capital)? Decentralized ledgers start here with a fundamentally paranoid foundation of 'trust minimization': asymmetric cryptography allows the validity of transactions to be confirmed by all participants at any time, with little effort required. The information technology system becomes immanently verifiable without any kind of transcendent authority.

Rather than marking the passing of seconds, minutes, and hours, these systems order transactions broadcast from anywhere in the topology of the network, agreeing upon discrete units of history as a method of mutual yet competitive time creation and the construction of a shared historicity. The passing of time is dictated not by institutions in control of atomic clocks, but *via* a variety of different protocols aimed—at least in theory—at decentralizing time-production away from a single point of control (and failure).

Can we see in these two architectural approaches to techno-capitalist temporality—*command-and-control,* and *peer-to-peer*—respective tendencies and affinities with Chronos' time of order and precision measurements, and Aeon as the emergent and immanent temporality of opportunity and subjective perception? It would appear that, in these realized networked timekeeping systems, both Chronos and Aeon co-exist in tension, in some form of spectral superposition, existing in mutual opposition, yet reciprocal necessity.

We propose that *distributed, consensus-based timekeeping technologies*—incorporating the mnemotechnics of what are commonly known as *blockchains,* but more fittingly referred to as *timechains*—can be apprehended as a realized instantiation of a generative substrate for the spawning of occurrences in virtual time as a by-product of their production of Chronic order. This 'ultimate abstract power,' and the concomitant shift in the temporal apparatuses at our disposal, has ramifications regarding the increasingly fragmented era of patchwork modernity that now delimits the preconditions for experience itself. This fragmentation is not merely a point of analytic interest, however. In the past, radical movements with temporal secessionism at the core of their manifestos include the May Fourth movement in China, French Revolutionary Time, and the rearchitecting of time-zones by nation states to distance themselves temporally, economically, and politically from their imperial and colonial oppressors.

> [M]odernity is expressed by and through the then new technologies of the clock and the calendar and the form of time that they produce. And I think that you could read the May Fourth Movement as, in some way, an acknowledgement of that. The May Fourth thinkers who wanted to embrace this particular mode of the Gregorian calendar, this particular mode of temporality, thought that this new form of time was the transcendental condition under which China could be modern. I don't think they were necessarily particularly Kantian, but they nevertheless understood that in some way.[xi]

Given that distributed ledgers are "an example of technology that doesn't happen in time, (instead) happen(ing) to time," this text may shed light on how we may organise within a new temporality, reconfiguring the delimitations of our conceptual apparatuses in the process.[xii]

Bitcoin: Capitalism's Transcendental Timechain Machine?

> Cyberspace's emphasis on temporal precision and accuracy is primarily due to the intimate interactive dynamics which have developed between technology and economic systems. In cyberspace, flows of capital—which are never anything other than digital code—are continuously subjected to virtual transactions that are sensitive to minute variations in time. As digital code, time and money have converged on a single numerical and technical plane, making the conversion between the two ever more immediate and immanent (116).

In the years since *Capitalism's Transcendental Time Machine* was written, instantiations of peer-to-peer networked computing architectures have emerged that can be understood as mediating between real and virtual temporal regimes, such as those of Aeon and Chronos. In keeping with the timekeeping systems of the past, revelatory and eschatological legends are projected upon these novel computational substrates by the faithful and critics alike, as humans strive to demystify and de-esotericize these nascent complex and headless technologies.

Much has happened in the reification of techno-materialities since Y2K, which can be retrospectively linked to, and rationalized by, the conceptual themes and trajectories explored in *Capitalism's Transcendental Time Machine*. The processes of techno-capitalist time-production, so pointedly characterized by Greenspan, have been exemplified by a novel technical system bridging the real and virtual, incorporating Deleuze and Guattari's transcendental materialism at its very core. In this section, approaches are explored that capture the material and conceptual implications of the Balkanization of timekeeping using a theoretical foundation built upon Greenspan's work. A particular focus will be placed on distributed ledger technologies such as the timechain. What roles do Chronos and Aeon play in the basic mechanisms of these emerging timekeeping concepts?

> For what is crucial in the convergence of time and money on the digital plane is not only the immanence and speed of quantitative conversion, but also the increasing importance of systems and transactions that are hypersensitive to the date (122).

On All Hallows' Eve, 2008, a short technical paper was circulated on the Cypherpunks Mailing List by the pseudonymous Satoshi Nakamoto, describing a novel peer-to-peer protocol design called Bitcoin. The system's design was intended to implement a network that would enable users to exchange messages. The network would satisfy its security, consensus formation, entropy generation, and coin distribution requirements *via* an energy-intensive process known as proof-of-work, also referred to as 'mining,' analogous to gold. Proof-of-work connects the virtuality of the inside of the network with the materiality of the outside 'real world' through a lottery-style race to compute 'costly' and otherwise useless hashes, producing large amounts of heat and e-waste as by-products.

> In this paper, we propose a solution to the double-spending problem using a peer-to-peer distributed timestamp server to

generate computational proof of the chronological order of transactions.[xiii]

3. Timestamp Server

The solution we propose begins with a timestamp server. A timestamp server works by taking a hash of a block of items to be timestamped and widely publishing the hash, such as in a newspaper or Usenet post [2-5]. The timestamp proves that the data must have existed at the time, obviously, in order to get into the hash. Each timestamp includes the previous timestamp in its hash, forming a chain, with each additional timestamp reinforcing the ones before it.

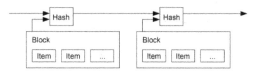

Satoshi Nakamoto, Bitcoin whitepaper §3, 2008

Cryptocurrencies are timestamping and event-ordering systems at their core. In addition to the network architecture and consensus mechanisms, Bitcoin also employs a noteworthy approach to record-keeping: a discretized, linear, append-only data structure most fittingly referred to as a *timechain* (also referred to as a *blockchain*). This data structure, and associated mechanisms to achieve decentralized network-wide consensus, provide a high degree of assurance that the network will respect a particular set of transaction orderings, which, when chained together in a precisely specified sequence, manifest a canonical historicity.

Bitcoin is a decentralized timestamping server, and the transactions are simply messages changing the effective balances that each network participant has access to. These balances are denominated in the native unit of the system, BTC, and are used to pay transaction fees to miners, functioning as the *de facto* currency with which value is redistributed amongst the users of the network. Satoshi Nakamoto used the word 'timestamp' on fourteen occasions in the Bitcoin whitepaper. Bitcoin is an abstract timekeeping daemon incarnated through cryptography, economics, and thermodynamics. After Kant, Deleuze and Guattari, and Greenspan, we can regard Bitcoin (and other timechain networks employing peer-to-peer consensus mechanisms) as a new form of time production that is ever more deeply connected to capitalist processes than anything that preceded it.

> Aeonic events do not occur in time not because they belong to a transcendent outside, but because they are flat with the single plane of immanence which collapses the distinction between time and that which populates it. Equally immanent within any

given moment of Chronos, in Aeon "everything happens at once." Operating with a mode of distribution that is incommensurable with the order of Chronos, Aeonic events cannot help but scramble the linear sequence of extensive time (104).

Timechain technology achieves its own temporal synthesis *vis-à-vis* the mediation of both a virtual and recorded event by way of a 'schizotemporal duality' extant in such peer-to-peer networks. Proof-of-work functions as a leaderless consensus mechanism whereby the recording of virtual events (transactions) towards a ledger takes place, creating a chronological, numerical order, thereby materializing the potential of an immanent peer-to-peer network through computation and energy.

Characterising this biphasic dualism is far from straightforward, but Greenspan's work relating to cyberspace time provides a sound baseline from which to make onto-epistemic approaches. Aspects of cyber-clock time and block-clock time were characterised by Greenspan in *Capitalism's Transcendental Time Machine* with reference to a more general conception of *"cyberspace time"* (115). Greenspan considered cyberspace time to be inhuman, mechanically simulatory, and implying quantisation. As cyberspace is nonlocalizable, its regime of time would be transglobal or post-global—today we might use the term decentralized. An immanent machinic culture (peer-to-peer), cyberspace-time would measure nothing outside of its domain of orientation (hard-bounded). As an abstract yet empirical method of timekeeping, cyberspace-time would require a larger paradigm shift than the clock was to the calendar.

The temporal production *via* Bitcoin's network, proof-of-work, and the timechain ledger proceeds in two modes. Firstly, a continuous cyber-clock mode exists where nodes propose transactions in 'real-time.' After being broadcast and propagated through the network by nodes relaying transactions to their peers, these 'unconfirmed transactions' are then held in mining nodes' working memory, typically traditional RAM. Collectively, this provisional memory is referred to as a network's 'mempool' (memory pool)—itself pure virtual potential—as the sequence of events to be confirmed and canonized has yet to be determined. This is an existence outside of time, in deep contingency.[xiv]

Secondly, a discrete block-clock mode ticks to the sequential cadence of confirmed blocks that is strictly under the regime of Chronos. In this sense, proof-of-work is the immanent timekeeping mechanism, which leaderlessly transmutes virtual network activity through the computational power of capital into ordinally sequenced batches of pure

Chronos. The affect of abstract virtualities such as capital itself leaches into the sequencing and ordering of time itself.

Invoking the neomillennial spirit, the thermodynamic costliness of proof-of-work might be regarded as a *burnt offering for an indifferent god*. In the collapsing of one temporal mode into the other, the opportunity for arbitrages, slippages, and other temporally adversarial behaviours emerge. Bitcoin transactions are confirmed by miners selecting the user-broadcast proposals they wish to include in an upcoming block, typically prioritized by the size of transaction fees paid. As exemplified by Greenspan at length in *Capitalism's Transcendental Time Machine* (with myriad historical references), in Bitcoin, the marshals of temporal production apparatuses once again wield outsized influence over which events are included within the timechain, and in what order. On the timechain, history will always be written by the winners, to paraphrase the tired cliché. The timestamps supplied by Bitcoin miners utilise the Unix Time format mentioned earlier, as 32-bit *unsigned* integers commencing in 1970. They are not vulnerable to the *Epochalypse* bug in 2038, when 32-bit *signed* integers using original Unix Time will overflow its limit. The Bitcoin network will instead 'run out of time,' *ceteris paribus*, in 2106.

The cyclically rhythmic and discretized temporality of cryptocurrency networks—the block-clock mentioned earlier—is hardly something to set one's watch by. As proof-of-work is a random, lottery-style process involving a search for a possibility space that iteratively uses brute-force computational repetition, the time between candidate blocks that fulfil the network-mandated validity conditions is variable. As a result, the time between blocks is unpredictable and can differ widely. The network periodically recalibrates difficulty: the probability of a given hash satisfying the conditions for block creation, which in turn serves to adjust the inter-block cadence. In Bitcoin, a median inter-block cadence of 600 seconds is targeted, but it is entirely feasible to take twice as long to find a block, with the next block following just a handful of seconds later.

A mitigation that is taken in Bitcoin to deter attacks employing deliberately false timestamps—a moving average of the most recent eleven confirmed blocks' timestamps, known as Median Time Past (MTP)—also has a side effect of helping make longer-term unions of block and clock times, such that temporal averaging measures are routinely used in slow-block networks such as Bitcoin. The miner-supplied timestamp of the latest block must always be greater than MTP. Thus, MTP is the monotonically incrementing temporal machinery facilitating the Chronic production of Bitcoin's timechain.

Conclusion: The Time Is Out of Joint

To conclude this introductory statement on *Capitalism's Transcendental Time Machine*, we usher the reader to bathe directly in the shifting tides of Anna Greenspan's transcendental materialism rather than in this mere diffraction of speculative extrapolation. Here we recap our attempt to bring *Capitalism's Transcendental Time Machine* into the 2020s as Greenspan so clearly and concisely dragged Kant, Descartes, Marx, Bergson, Deleuze, Guattari, Foucault, and others beyond the threshold of the third millennium.

Capitalism's Transcendental Time Machine's arrow of time begins with Kant's Copernican Revolution, twisting the Platonic vision of transcendent eternity through the newfound primacy of time over space achieved *via* pure interiority, with the epistemological status of a synthetic *a priori* form. Employing Kant's transcendental aesthetic, Greenspan yields a dualistic sense of time. This sets up a discontinuity between the insideness of time, which can be measured, and the experience of duration as the passage of time as an outsideness.

Contorting this through Deleuze's exotic interpretation of Kant's theory of time, Greenspan invokes the Deleuzean concept of Aeon to flatten the outside of a somewhat Kairotic or Bergsonian duration into an extensive plane of immanent intensities. Greenspan then brings this into the era of computation, digitalia, machinery, and cyberspace-time. Through an examination of the events incident with the nascence of the third millennium, Y2K is proffered as a then-present example of an Aeonic occurrence. Such manifestations of Aeon present themselves as ruptures, caesuras, and discontinuities in the metaphysical fabric of time. Y2K unfolded a new temporal regime, a new techn(e)o-millennialism, with eschatological undertones of apocalyptic prophesies harking back to the myths and spiritual technologies of Abrahamic faiths. Heralding the dawn of the age of cyberspace, machinic temporality takes precedence over the time of clock and calendar from here onwards.

In the orbit of the temporal rupture and virtual catastrophe of Y2K, Greenspan's account arrived at its *"teleological termination point"* (109) as her doctoral dissertation was submitted to the University of Warwick. Our wish for this supplementary text is to situate and further develop Greenspan's theories of time in the context of the present day (2022).

Ultimately, we conclude that the non-event of Y2K paved the way for the ascendancy of machine time. The rapid proliferation of networked modes of being—not least the Internet itself—was accompanied by a concomitant increase in importance in modes of temporality which facilitate and govern the synchronization of widely distributed computational apparatuses. These approaches take varying flavors and architectures, with some protocols resembling the hierarchies of authority that human societies have taken since time immaterial, and others that instead opting for the immanent flatness of a peer-to-peer structure without intermediaries. Arguably the most evocative and provocative exemplification of the new affordances of contemporary chronotechnics is what we refer to as timechain technology, the linear and append-only data structure that gives decentralized networks such as Bitcoin their vertebral historicity. Timechain-architected distributed systems—and the mechanisms by which peer consensus in the absence of trusted authorities is achieved—can be regarded as a process of transforming virtual network activity, through the computational power of capital, into ordinally sequenced batches of *pure Chronos*. The timechain instantiates a new clock, *a new kind of time*, far more removed from that of the diurnal clock and solar calendar than has ever been witnessed before.

What can we imagine to be the next part of this story? Does this trajectory end here, with the prophesy of *Capitalism's Transcendental Time Machine* seemingly fulfilled? We suppose not. But unlike Bitcoin's radical mechanism of synthesizing historicities, as mere humans we have no way of peering beyond the veil and seeing which of our possible futures may be borne out. This is perhaps the most reassuring matter of all: that in the age of ultra-precision and Chronic segmentation, the future is anything but certain. One speculation seems uncontroversial: that capital, and those entities in the service of it, will continue to desire, enact, and exploit ever-grander conceptions and architectures of temporal engineering. For as long as there is value to be redistributed, there will be incentives to engineer more sophisticated machinery with which to manipulate the nature and flow of time. Today, whether we acknowledge it or not, we all live inside Capitalism's Transcendental Time Machine.

Wassim Z. Alsindi, Max Hampshire, and Paul Seidler

Berlin, Germany and Vienna, Austria

2022

Summary

This thesis seeks to establish a connection between abstract thought and material practice. It does so by focusing on the relation between the transcendental philosophy of time and the socio-technics of timekeeping practices.

The thesis begins with a discussion of Kant's philosophy of time as outlined in the *Critique of Pure Reason*. It argues that Kant's discovery of the transcendental coincides with the development of an entirely new conception of time. This new conception overturns classical thought by making a distinction between the abstract form of time and the empirical phenomena of movement and change.

The second chapter maps the transcendental philosophy of time on to the history of capitalist timekeeping. This history includes the invention and development of the mechanical clock, temporal standardization, and the increasing importance of the equation 'time = money.' The aim in bringing these two spheres together is to show both that Kant's philosophy of time owes much to his empirical surroundings, and also that capitalist time can only be understood through the temporal abstraction of transcendental thought. This link between Kant and capitalism is blocked, however, by a dividing line which separates the philosophical nature of time from the empirical changes of history.

In order to surpass this problem, the thesis turns to the work of Deleuze and Guattari whose 'transcendental materialism' connects the abstract production of time with empirical innovations. This is accomplished by replacing the classical conception of a transcendent eternity with the immanent materiality of an exterior plane. This plane—which they call Aeon and is composed of thresholds, or singular events—makes no distinction between time and that which occurs in time. The final chapter explores the dawn of the third millennium—or Y2K—as constituting one such Aeonic event.

0 — Introduction

In colloquial language, the terms inside and outside are used to demarcate simple, spatial relations. The boundaries between them are physical and the passage which connects one to the other, though not always easy to negotiate, is never completely blocked. For no matter how secure, walls can always be scaled, doors opened, and gates unlocked. In philosophical language, however, the terms inside and outside designate a relation that is altogether more impermeable. Whether of an individual subject or organism, or of a social code or structure, interiority, as a philosophical concept, indicates an absolute segregation.[1] The inside, in this context, is a mode of containment that operates not through physical boundaries but by an imperceptible border which draws the contours of all that can be thought and perceived. It is a contention of this thesis that, when used in this absolute sense, the division between inside and outside is not a spatial determination but a temporal one. Existence is an enclosure not because it happens in space but because it locks us in time.[2] It is for this reason that one can detect a tendency in both philosophy and religion to oppose the concept of time with notions of liberation, escape, and exteriority, for an inside that is bounded by temporal rhythms must find its outside in a realm which is exterior to time.[3]

In the classical Western tradition, this connection between the philosophy of time and the notion of inside and outside is based on a disjunction which opposes time to eternity. This disjunction is articulated most famously by Plato who defines time as "the movable image of eternity," a definition which establishes the interiority of time in opposi-

---

1: Much contemporary or postmodern thought has dealt with the segregation between inside and outside by concentrating on the interiority of language. Deconstruction, in particular, has held that this zone of interiority is so all encompassing that it renders an occupation of the outside impossible (note Derrida's famous phrase: *il n'y a pas de hors-texte*). Subversion, from this point of view, can only occur as a disruption from within.
2: This claim, that interiority has more to do with time than with space, is one of the crucial insights of transcendental philosophy and will be discussed in detail in chapter one.
3: Though extremely widespread, the notion that liberation is an escape from time is perhaps most clearly expressed in the religions of the East such as Hinduism and Buddhism. Both these religions have developed meditative techniques (yoga) that aim to release the practitioner from the never-ending cycle of time, and both maintain that enlightenment is reached through an escape from the illusion of time, or Maya. The details of this line of thought and its relation to the arguments which follow are, however, beyond the scope of this thesis.

tion to an exteriority which is eternal.ⁱ Though immensely widespread, this contrast between time and eternity rests, at least in its classical formulation, on a very specific understanding of both the nature of time and of the relation between inside and outside.[4]

The classical tradition equated time with astronomy. Conceived of as a "movable image," time was thought to be perceived in the cyclical changes of the heavenly spheres.[5] Equivalent to celestial movement, time was made the very principle of variation.[6] Manifesting itself as a never-ending process of change and activity, it governed the continuous flow of becoming in which all existence was trapped.

Thus, it was precisely due to its associations with variation that time was considered to be a mode of capture. The classical tradition considered temporal rhythms, the passage of the seasons, and the changes of day into night as an elaborate simulation which belonged only to the created world of phenomena. It held that the processes of movement and change were but a shadow of a timeless realm that lies beyond, and it was inside this world of shadow and mirage that the subject was caught.[7] Governed by the variations of matter, entangled in the multiplicity of becoming, humans were held prisoner, duped by the illusory movement of time.

This vision of time found its direct opposition in the concept of eternity. Differentiated from the temporal image of movement and variation, the eternal was conceived of as a realm of constant stasis. In contrasting change with identity, multiplicity with unity, and becoming with being, eternity offered an alternative to the world of sensible appearance, and thus constituted a realm which existed outside the phenomenon of time.

It is within this dualistic framework, then, that the exteriority of the

---

4: In what follows, I offer a brief outline of the classical conception of time and eternity. Though this could undoubtedly be criticized for passing over many of the complexities of classical thought, the purpose here is only to sketch the basic contours of this philosophical tradition so as to provide a clearer means of understanding the temporal revolutions which constitute the main focus of this thesis. To this end, both Plato's and Aristotle's philosophies of time are discussed in more detail in chapter one.
5: See Plato, "Timeaus," in *Plato: The Collected Dialogues*, especially sections 38–39. Also note the following from *Definitions*: "(chronos) time: the motion of the sun, the measure of its course" (Plato, "Definitions," 1678).
6: As we will see, both Plato and Aristotle tie time directly to movement. Though Plotinus argues against this formulation, his notion that time is an activity of the soul shows that he too conforms to the classical tradition in linking time with the variable processes of becoming and change.
7: I am referring here, of course, to the writings of Plato. It is interesting to note that in the most famous section of these writings, Plato uses a spatial metaphor—the image

eternal must be understood. Eternity, conceived of in opposition to temporality, should not be confused with the everlasting, which is a continuous extension of time.[8] Situated neither in the deep past nor in the distant future, eternity is not a stretch of time but a timelessness. Co-existing simultaneously with each and every moment, it is the essence of appearances, the constant form which the variations of time can only represent in a shadowy fashion.

As the essence of time, the eternal was revered as the divine archetype. Operating from above, it was eternity that created time. Considered to be the essence of transcendent production, it was able to create without getting involved in the matter of its creation.[9] "Eternity," writes Plotinus "is a majestic thing and thought declares it identical with God."[10]/ii

With this quotation, the obvious convergence between the classical notion of eternity and the conception of the deity produced by the monotheistic traditions of the West is clearly revealed. The form of the eternal—as the genesis of the image of time—is paralleled in the opening section of the Old Testament where we encounter God, as the eternal, who is presented as the creator of time.

> And God said, Let there be light: and there was light. And God saw the light, that it was good: and God divided the light from the darkness. And God called the light day, and

---

of an underground cave—to illustrate his conception of interiority. Even here, however, the prisoners are captured not so much by spatial boundaries, but rather by their incapability of breaking free from the entrapment produced by a fascination with the moving images of time. See Plato, "The Republic," in *Plato: The Collected Dialogues*.

8: "Because eternity touches each and every time, it is easily confused with the closely related concept of what 'always was, is, and will be,' or, in a word, the everlasting. But in its own proper concept, the eternal only 'is'; only in the present tense can it be said to be or act in any way. Exempted from all having-been and going-to-be, eternity is familiarly defined as timelessness, in distinction from the everlasting (sometimes also called the sempiternal)" (Elade, *Encyclopedia of Religion: Volume 5*, 167).

9: Drawing on the work of such feminist thinkers as Luce Irigaray (esp., *Speculum of the Other Woman*), it appears that the classical distinction between the phenomenon of time and the transcendence of eternity is essentially masculine in nature. The notion of a transcendent eternity, beyond or above the enclosure of time, only occurs by differentiating the eternal from matter, creation, becoming, and multiplicity—that is from all things traditionally thought of as female. It is interesting to note in this respect that in Hinduism, Shakti, the principle of female power, is sometimes conceived of as time. See Heinrich Zimmer, *Myths and Symbols in Indian Art and Civilization*.

10: The influence of Neoplatonism on monotheistic religion, and in particular on Christianity, is much too vast a subject to address here. Suffice it to note that it is clear—even from this minimal exposition—that the philosophical understanding of the eternal converges with the Judeo-Christian God.

the darkness he called night. And the evening and the morning were the first day (Gen. 1:3–4).

According to the Bible, then, time originates with the first act of creation. Moving across the waters of the unformed void, God acts initially to generate light and begin the passage of time. This primordial event is the singular occurrence which takes place outside the confines of temporality, for once it is established, a time determined by the passage of day into night structures and conditions the rest of the week of creation. Eternity, as an exterior and transcendent dimension, appears in its pure form only once again, at the end of the Bible, with the promise of messianic redemption.

Thus, in both classical philosophy and in the scriptures of the Abrahamic traditions, life's entrapment in the continuous process of temporal change, becoming, and multiplicity was opposed to the wholeness and unity of an eternal being who, untainted by the material world, existed as complete perfection contained within itself.[11] The outside was thus equated with transcendence, a mode of escape that led out of the enclosure of time and allowed one to reach—whether through faith or through knowledge—a higher and more primary inside.

This thesis is an exploration of two revolutions, one philosophical, the other socio-economic, which together have fundamentally altered the philosophy, culture, and technics of time.[12] The first of these is philosophy's 'Copernican Revolution' which was instigated by Immanuel Kant in the *Critique of Pure Reason*. The second occurs with the onset of capitalism and involves the invention—and subsequent innovations—of a timekeeping system that is based on the clock. By bringing these two revolutions together, this thesis seeks to establish a connection between abstract conceptual thought and concrete material practices, a connection which is exemplified by the convergence between the transcenden-

11: Note the following quotation from Plotinus: "That which neither has been nor will be, but simply possesses being; that which enjoys stable existence as neither in process of change nor having ever changed—that is Eternity. Thus we come to the definition: the Life—instantaneously entire, complete, at no point broken into period or part—which belongs to Authentic Existent by its very existence, this is the thing we are probing for—this is Eternity" (Plotinus, "Time and Eternity," 225).

12: In order to achieve focus, much that relates to the main theme of this thesis—that is, revolutions in the nature of time—was of necessity left out. The two most obvious exclusions are, on the 'materialist side,' the recent changes in the physics of time (a topic that is introduced in an interesting and comprehensive manner by Ilya Prigogene and Isabelle Stengers in *Order out of Chaos* and, on the 'philosophical side,' in the work of Henri Bergson (who is undoubtedly an important influence on the philosophy of time found in the writings of Deleuze and Guattari; see Deleuze's *Bergsonism*). To incorporate these topics would require much more time and space than is available here.

tal philosophy of time and the socio-history of timekeeping practices. Establishing this connection, however, requires not only a reformulation of the classical conception of time—produced, as we will see, through the creation of a split between, on the one hand, the constant structure of formal time, and, on the other, empirical change conceived of as history—but also a reinvention of the classical notion of eternity. This latter is found in the work of Deleuze and Guattari who substitute the transcendence of eternity with the immanent concept of Aeon, or the absolute outside, conceived of as the continuous variation of an intensive temporality. It is by way of this concept of Aeon that we will find, in what appears as the 'history' of capitalist time, Aeonic events which are at once entirely abstract yet fully material. The abstract materiality of these events, as we will see, transfigure the boundaries between inside and outside, for though they are in no way eternal, they nevertheless occur on an exterior plane outside of the interior confines of time.

From the point of view of the philosophy of time, the revolutionary break brought on by both Kant and capitalism rests on a transformation which occurs in how time is mapped on to the distinction between constant and variable.[13] As we will see in the chapters which follow, both critique and clock time differentiate themselves from the classical tradition by insisting that it is not time itself which varies, but rather that variation inheres in that which exists in time. This distinction between time and that which is in time arises from the fact that both Kant and capitalism separate temporality from the changing patterns of astronomical cycles. Split off from the concrete rhythms of the phenomenal world, time becomes an abstract grid, the *a priori* frame which structures both philosophical thought and the socio-economic and cultural milieu. Time is no longer variable since it has become the very presupposition of change. The stasis of eternity is thus replaced by the constant fixture of formal time.

This transformation in the nature of time is, as will be made clear, of fundamental importance to the whole of the Kantian system. For it is this division between time and what occurs in time that ultimately distinguishes the empirical (*a posteriori*) from the transcendental (*a priori*). In the first section of the First *Critique*, the 'Transcendental Aesthetic,' Kant insists that time cannot be equated with alteration. "Alteration is an empirical phenomenon,"[†] claims Kant, and is thus "only possible through and in the representation of time."[iii] This paves the way for

---

13: This distinction corresponds to a set of oppositions—including quantity and quality, and content and expression—which will be discussed throughout this thesis. It is a contention of this thesis that these oppositional couples—or stratified distinctions—are what constitute the interiority of time.

what Deleuze called the "first great Kantian reversal" which frees time from its age-old subordination to movement. Unhinged from its ties to change and activity, time becomes an abstract condition of experience, the *a priori* structure within which all change and movement takes place.

In capitalism, this differentiation—a differentiation between a constant temporality and the variation of that which occurs in time— receives concrete expression through the division between clocks and calendars. Though this split has existed for thousands of years,[14] it is only within capitalism that the distinction between these two types of timekeeping devices has become an abstract distinction in the nature of time itself. Through the continuous innovation and growing ubiquity of the clock, capitalism contrasts the qualitative time of the calendar (with its differences in seasons, light, temperature, etc.) with the precise, homogeneous, standardized, and purely quantitative ticking of the clock. It is within the former's qualitative time that variation takes place. Change in time is recorded by the calendar which has ceased to measure the rhythms of everyday life and become instead a mechanism subordinated to the developmental narrative of history. Though capitalism makes use of these variations in calendric time,[15] it is also essential for the capitalist mode of production that time be treated as an abstract quantity that does not vary. It is this that is provided by the time of the clock.

By establishing the difference between the structure of a constant temporality and the variable experiences of history, both Kant and capitalism have created a fracture in the appearance of time. It is by way of this fracture (and its coinciding synthesis) that these two revolutions have managed to overturn the classical tradition and inaugurate what may be called the modern conception of time.[16]

Yet despite the fact that the critical understanding of temporality finds its parallel in the culture and technics of capitalism, there is an adamant insistence, on both sides, that a fundamental distinction be maintained between the philosophy of time and its socio-economic and cul-

---

14: Sundials have been in use since the third millennium B.C., and evidence of water clocks (or clepsydra) have been found as early as the sixth-century B.C.; see Dohrn-van Rossum, *History of the Hour: Clocks and Modern Temporal Orders*, 20–21.

15: This is a crucial point that will be made clear in our discussion of the economist Böhm-Bawerk found in chapter two.

16: Deleuze uses this phrase when describing the Kantian conception of time. Though I have not included any strict definition of modernity, I have used the term to describe both the Kantian philosophy of time and the timekeeping practices that developed with the clock. Used in this manner, it is meant to differentiate both Kant and clock time from, on the one hand, the philosophy of time upheld in the classical tradition, and, on the other, from the contemporary or 'postmodern' timekeeping practices that have emerged within cyberspace.

tural manifestations. This distinction rests, as we will see, on the apparent divergence between transcendental and historical production. The explicit aim of the *Critique of Pure Reason* is to establish, through immanence of criteria, the legitimate domain of reason and thereby dismiss the 'groundless pretensions' of metaphysical speculation.[17] From the point of view of critique, therefore, it is strictly illegitimate to hold that time is the product (or the image) of eternity. In revolt against this classical doctrine, Kant replaces transcendent creation with the immanent synthesis of the understanding. Operating in a realm which is constitutive of experience, these synthetic processes construct time as an *a priori* epistemological representation. This representation, which Kant calls the form of inner sense, is the universal and necessary precondition for all empirical phenomena. Put simply then, time, for Kant, is a mental construct within which empirical reality takes place. History, which develops in time, cannot be equated with transcendental synthesis since the very existence of history presupposes, and is dependent upon, the transcendental construction of time.

Karl Marx, the most famous philosopher of capitalism, shares Kant's insistence of the need to develop an account of production which does not seek recourse to divine transcendence.[18] However, unlike Kant, Marx maintains that the ultimate realm of production lies not in the synthetic processes of reason, but rather in the dialectical forces of history. Thus, for Marx, the *a priori* are themselves subject to change. Produced by the dynamic forces of history, formal time is not an epistemological representation but a contingent, historical formation. Marx's historical materialism[19] (his 'Hegelianism turned on its head') thus maintains that outside the particularities of the capitalist time machine is a form of variable time with a logic of its own. The exteriority of this

---

17: To quote Kant's famous passage: "It is obviously the effect not of levity but of the matured judgment of the age, which refuses to be put off with illusory knowledge. It is a call to reason to undertake anew the most difficult of all its tasks, namely that of self-knowledge, and to institute a tribunal which will assure to reason its lawful claims, and dismiss all groundless pretensions, not by despotic decrees, but in accordance with its own eternal and unalterable laws. This tribunal is no other than the *critique of pure reason*" (*Critique of Pure Reason*, 9 [Axii]).

18: This is obvious from the famous Marxist contention that religion is the opiate of the people.

19: "According to Engels' 1892 introduction to *Socialism: Utopian and Scientific*, 'historical materialism designate[s] that view of the course of history which seeks the ultimate cause and the great moving power of all important historical events in the economic development of society, in the changes in the modes of production and exchange, in the consequent division of society into distinct classes, and in the struggle of these classes against one another'" (Shaw, "Historical Materialism," 234).

temporality—which is not exhaustively structured by any specific mode of production—is ultimately responsible for creating the time of capitalism (conceived of as both the duration of the capitalist mode of production and the structure of time prevailing within it).

Thus, both critical thought which refuses to acknowledge its socio-economic surroundings, and Marxism which denies the possibility of transcendental synthesis, insist that—despite their obvious connections—the philosophical and socio-technical revolution of time be kept separate and opposed. This opposition, as we have seen, ultimately rests on the fact that the privilege given by transcendental production to the ahistoricity of a constant time comes into conflict with the primacy that historical materialism grants to the variations of a temporality governed by the logic of events. With this conflict, the path to exteriority—on both sides—is lost, as each revolution seeks to contain the other by presenting itself as a higher and more primary inside. Neither Kantian thought, nor the Marxist analysis of capitalism, will accept that the exterior realm productive of time is constituted by the eternal transcendence of God. Nevertheless, they come into conflict over what should be substituted for eternal creation in the modern conception of time. Transcendental critique, the critique of political economy, and the secular time of capitalist societies thus converge in their understanding of time but diverge in their accounts of what lies outside it as the ultimate force of production. The modern revolution in the nature of time is thus only partially complete. For though the classical conception of time has been overturned, the notion of eternity—the traditional zone exterior to time—has been left basically unchanged (if only by being ignored).

Deleuze and Guattari's *Capitalism and Schizophrenia* presents itself as a revolution in transcendental thought which seeks to replace Kantian idealism with a type of Spinozistic materialism.[20] This involves, as we will see, a critique of the Kantian system itself. For according to Deleuze and Guattari, the Kantian notion that transcendental production occurs under the unity of the subject and is therefore epistemological in nature is strictly illegitimate from the viewpoint of critique. Refusing to see *a priori* synthesis as an idealist representation, they reconstruct transcendental philosophy on the basis of an immanent materialism.

20: Deleuze and Guattari's involvement with Spinozistic philosophy is hard to overestimate. Spinoza's non-reductive, immanent, cosmic, and ethical materialism could be said to be the single most important influence in their work. Though the philosophy of Spinoza will be touched upon in chapter three, to explore it in detail is beyond the scope of this thesis. To fully engage with this topic, see Deleuze's two books on Spinoza (listed in the bibliography) and the numerous references to Spinoza found throughout *A Thousand Plateaus*.

This combines the critical method with a Spinozistic vision of a world laid out on a single plane (substance or Nature).[21] Transcendental syntheses thus cease to function as the interior operations of reason and become instead machinic[22] diagrams for the intensive multiplicities that compose and populate an exterior body which Deleuze and Guattari call the plane of consistency, planomenon, or body without organs.

Whereas Kant's Copernican Revolution involved a reformulation of the nature of time, *Capitalism and Schizophrenia*'s materialism involves a revolution in the nature of eternity. This requires, as we will see, that the opposition between an interiorized notion of time associated with change, multiplicity, and becoming, and the conception of the outside as a divine, transcendent, and unified eternity, be overturned. Transcendental materialism thus substitutes the classical disjunction between time and eternity with the difference between two planes of composition which function machinically to produce the distinction between extensive and intensive time. The former of these—named Chronos—is attributed to the plane of organization and development, while the latter belongs to the immanent plane of consistency and is given the name of Aeon. With the concept of Aeon, Deleuze and Guattari bring to philosophy a notion of eternity which is not based on the wholeness and unity of a transcendent beyond, but on the flat multiplicity of an immanent outside.

In the Biblical tradition, the eternal cuts into time through singular events that are explosive and highly dramatic in nature. At the limit, it appears as genesis and apocalypse, the beginning and end of creation. Beyond these points, the eternal is encountered only after death, on Judgment Day, where it carries the threat or promise of damnation or salvation, or when it crashes into history, interrupting the linear order of time through miracles and divine revelation.

We will see that—though no less intense—the connection between Aeon and Chronos is much more quiet and subtle, for Aeon does not manifest itself in time. Though it is itself composed of singular events

---

21: To quote from Deleuze: "Everyone knows the first principle of Spinoza: one substance for all the attributes. But we also know the third, fourth or fifth principle: one Nature for all bodies, one Nature for all individuals, a Nature that is itself an individual varying in an infinite number of ways. What is involved is no longer the affirmation of a single substance, but rather the laying out of a *common plane of immanence* on which all bodies, all minds and all individuals are situated" (*Spinoza*, 122).

22: The term machine will be used throughout this thesis as it is crucial to the work of Deleuze and Guattari and will be explained in more detail in chapter three. Briefly though, Deleuze and Guattari use the term machine not to signify a technical apparatus, but rather to designate the immanent circuits of production that constitute any flat assemblage (regardless of its particular form or substance).

(which can be precisely dated and named) these events compose a virtual plane of intensity that positively avoids climactic actualization. Deleuze and Guattari call these Aeonic occurrences plateaus, and show how they constitute an exteriority that haunts the successive order of extensive temporality.

The final chapter of the thesis takes the pervasive sense of anticlimax that accompanied the dawn of the third millennium as indexing one such event and explores Y2K—a sign that operates as both a date and a name—as a singular Aeonic occurrence. While this may first appear farfetched, we will see that, though it has now been dismissed as irrelevant, Y2K is crucial to the transcendental philosophy of time. This is primarily due to the fact that, as a singularity, it shares all the characteristic features of Aeon, including an affective virtuality, a non-signifying semiotic, a disruption—or positive avoidance—of extensive succession, and an immanent, machinic abstraction.

Cutting across the stratified segmentation of Chronos, Y2K thus functions as a mutation (or accident) both in the structure of formal time and in the empirical development of history. It collapses the distinction between time's formal expression and the content which happen to fill it, dissolving the rigid opposition between technics and culture, constant and variable, and temporality and change. In this way, Y2K constitutes an event—not in time but of time—that allows the capitalist production of temporality to escape from the interiority of history, and thus exemplifies the convergence between the material practices of timekeeping systems, and processes of abstraction which are conventionally located in the philosophy of time.

1 — Philosophy's Copernican Revolution

The history of Immanuel Kant's life is difficult to portray, for he had neither life nor history [...] I do not believe that the great clock of the cathedral performed in a more passionless and methodical manner its daily routine than did its townsman, Immanuel Kant. Rising in the morning, coffee-drinking, writing, reading lectures, dining, walking, everything had its appointed time, and the neighbours knew that it was exactly half-past three o'clock when Immanuel Kant stepped forth from his house in his grey, tight-fitting coat, with his Spanish cane in his hand, and betook himself to the little linden avenue called after him to this day the "Philosophers walk." [...] What a strange contrast did this man's outward life present to his destructive, world-annihilating thought! In sooth, had the citizens of Königsberg had the least presentiment of the full significance of his ideas, they would have felt a far more awful dread at the presence of this man than at the sight of the executioner, who can but kill the body. But the worthy folks saw in him nothing more than a Professor of Philosophy, and as he passed in his customary hour, they greeted him in a friendly manner and set their watches by him.

—Heinrich Heine, *Religion and Philosophy in Germany*, 108–109

Fire in the water. The image of REVOLUTION.
Thus the superior man sets the calendar in order and
makes the seasons clear.

—I Ching Hexagram 49: Ko / Revolution (Molting)

1.0 — The Discovery of Transcendental Time

In 1781, Immanuel Kant published the first edition of the *Critique of Pure Reason*. The history of philosophy registers the date as the moment of Kant's 'Copernican Revolution,' a moment in which Kant is said to have accomplished in the realm of thought what Copernicus had accomplished, over two centuries earlier, in the realm of astronomy. Traditionally, the story of Kant's revolution emphasizes epistemology and concentrates on the role of human intellect in constituting the external world. It is here, we are told, that one should locate the dramatic shift that is at the core of Kantian philosophy.[23] What this chapter will

---

23: In the following section, this position will be illustrated through the writings of Heinrich Heine. Though Heine's poetic and lyrical language is unique amongst the commentators on Kant, his views are not at all unconventional. In the *Past Masters* text on Kant, for example, Roger Scruton writes that the essence of the Copernican Revolution is that "self-consciousness requires that the world must appear to conform to the categories" (Scruton, *Kant*, 28). The *Encyclopedia of Philosophy* concurs that this epistemological view is the key to understanding Kantian thought: "Kant's principal task in the *Critique of Pure Reason* was to determine the cognitive powers of reason, to find out what it could and could not achieve in the way of knowledge" (Walsh, "Immanuel

argue, however, is that this emphasis on the role of the intellect mistakes what is truly revolutionary in critical thought. The argument, which draws on Deleuze's reading of Kant,[24] consists of two main points. First, that the transformation of the human subject is merely a consequence of Kant's more fundamental innovation, the discovery of the realm of the transcendental, and second, that to appreciate the truly revolutionary nature of this discovery, we must turn our attention away from the enlightened subject of reason and focus instead on the occulted nature of time.

The most common approach to Kant is to read him as an epistemologist, a philosopher who is predominantly concerned with how knowledge can be justified. According to this account, the *Critique of Pure Reason* centres around the question: "How are *a priori* synthetic judgements possible?"[i] To answer this question, Kant must begin by defining what he means by the synthetic *a priori*.

"In the order of time," writes Kant in the preface to the First *Critique*, "we have no knowledge antecedent to experience, and with experience all our knowledge begins. But though all our knowledge begins with experience it does not follow that it all arises out of experience."[ii] With this distinction between knowledge that is based in experience and knowledge that is independent of it, Kant separates the *a priori* from the *a posteriori*. This difference is absolute and rigorously determined. Empirical knowledge "which has its sources *a posteriori*, that is, in experience" gives rise to judgments which are particular and contingent (*e.g.*, 'the sun rose today') while *a priori* knowledge, on the other hand, gives rise to judgments which are universal and necessary (*e.g.*, 'today succeeded yesterday').[iii] Since knowledge gained from experience is always particular and contingent, it can never be the basis for judgments which are universal and necessary. Thus, Kant writes that "necessity and strict universality are the sure criteria of *a priori* knowledge."[iv] This difference between the *a priori* and the *a posteriori* is the first basic division which allows Kant to demarcate the singular zone of knowledge that he is concerned with in the First *Critique*.

Yet this distinction between knowledge that is based in experience and knowledge that is independent of it is not in itself sufficient for understanding the central problematic of Kantian thought. In order to discover the transcendental, yet another distinction was required. The two sides of the table had to be split in half. To accomplish this, Kant drew

---

Kant," 308).
24: This reading stems from both of Deleuze's book on Kant, and a series of lectures on Kant that have been reprinted on the Internet (see bibliography).

another line on a different axis, cutting across both the *a priori* and the *a posteriori*. This line corresponds to the difference between knowledge that is analytic and knowledge that is synthetic.

Synthetic *a priori*	Analytic *a priori*	Synthetic *a posteriori*	Analytic *a posteriori*
Transcendental	Logic	Experience	N/A

Table 1. Kantian Axes

Analytic *a priori* knowledge covers logical truths. By drawing out "something which is (covertly) contained in [a] concept," analytic *a priori* truths analyze, elucidate, or explicate what is already implicitly known.[v] Kant's example is as follows: "If I say, for instance, 'All bodies are extended', this is an analytic judgment. For I do not require to go beyond the concept which I connect with 'body' in order to find extension as bound up with it."[vi]

Analytic knowledge is restricted to the domain of the *a priori*. It does not arise empirically. "Judgments of experience," writes Kant, "are one and all synthetic."[vii] By the term 'synthetic,' Kant is referring to knowledge that 'goes beyond the concept.' To make the judgment, 'this body is heavy,' for example, is to connect concepts 'synthetically.' Since not all bodies are heavy, one cannot arrive at the concept 'heavy' from an analysis of the concept 'body.'[25]

Transcendental philosophy concerns itself with the first box in the table—the 'synthetic *a priori*.' The puzzle which it sets for itself is how synthetic knowledge can be produced independently of experience. The prime examples of synthetic *a priori* knowledge are found within the realm of mathematics. As the commentator Alfredo Ferrarin writes, "[i]f what the Critique shows is the possibility of synthetic apriori judgements, it is mathematics that takes advantage of this ampliative principle with greatest confidence and success."[viii] '7 + 5 = 12,' to stick with the example that is repeated throughout the secondary literature on Kant, is a synthetic *a priori* judgment.[26] It is *a priori* since it, like all mathematical propositions, is both universal and necessary. It is synthetic since neither the number 7 nor the number 5 has contained within it the number 12. "The concept of 12," writes Kant, "is by no means already thought in merely thinking the union of 7 and 5; and I may analyze my concept

---

25: On page 49 [B11] of the First *Critique*, Kant uses this example to explain synthetic judgements which are made from experience.
26: Kant himself uses this example himself both in the First *Critique* and in the *Prolegomena to Any Future Metaphysics*.

of such a possible sum as long as I please, still I shall never find the 12 in it."[ix]

Though philosophers had long been concerned with such *a priori* truths as are found in mathematics, it was Kant who first recognized them as being synthetic.[27] Thus, transcendental philosophy, even when confined to epistemology, is far from being a mere exercise in the catalogue of knowledge. For in questioning the tendency to divide everything between *a priori* analytic judgments and *a posteriori* synthetic judgments, Kant "explode[ed] the insufficiency of certain philosophical categories."[x] Focusing his attention on the synthetic *a priori*, he exploded old distinctions and in so doing discovered a powerful new machine.

According to Kant, synthesis is "a blind but indispensable function of the soul." Though "we are scarcely ever conscious" of its power, without it, he insists, "we should have no knowledge whatsoever."[xi] In focusing on the connections and constructions of this hidden realm, the *Critique of Pure Reason* develops a 'synthesized way of handling philosophy'[28] which is not based on an analysis of that which is already given but on an "extension of our previously possessed concepts."[xii] It is, writes Kant, "a genuinely new addition to all previous knowledge."[xiii]

It is this 'new addition' that accounts for the shift in the subject's position which occurs in Kantian thought. What is important to recognize here is that this shift is a result—a corollary—of the more fundamental discovery of this abstract and productive realm of knowledge. Before Kant, the subject was found buried, submerged underground, and chained in the darkness of Plato's cave. According to this traditional vision, the subject was trapped in the body, forced to access the world through the unreliability of the perceptual apparatus. An unfortunate fool blinded by ignorance, duped into mistaking shadows for reality, the subject could not help but deform the world, mutating it into the falsity of illusion. Philosophy's striving consisted in its promise to provide the escape route. Operating with a truth that depended on a "harmony between the subject and the world,"[†] philosophy struggled to cut the chains, to correct the inherent deformity, to free the prisoner from the world of shadows and illusions.

Through his discovery of the transcendental, Kant replaces harmony with circuitry. The subject, no longer deceived and defective, be-

---

27: As Deleuze writes, "analytic a priori judgment, that meant something, synthetic a posteriori judgment, that meant something, but synthetic a priori judgment – that's truly a monster" ("Kant: Synthesis and Time," 10).

28: This phrase comes from a question raised by Deleuze in an introductory lecture on Kant. "Why," Deleuze asks, "wouldn't there also be a synthesized or electronic way of handling philosophy" ("Kant: Synthesis and Time," 19).

comes productive and constitutive. Having given up the impossible attempt at conforming to the objects of the world, "the rational being thus discovers he has new power."[xiv] After Kant, the objects of the world must conform to us. "The first thing the Copernican Revolution teaches us," writes Deleuze, "is that it is we who are giving the orders."[xv] The prisoner has become a legislator.

As previously noted, it is this shift in the subject's position which is traditionally taken to be at the core of Kant's revolutionary thought. In a dramatic passage, the poet Heinrich Heine described this, philosophy's Copernican Revolution, as follows:

> Formerly, when men conceived the world as standing still, and the sun as revolving round it, astronomical calculations failed to agree accurately. But when Copernicus made the sun stand still and the earth revolve round it, behold! Everything accorded admirably. So formerly reason, like the sun moved round the universe of phenomena and sought to throw light upon it. But Kant, bade reason, the sun stand still, and the universe of phenomena now turns round, and is illuminated the moment it comes within the region of the intellectual orb.[xvi]

Yet, while Heine has captured the drama of Kant's discovery, his account reveals a certain problem. For if the stress is on human reason, Kant's allusions to Copernicus are somewhat puzzling. Before Copernicus, Heine reminds us, the earth stood as the central pivot or axis around which everything else revolved. Modern astronomy, which is based on the Copernican system, removed the earth from this central position, making it equal to any other planet. The Copernican Revolution thus derailed us from our privileged status in relation to phenomena. Kant, on the other hand, is said to have done the exact opposite. Whereas Copernicus displaced us from the centre of the universe, Kant put us there. Why, then, does Kant speak of his philosophy as Copernican? It would seem that the emphasis on the human intellect is not a sufficient explanation. Perhaps, if we look more closely, we might find some other reason for this seemingly confused analogy.

In the early years of the sixteenth-century, Nicolaus Copernicus, a Polish astronomer, attained immortal fame by overthrowing the Ptolemaic universe of the ancient world. Frustrated with the impossibility of achieving accurate measurements of astronomical movements, Copernicus began to question Ptolemy's geocentric vision. Instead of assuming that the stars revolved around a static earth, Copernicus thought, to quote Kant, "whether he might not have better success if he made the spectator to revolve and the stars to remain at rest."[xvii] Copernicus posited a heliocentric world in which the stars no longer measured time. He explained the day by the earth's rotation on its own axis and the year by its annual cycle around the sun. In the Copernican system, then, it is the movement of the earth which marks out the temporality of the astronomical calendar.

The *Critique of Pure Reason,* writes Kant, proceeds "precisely on the lines of Copernicus' primary hypothesis."[xviii] Inspired by the astronomer's method, Kant attempted an analogous experiment in philosophy. Frustrated by the inherent instability of metaphysics, critical thought seeks to attain more solid foundations by focusing not on the authority of experience but on the conditions which make experience possible.

It is well known that Copernicus' discovery met with fierce resistance, both from natural philosophy and from the Church, for these two institutions were allied in their commitment to maintaining the authority of Aristotle who had insisted that the earth stood still. This resistance was heightened by the fact that despite Copernicus' findings, the world still appeared to conform to Ptolemy's ancient vision. Copernicus was thus responsible for a strange and mysterious revolution in which nothing seemed to change but through which everything has been transformed. It is in this way, as we will see, that Kant is a true Copernican. The Copernican Revolution, whether in astronomy or philosophy, changes nothing at the level of experience. Our perceptions, and even the way we talk about those perceptions, have not been altered. Phenomena remain the same. The sun still appears to revolve. The earth still appears to stand still. External bodies still appear to be in motion. We still say that the sun rises and sets. The difference is, and this is the revolution, that now 'everybody knows it is only a manner of speaking.'

In a series of lectures on the *Critique of Pure Reason,* Gilles Deleuze maps out a singular and original account of Kant's Copernican Revolution which is based neither on epistemology nor on a change in the position of the intellect, but on a shift in the nature of appearance itself.

According to Deleuze, the classical tradition structured the world around a basic opposition. "The whole of classical philosophy from Plato onwards," he writes, "seemed to develop itself within the frame of a duality between sensible appearances and intelligible essences."[xix] Thus, before Kant, the world was divided between, on the one hand, the degraded realm of sensation which was based on bodily knowledge and experience and, on the other hand, the realm of ideas, pure forms or essences which were transcendent and therefore untainted by the blemishes of sensation.

For Plato, *a priori* knowledge was proof of transcendence. His dialogues insist that the very fact that there is knowledge independent of experience shows that reason remembers a time when it was unfettered by the body's cage and was free to gaze upon the pure essence of things.[29] The philosophical distinction between *a posteriori* and *a priori* knowledge was thus, for Plato, evidence of the fact that our capture in the illusory realm of phenomena could be opposed to an exteriority characterized by the transcendent truth of the idea.

The *Critique of Pure Reason* overturns the classical tradition by developing a philosophy that is no longer grounded in this basic opposition. "For the disjunctive couple appearance/essence," writes Deleuze, "Kant will substitute the conjunctive couple what appears/conditions of appearance. Everything is new in this."[xx]

With Kant, then, phenomena cease to be trapped by the ancient duality. "It's like a bolt of lightning."[xxi] The world of appearances vanishes and what is left instead, according to Deleuze, is the apparition. "The apparition is what appears in so far as it appears. Full stop. I don't ask myself if there is something behind, I don't ask myself if it is false or not false. The apparition is not at all captured in the oppositional couple, in the binary distinction where we find appearances distinct from essences."[xxii]

No longer bound by the fundamental distinction of classical thought, Kant transforms the meaning and implications of *a priori* knowledge. "In the case of the *a priori*," writes Deleuze, "Kant borrows a word but he completely renews its sense."[xxiii] For unlike Plato, in Kant, the *a priori*, as we will see, is associated with the immanence of abstraction and not the transcendence of the eternal forms. To quote Deleuze: "Kant is the one who discovers the prodigious domain of the transcendental. He is the analogue of the great explorer – not of another world, but of the upper and lower reaches of this one."[xxiv] In opposition to the transcendent ideas and logic of the analytic *a priori*, the synthetic *a priori* constitute a continuous process of production that is both exterior and immanent to our experience of the world. The basic question of transcendental philosophy, 'how are *a priori* synthetic judgments possible?' can thus be restated as follows: given a certain experience what are the conditions that went in to producing it? Kant's answer, as we will see, shows that that which is exterior—or independent—of experience is not a transcendent world above us, but rather an immanent outside. It is this which he calls the transcendental.[30]

29: One of the most famous examples of the Platonic view of the *a priori* occurs in the *Meno*, where Socrates infers the transcendence of the Forms through a slave's knowledge of geometry. See Plato, "Meno," especially pages 363–374.
30: According to Deleuze, "[t]he whole Kantian notion of the transcendental is created in order to refute the classical notion of the transcendent. The transcendental is above

As was noted in the introduction, the classical disjunction between essence and appearance corresponds to the distinction in the philosophy of time between, on the one hand, the phenomena of temporality and change, and, on the other, the essence of eternity. Overturning this classical duality between essence and appearance requires not only a transformation in way we approach phenomena, but also a fundamental reinvention of the philosophy of time. As we will see in this chapter, the discovery of the domain of the transcendental ultimately rests on this reinvention—or revolution—in the nature of time. Deleuze, recognizing this, writes in an introduction to Kant that "all the creations and novelties that Kantianism will bring to philosophy turn on a certain problem of time and an entirely new conception of time."[xxv] It is to this new conception of time which this chapter now turns.

1.1 — The Transcendental Aesthetic: Time as the Form of Inner Sense

'Till now the task we have given ourselves was to represent space, the moment has come to think time.

—Gilles Deleuze, "Kant: Synthesis and Time," 1

With its central divisions, parts, sections, chapters, books, sections of chapters, and chapters of books, the structure of the *Critique of Pure Reason* seems more like the work of a ramshackle artificial intelligence than that of a human being.[31] The immense scale and complexity of Kant's 'thinking machine' is revealed with one glance at the table of contents.

The bulk of the text is divided into two main parts, the 'Transcendental Aesthetic' and the 'Transcendental Logic.' This split corresponds to the central distinction in Kantian thought which divides the intuition from the understanding. Intuition deals with the realm of sensation. Receptive and immediate, it is the form in which the diversity of sense material is presented to the mind. Understanding, on the other

---

all not transcendent" ("Kant: Synthesis and Time," 27).

31: Thomas De Quincey's text, "The Last Days of Immanuel Kant," gives further evidence for this seemingly preposterous claim. Besides the meticulous order of his daily schedule, Kant never perspired, evoked rigorous numerological arrangements for the guests at his dinner table, and, at his deathbed, when all human faculties had left him, was still able to speak at length on any problem in history, philosophy, or mathematics.

hand, is defined as the "spontaneity [in the production] of concepts" (brackets in original).[i] An active mediation rather than a receptive and immediate presentation, understanding serves to represent the perceptions that are given to us in intuition in accordance with the categories of reason. Time appears first in the former category and is defined in the opening section of the *Critique of Pure Reason* as a 'pure intuition,' or the "form of inner sense."[ii]

The 'Transcendental Aesthetic,' "[t]he science of all principles of *a priori* sensibility," begins with a strict process of elimination.[iii] It is concerned only with what is left after both the concepts of the understanding and the matter of sensibility have been stripped away. What remains are what Kant calls the 'pure intuitions,' or 'the form of appearances.' These are defined as the underlying conditions that constitute our perception of the world. The transcendental media for the reception of sensible content, they constitute the structure and form which the apparition must take. For Kant there are only two such forms: space and time.

Kant defines space as "the form of outer sense." It is "the property of our mind" through which "we represent to ourselves objects which are outside us."[iv] Thus, for Kant, space is the form in which the external world is presented to the senses—that is to say, everything that we sense as external to us, we necessarily perceive of as being in space. To quote Kant:

> In order that certain sensations be referred to something outside me (that is, to something in another region of space from that in which I find myself), and similarly in order that I may be able to represent them as outside and alongside one another, and accordingly as not only different but as in different places, the representation of space must be presupposed.[v]

Time, on the other hand, is defined as "the form of inner sense, that is of the intuition of ourselves and of our inner state."[vi] In the 'Transcendental Aesthetic' then, time provides the underlying structure of all our states of mind. It is what conditions the very experience of thought, including our awareness of outer perceptions and the consciousness we have of ourselves. As Kant writes, "everything which belongs to inner determinations is therefore represented in relations of time."[vii]

In the following section we will see that in making time the form of inner sense, Kant revolutionizes the classical philosophy of time both by liberating it from its dependence on change, and by releasing it from an implicit spatial bias.

According to Deleuze, the first great Kantian reversal in the *Critique of Pure Reason* was to free time from its subordination to movement. Taking Hamlet's phrase that 'time is out of joint' and applying it to Kant,[32] Deleuze shows how, in taking time off its hinges, Kant develops a "sort of modern consciousness of time."[viii] In this "modern consciousness," time is separated from the external world of space, and thus undergoes a sort of topological twist. What was once located in the external world is folded in.[33] Time, detached from the movement of that which is outside us, becomes the structuring principle which conditions the inside. Thus, as we will see, in making time the form of inner sense, Kant not only redefines the classical conception of time, but he also transforms the traditional understanding of interiority and its relation to the outside.

In Plato's dichotomized world, time exists only on one side of the mirror. Essences, which are eternal and real, exist in a transcendent realm outside time. Time, on the other hand, belongs to the world of appearances which, according to Plato, is governed by a continuous process of change and movement. For Plato, then, it is change and movement that are the defining features of time.

In his dialogue, *Timaeus*, Plato describes time as the "image of eternity."[ix] He perceives this image in the movement of the stars, and thus equates the production of time with the 'perfect and immutable' cycles within which the planets revolve. "Such was the mind and thought of God in the creation of time. The sun and the moon and five other stars which have the name of planets were created by him in order to distinguish and preserve the numbers of time."[x] In the 'curved time' of a circular universe, Plato's God has bent the sky into an arc. "A Demiurge which makes circles," as Deleuze puts it, has created a world whose map is observed in the heavenly spheres.[xi] Thus, for Plato, 'the name' and 'the number' of time can be found in the changes and motion that take place in the sky.

32: In his text, "On Four Poetic Formulas That Might Summarize the Kantian Philosophy" (found in both *Kant's Critical Philosophy* and in *Essays Critical and Clinical*) Deleuze uses this Shakespearean quotation, 'the time is out of joint,' to explore Kantian thought. To quote Deleuze: "Hamlet is the first hero who truly needed time to act, whereas earlier heroes were subject to time as the consequence of an original movement (Aeschylus) or an aberrant action (Sophocles). The *Critique of Pure Reason* is the book of Hamlet, the prince of the north" (28).

33: To quote Kant: "Time is not something which exists of itself, or which inheres in things as an objective determination, and it does not, therefore, remain when abstraction is made of all subjective conditions of its intuition. [...] Time is nothing but the subjective condition under which alone intuition can take place in us" (*Critique of Pure Reason*, 76 [A33/B49]).

Kant's break with Plato is absolute. For according to the First *Critique*, movement is empirical, which is to say it exists at the level of experience. Transcendental philosophy, Kant writes, "cannot count the concept of change among its *a priori* data."[xii] For Kant, the revolutions of the stars, the swing of a pendulum, and the sand in an hourglass all occur *in* time and, as such, fall outside the problematic of critique. Plato's perfect image cannot be time, for "time itself does not change, but only something which is in time."[xiii] According to Kant, time explains the possibility of movement, but movement is not time. "The concept of alteration, and with it the concept of motion, as alteration of place," he writes, "is possible only through and in the representation of time."[xiv]

Thus, Kant liberates the form of time from the endless cycle of the Platonic world. Time is no longer contained within the circular revolutions of the planets. Instead, it is the relation of time to motion itself that revolves. In Kant, writes Deleuze, "time is no longer related to the movement which it measures, but movement is related to the time which conditions it."[xv] The *Critique of Pure Reason* conceives of a 'straight line' of time that is cut off from its subordination to all that exists in time.[34] To quote from Deleuze:

> Time is no longer coiled up in such a way that it is subordinated to the measure of something other than itself, such as, for example, astronomical movement. Everything happens as if, having been coiled up so as to measure the passage of celestial bodies, time unrolls itself like a sort of serpent, it shakes off all subordination to a movement or a nature, it becomes time in itself for itself, it becomes pure and empty time. It measures nothing anymore. Time has taken on its own excessiveness. It is out of its joints, which is to say its subordination to nature; it's now nature which is subordinated to it.[xvi]

34: It is interesting to note that Foucault, when writing of Deleuze, evokes the 'straightening' of time that is initially produced by the First *Critique*. "The circle must be abandoned as a faulty principle of return; we must abandon our tendency to organize everything into a sphere. All things return on the straight and narrow by way of a straight and labyrinth line" ("Theatrum Philosophicum," 166). This notion of the straight labyrinth of time is used by Deleuze to designate the transcendental form of time. In the preface to *Kant's Critical Philosophy*, he writes as follows: "We move from one labyrinth to another. The labyrinth is no longer a circle, or a spiral which would translate its complications, but a thread, a straight line, all the more mysterious for being simple, inexorable as Borges says, 'the labyrinth which is composed of a single straight line, and which is indivisible, incessant'" (vii). Deleuze also uses the notion of a straight labyrinth to describe the time of Aeon (a concept that will be discussed in detail in chapter three).

Since time is already presupposed in motion, Kant, 'the great explorer,' must begin to search elsewhere. Looking behind objects to discover the conditions of their production, Kant finds that time is "not an empirical concept that has been derived from any experience."[xvii] In the abstract realm of the transcendental, Kant discovers a form of time that is independent of the experience of motion.

It would first appear that Kant finds a predecessor in Aristotle, who modifies the Platonic vision by making a distinction between motion and time. Though Aristotle connects time to the cycles of astronomical change, he does not equate it with them. His argument instead rests on two points. First, while time exists everywhere, movement only occurs in particular things, and second, while things that move can be either fast or slow, time itself does not shift in speed. "It is evident, then," writes Aristotle, "that time is neither movement nor independent of movement."[xviii]

In order to discover the precise relation between motion and time, Aristotle turns to numbers. To quote his famous formula, "time is just this—number of motion."[xix] The circular revolutions, the heavenly spheres are still linked to time, but the two are no longer directly equivalent. "Time is not movement, but only movement," writes Aristotle "in so far as it admits of enumeration."[xx] Change must be numbered for it to be time.

"Time, then," for Aristotle, "is a kind of number."[xxi] The kind of number that it is, however, rests on a distinction made in the *Physics* between the "number with which we count," and "the number of things which are counted."[xxii] To quote from the *Physics:* "Number, we must note, is used in two ways—both of what is counted or countable and also of that which we count. Time, then, is what is counted, not that with which we count: these are different kinds of thing."[xxiii]

Thus, Aristotle, like Kant, seeks to discover time by shifting focus away from the concreteness of astronomy. However, as we will see, the abstraction he makes in the direction of number is ultimately subordinated to empirical movement. For according to Aristotle, the numbers of time are determined as "the measure of a quantity of change."[xxiv/†]

For Kant, as for Aristotle, time is conceived as being fundamentally numeric. Kant recognizes that any representation cannot help but serve to spatialize time, and since time "yields no shape," it cannot be represented.[xxv] Still, he focuses on a single spatial image that will function as an analogy for his new form of time. In Kant, the closest we get to time in space is the image of the real number line.[35] "We represent the time

---

35: Commentator Alfredo Ferrarin makes much of this, arguing that in Kant, numbering and arithmetic are practically synonymous with the generation of time.

sequence," he writes, "by a line progressing to infinity, in which the manifold constitutes a series of one dimension only; and we reason from the properties of this line to all the properties of time."[36/xxvi]

Yet despite the fact that both Kant and Aristotle link time to number, Kant breaks with Aristotle no less than with Plato. For in freeing time from its subordination to movement, Kant had to uncouple number from measurement. In the domain of the transcendental, the numerical processes of time are unhinged from the concreteness of change. With Kant, the number of time thus breaks from Aristotle's classical formula, ceasing to function as 'the quantity of motion'; the 'things that are counted' become 'that with which we count.'

It is easier to understand what is at stake in this reversal if we map Aristotle's distinction in the philosophy of numbers on to the difference between cardinal and ordinal numbers. Cardinal numbers (*e.g.*, one, two, three...) are used to express amount or quantity. Ordinal numbers, on the other hand, are used to express position (*e.g.*, first, second, third...). Bound to keep track of that which it belongs to, the cardinal number is tied down, attached to what is in time. "Cardinal," writes Deleuze, "comes from cardo; cardo is precisely the hinge, the hinge around which the sphere of celestial bodies turns, and which makes them pass time and again through the so-called cardinal points."[xxvii] Ordinal numbers, on the other hand, are indifferent to the space of measurement. What counts, for them, is order not measure.[37] In unchaining time from its bonds to what is in time, Kant simultaneously freed numbers from their subordination to measurement. As Deleuze writes, in Kant's 'new definition of time,' number "ceases to be cardinal and becomes ordinal, a pure *order* of time."[xxviii]

In the end, therefore, despite the differences between Plato's and Aristotle's conceptions of time, from the perspective of transcendental

---

36: This sentence continues as follows: "with this one exception, that while the parts of the line are simultaneous the parts of time are always successive" (Kant, *Critique of Pure Reason*, 77 [A33/B50]). Yet, it is important to note that while the parts of time are successive, time itself, for Kant, is not. Deleuze is insistent on this point. "Time," he writes, "is no longer defined by succession because succession concerns only things and movements which are in time. If time itself were succession, it would need to succeed in another time, and on to infinity. Things succeed each other in various times, but they are also simultaneous in the same time, and they remain in an indefinite time. It is no longer a question of defining time by succession, nor space by simultaneity, nor permanence by eternity. Permanence, succession and simultaneity are modes and relationships of time" (*Kant's Critical Philosophy*, vii–viii).

37: A familiar example of ordinal numbering is that used by the library cataloguing system. It is clear, in this case, that what is important is the order of the books and not the amount of space between them.

philosophy, they are basically alike, for both belong to "a certain tradition of antiquity, in which time is fundamentally subordinated to something which happens in it, and this something can be determined as being change."[xxix] By separating time from the heavenly spheres and making number independent of motion, Kant thus splits with an entire tradition. Operating with the conjunction 'what appears/conditions of appearance,' Kant creates (or discovers) a disjunction between the form of time itself, and the changes which occur in time.

This distinction between the abstract form of time and the changes which occur within it requires that time be released from its spatial determinations. In the *Critique of Pure Reason*, time is no longer located in the objects of the world (or in their relations) but is situated instead in an abstract realm that is independent from our perceptions of space. The transcendental form of time, as we have seen, is an empty form, conceived of as nothing but a pure, ordinal sequence. Since time has no spatial dimension, even the number line is but an analogy.

In the 'Transcendental Aesthetic,' space, as we have seen, captures the whole of exteriority inside itself. Thus, in order to separate time from space, time, which was once located in the external world, must be folded in. For according to the First *Critique*, the only thing that is not in space is the inner determinations of our mind. In making time the 'form of inner sense,' Kant thus locates time in the singular domain which exists outside the representation of space.

This process of interiorization gives time a certain dominance over space. For according to Kant, everything that we represent as in space must also be processed by time precisely insofar as it is experienced (and thus belongs to our inner states). "Appearances," writes Kant, "may, one and all, vanish; but time (as the universal condition of their possibility) cannot itself be removed."[xxx] Thus, for Kant, while everything that exists is in time, time is the one thing that does not exist in space, since everything in space 'already' presupposes time.[38] To quote from the First *Critique*:

> Time is the formal *a priori* condition of all appearances whatsoever. Space, as the pure form of all *outer* intuition, is so far limited; it serves as the *a priori* condition only of outer appearances. But since all representations, whether they have for their objects outer things or not, belong in themselves, as determinations of the mind, to our inner state; and since this inner state stands

---

38: From the perspective of transcendental philosophy, then, William S. Burroughs' formula, "The only way out of time is into space" can only be a trick (*Ah Pook Is Here*, 19).

under the formal condition of inner intuition, and so belongs to time, time is an *a priori* condition of all appearances whatsoever. [...] Just as I can say *a priori* that all outer appearances are in space, and are determined *a priori* in conformity with the relations of space, I can also say, from the principle of inner sense, that all appearances whatsoever, that is, all objects of the senses, are in time, and necessarily stand in time-relations.[xxxi]

Once abstracted and interiorized, time takes on enormous new powers. Productive of the actual rhythm of thought and sensation, it gains control over the whole of experience. Time, as the form of interiority, is thus absolutely inescapable. Everything we see, think, feel, hear, and know has already been given a speed, an order, and a rhythm in time. With Kant, then, the inside ceases to be conceived of as an empirical container and is instead thought transcendentally, as an interiority over against space and not merely in space. One can never escape time, since time is a limit that works us from the inside. Yet, as Deleuze notes, there is something very strange in this notion of time as interior limit.

To think time means to substitute for the classical schema of an exterior limitation of thought by the extended, the very very strange idea of an interior limit to thought which works it from the inside, which doesn't at all come from outside, which doesn't at all come from the opacity of a substance. As if there was in thought something impossible to think. As if thought was worked over from the inside by something that it cannot think.[xxxii]

In moving from transcendence to the transcendental, Kant reworks both the inside and the outside. Time conditions an inescapable interiority, but in doing so opens a new and more radical exteriority since the production of time itself cannot be captured 'within' time. In other words, the one thing that is not interior to time is the transcendental form of time itself. Thus, in discovering the abstract realm of the transcendental, Kant unmasks an unanticipated, immanent exteriority—an outside that does not transcend the world but that is no less alien for that. "The greatest initiative of transcendental philosophy," writes Deleuze, "was to introduce the form of time into thought."[xxxiii] Yet, as the next section will show, it is only a very particular mode of thought that can process Kant's modern consciousness of time, for Kant revolutionizes the interiority of thought only by immersing it in the exteriority of time.

1.2 — The Transcendental Deduction: Time and the 'I Think'

How can man think what he does not think, inhabit as though by a mute occupation something that eludes him, animate with a kind of frozen movement that figure of himself that takes the form of a stubborn exteriority?

—Michel Foucault, *The Order of Things*, 323

It's wrong to say: I think. Better to say: I am thought. Pardon the pun. *I* is an *other*.

—Arthur Rimbaud, *Complete Works*, 113

I am separated from myself by the form of time.

—Gilles Deleuze, *Kant's Critical Philosophy*, ix

In modern philosophical thought, it is Descartes who first secures the borders which separate the inside from the outside. His book, *The Meditations*, assures the divide by devising what has become one of philosophy's most familiar horror stories.[39] Deeply suspicious of appearances, Descartes speculates that God has been replaced by an evil demon who tricks us into taking the exterior world for reality. Determined to escape these demonic delusions, Descartes supposes "that the heavens, the air, the earth, colors, figures, sounds and all external things are nothing other than the playful deceptions of dreams by means of which he [the demon] has set traps for my credulity."[i] Stripped of all faith in reason and truth, Descartes imagines the external world as a mad and uncontrollable experiment. The senses, which grant us access to this outside world, must no longer be trusted. Even the certainties of abstract truths as are found in mathematics and geometry must be questioned. For once the demon has been let in, there is no telling how far his influence extends. Plagued by a powerful and cunning entity bent on deception, Descartes tries to flee from the demon, demarcating the outside by a rigorous process of philosophical doubt.

Yet, as time passes, Descartes manages to gain control and dispel the horror which torments him. Turning in on himself, Descartes discovers that the doubt which haunts the outside serves to ground the

---

39: As Slavoj Žižek writes, the Cartesian *cogito* "opens up, for a brief moment, the hypothesis of the Evil Genius who, behind my back, dominates me and pulls the strings of what I experience as reality" (*Tarrying with the Negative*, 12).

inside in an undeniable certainty.[40] The fact that I doubt, *The Meditations* famously conclude, assures me that I exist. For "when I doubt, there is one thing which I cannot doubt, which is that as a self that doubts, I think."[ii] In doubting the objects, properties, truths, and sensations of the external world, Descartes thus carves out a secure container for the subject's insides. The famous formula, 'I think therefore I am,' guards us against the demonic games that threaten our perception and knowledge of the outside world.

Separated from the dubious nature of exteriority, the Cartesian subject thus finds its protection by folding in. For though everything outside us may be a trick, nothing, Descartes contends, can fool us about what exists inside. Guarded by the security of self-consciousness, Descartes uses the boundaries of a conscious interiority to rebuild his faith in the external world. After Descartes, it is this certainty of interiority which has become the sure foundation for philosophical inquiry.[41] Schopenhauer describes it as follows:

> By his taking *cogito ergo sum* as the only thing certain, and provisionally regarding the existence of the world as problematical, the essential and only correct starting point, and at the same time the true point of support, of all philosophy was really found. This point, indeed, is essentially and of necessity the *subjective, our own consciousness*. For this alone is that which is immediate; everything else, be it what it may, is first mediated by consciousness, and therefore dependent on it. It is thus rightly considered that the philosophy of the moderns starts with Descartes as its father.[iii]

It would seem from the traditional account of the Copernican Revolution, with its emphasis on the synthetic powers of the human intellect, that the *Critique of Pure Reason* is a continuation of this basic line. In focusing on the constitutive inner powers of human subjectivity, Kant, according to this interpretation, outlines a philosophical position that—in Cartesian fashion—prioritizes the inside. By positioning reason at the

---

40: To quote Descartes: "Yet there is a deceiver—I know not who he is—, most highly powerful and most highly cunning, who always industriously deceives me. If he is deceiving me, then without doubt *I* also am. And he might deceive me as much as he can, he will still never effect that I would be nothing, so long as I shall cogitate that I am something. So that—all things having been weighed enough, and more—this statement were, finally, to be established: '*I am, I exist*' is necessarily true, so often as it is uttered by me or conceived by the mind" (*Meditations*, 101).

41: As Land notes, "doubt was only a detour to a more secure edifice of knowledge" ("Delighted to Death," 77).

centre of the universe and concentrating on the legislative powers of the understanding, critique, according to this reading, reinforces the subject discovered by Descartes. Kant's 'modernity,' from this perspective, consists in his belief that the external world of representations is generated by the productive powers of interiority.

All this dissolves, however, with the contention that Kant's 'modern consciousness' stems not from his repositioning of the subject, but from his redefinition of time. For in making time the form of inner sense, Kant subordinates the certainty of interiority to the productive forces of temporalization. Transcendental philosophy, as we will see, abandons the Cartesian line by conceiving of an inside that is passive in relation to the immanent exteriority of time. Dismantling the security of interiority by discovering an outside line that divides the inside from within, the *Critique of Pure Reason* riddles interiority with the difference between the receptive nature of what exists in time, and the synthesizing processes of the form of time itself. With Kant, then, the certainty of self-consciousness dissolves into questions about the relation of time to itself. Critical thought thus not only differentiates itself from the tradition of modern philosophy which stems from Descartes, it fractures its very foundations.

As we have seen in the discussion of the 'Transcendental Aesthetic,' the First *Critique* divides the inside from the outside through the distinction that it makes between space and time. Space, for Kant, as the form of outer sense, constitutes the structure in which the objects of the external world are presented to the mind. The form of interiority, on the other hand, is time. Kant here defines the outside as that which exists in space and the inside as that which occurs in time. Yet, as we have already noted, since the exteriority of space is mediated by the inner determinations of the mind, everything that is in space is also in time. For Kant, then, all our experiences, whether internal or external, are inescapably conditioned by the order and relations of time.

From the perspective of transcendental philosophy, Cartesian doubt has an implicit spatial bias. Descartes seems far more concerned with the ways in which the evil demon may be deceiving us about the external world of space than he is with the deception that might be taking place in the internal realm of time.[42] This becomes startlingly apparent

---

42: Though Descartes claims that amongst the things which he doubts is the "time through which they [things] may endure," this has little practical consequence, for Descartes' reconstruction of certainty occurs inside the passage of temporal succession—that is, the days in which *The Meditations* unfold (*Meditations*, 93). Thus, though Descartes claims he is questioning time, his philosophical method does little to challenge the interior structure of time.

when one recognizes that *The Meditations*, structured around a series of successive days, is governed by a strict temporality.[43] Duped by the comfort of self-consciousness, Descartes seems blind to the fact that his entire philosophical method unfolds inside a structure that is conditioned by time. Kant's break with Descartes must be located here. It is impossible for Kant to make the inside the 'true point of support for philosophy' since the thought of the transcendental insists that the inside is produced by the alterity of time.

This notion of time as the productive force of interiority depends, first of all, on shifting the line which separates the inside from the outside. The border which Descartes locates at the break between the certainty of self-consciousness and the doubt which haunts our knowledge of the outside world is radically altered by the First *Critique*. With Kant, the division between interiority and exteriority, as we have seen, ultimately corresponds to the distinction between the empirical realm of experience and the transcendental plane, which is to say that in Kant, the inside is defined as that which occurs in time, while the outside is left to the only thing which escapes this interiority, that is the abstract and productive forces of time itself.

In focusing on this distinction—between time and what is in time—Kant dramatically diminishes the importance of self-consciousness. For consciousness of ourselves, to use Schopenhauer's term for the basis of Descartes' philosophy, is, for Kant, relegated to the level of the empirical. It is an experience which happens in time. Recognizing that 'I am' is a verb conditioned by temporality,[44] Kant thus questions the very core of the Cartesian formula. "The proposition 'I think' or 'I exist thinking,'" writes Kant, "is an empirical proposition."[iv] To quote from the First *Critique*:

43: Deleuze claims that this structure of *The Meditations* makes it "the first text to introduce time into philosophical discourse." For unlike previous philosophical texts, with Descartes, the unfolding of temporal succession has positive implications for what can or cannot be said. In Descartes, says Deleuze, "there is a temporality which has unfolded which meant that he could not say in the second what he will say in the fifth [Meditation]" ("Kant: Synthesis and Time," 37). There is undoubtedly an irony here, for despite the fact that time operates in *The Meditations* as a positive structuring principle, Descartes nevertheless ignores the operations of time when securing his philosophical foundations.

44: As Deleuze writes, the assertion 'I am a thing which thinks' serves—however implicitly—to bind the 'I think' to a determinate entity in time: "We cannot say with Descartes 'I think, therefore I am. I am a thing which thinks.' If it is true that the *I think* is a determination, it implies in this respect an indeterminate existence (*I am*). But nothing so far tells us under what form this existence is determined by the *I think*: it is determinable only in time, under the form of time, thus as the existence of a phenomenal, receptive or changing ego" (*Kant's Critical Philosophy*, viii).

> Consciousness of self according to the determinations of our
> state of inner perception is merely empirical, and always chang-
> ing. No fixed and abiding self can present itself in this flux of
> inner appearances. Such consciousness is usually named *inner
> sense*, or *empirical apperception*.[v]

Therefore, what Descartes perceived as an asylum from doubt becomes in Kant, a constantly changing "flux of inner appearances" which
constitutes not the stability of the I think, but the superficiality of the
empirical ego.

The ego, then, according to Kant, is in a passive or receptive relation to the structuring principles which condition it. As Deleuze writes,
"the Ego itself is in time, and thus constantly changing: it is a passive or
rather receptive Ego, which experiences changes in time."[vi] No longer
transparent to itself, the subject becomes an entity continually affected
by something which it cannot reach. For the experience of interiority,
like all inner determinations of the mind, has necessarily been structured
by time as the form of inner sense. The primary position granted to the
self as an object of awareness is thus subordinated in Kant to the synthesizing processes of time. Caught inside the web of temporality, the
being which doubts cannot serve as a foundation since, according to
critical thought, we only know the ego after it has already been given a
sequence, an order, and a rhythm by time. Critical philosophy is thus led
to an extremely strange assertion. According to Kant, the 'spontaneous'
activity of the synthetic *a priori* which characterizes the subject of the
Copernican Revolution must be separated entirely from the knowledge
of what goes on in our minds.

In the *Critique of Pure Reason*, Kant describes this curious consequence as the paradox of inner sense. Foreshadowed in the
'Transcendental Aesthetic,' but only fully brought to light in the
'Transcendental Deduction,' the paradox of inner sense, writes Kant,
arises from the fact that "this sense represents to consciousness even
our own selves only as we appear to ourselves not as we are in ourselves. For we intuit ourselves only as we are inwardly affected, and this
would seem to be contradictory since we would then have to be in a
passive relation [of active affection] to ourselves" (brackets in original).[vii] The self of transcendental philosophy is paradoxically split, fractured by a line that separates the consciousness of an empirical ego
from an unconscious, 'Transcendental I.' Moreover, the riddle continues, we are only conscious of ourselves after we have been worked over
by that part of ourselves that we can never know, for one only becomes
aware of the ego after it has affected itself from within. For Kant, then,

inner sense is governed by a complicated circuit in which the self is 'auto-affected' by 'another.'

This paradox which haunts Kant's notion of interiority is, as we have seen, a necessary consequence of the transcendental method, for the fundamental conjunction of critical thought—'what are the conditions of appearance?'—demands that one look behind empirical reality to the abstract forces which condition it. According to Kant's Copernican Revolution, our experience of ourselves is not given, it is produced. Thus, for Kant, knowledge of the empirical ego is not an answer but a riddle, for the concrete experience of interiority is incapable of revealing the abstract transcendental conditions of its own production. Thus, it is the very nature of transcendental production that ensures the shift away from the subject to time, for the only thing that can produce the experience of being in time is the operation of time itself.

Thus far, the transcendental notion of time has been described as an abstract and empty form defined as nothing but a pure, ordinal sequence. Taken on its own, however, this description is severely limited, and it is in danger of missing the fundamentally productive nature of the transcendental. Spontaneous and active, time at its most abstract is characterized by a continuous process of production. The form of temporality, for Kant, is, above all, not a static eternity. For as we will see, time, in transcendental philosophy, is made up of blind acts of synthesis continually at work producing the experience of a world that exists in time.

These productive capacities of the transcendental form of time are outlined by Kant in his discussion of the threefold synthesis set out in the first part of the 'Transcendental Deduction.' Before exploring these syntheses in detail, it is important to stress, once again, that Kantian synthesis occurs in a realm independent of experience. The threefold synthesis outlined in the 'Transcendental Deduction' comprises *a priori* machines that underlie experience. As Deleuze writes, they do "not bear on diversity as it appears in space and time, but on the diversity of space and time themselves. Indeed, without them, space and time would not be 'represented.'"[viii]

Kant's discussion of the threefold synthesis, then, is an attempt to uncover the productive, constituting forces of the form of time itself. "All our knowledge," writes Kant in the introduction to the section, "is thus finally subject to time, the formal condition of inner sense. In it they must all be ordered, connected and brought into relation."[ix] The synthetic processes of the 'Transcendental Deduction' are meant to explain the means through which this occurs, and Kant's goal is to explain how the transcendental form of time functions to put the world in time. The focus, then, is not on a realm of production that occurs in time, but rather on the 'spontaneous' activity that accounts for the abstract possibility of the very experience of time.

After cautioning the reader of the difficulties which will inevitably beset an enterprise "never before attempted," Kant begins his discussion with what he calls 'the synthesis of apprehension in intuition.' "Directed upon intuition," the 'synthesis of apprehension,' is located in the receptive domain of sensibility.[x] It transforms our intuitions into a grid that renders them capable of being perceived. For according to Kant, as Deleuze makes clear, there is not only a diversity that exists in time, but a diversity of time itself. The very possibility of perception thus requires that this diversity be synthesized. For intuition to take place, the unrepresentable multiplicity of time must be made representable. The 'synthesis of apprehension' fulfills this requirement by combining the manifold of intuition into the units that constitute moments in time. It thus operates, as Deleuze writes, to "produce the different parts of time."[xi]

The second synthesis, the 'synthesis of reproduction in the imagination,' is the act through which the imagination ensures the *a priori* rules which determine the "sequence or coexistence"† of appearances. It is, according to Deleuze, "the means by which we reproduce the preceding parts as we arrive at the ones following."[xii] Without this second synthesis, the order and association of representations would be completely random.

> If cinnabar were sometimes red, sometimes black, sometimes light, sometimes heavy, if a man changed sometimes into this and sometimes into that animal form, if the country on the longest day were sometimes covered with fruit, sometimes with ice and snow, my empirical imagination would never find opportunity when representing red to bring to mind heavy cinnabar.[xiii]

'The synthesis of reproduction' is thus the transcendental ground which ensures the reproducibility of experience. It is the means through which past appearances are duplicated and thus assures the coexistence and order of that which appears in time.

The third and final synthesis Kant calls 'the synthesis of recognition in a concept.' By relating the synthesized manifold to the concepts of the understanding, 'the synthesis of recognition' allows one to recognize what has been intuited and reproduced by the other synthetic operations. According to Kant, it is only through this final synthesis that one gains knowledge of the objects of experience. For "that which constitutes knowledge," writes Deleuze, "is not simply the act by which the manifold is synthesized, but the act by which the represented manifold is related to an object (recognition: this is a table, this is an apple, this is such and such an object)."[xiv] In the *Critique of Pure Reason*, it is 'the synthesis of recognition' which ensures the continuity of time, for in order to recognize any given object as identical in different times, there must be a synthesis capable of guaranteeing identity through time.

Through this final synthesis, Kant deduces what is known as 'the synthetic unity of apperception': the "pure original unchangeable consciousness" which constitutes the Kantian 'I think.'[xv] The ability to recognize the same object as identical in different times requires, according to Kant, a unity of consciousness—an unchanging identity—which ensures the temporal continuity necessary for recognition to take place (from the side of the transcendental subject). Transcendental apperception, then, is the necessary "condition which precedes all experience, and which makes experience itself possible."[xvi] Defined simply as "numerically identical," it is the synthetic operation which explains the continuity of experience, guaranteeing that all my experience belongs to me.[45/xvii]

As we have seen, it is with the notion of the 'Transcendental I' that Kant most clearly reveals his radical departure from the modern philosophical line that has its roots in Descartes. The security of self-consciousness which serves as the ground for Cartesian thought rests on the identity that exists between the knowledge of the *I think*, and the temporally determined, conscious entity that *I am*. The Kantian 'I' on the other hand, does not correspond to any determinate entity.[46] For, as has already been noted, the self of transcendental philosophy is paradoxically split, fractured by a line that separates the consciousness of empirical experience from the unconscious realm of the synthetic *a priori*. As Deleuze writes, "the I and the Ego are thus separated by the line of time which relates them to each other, but under the conditions of a fundamental difference."[xviii] By defining interiority through the split be-

---

45: As Deleuze writes, "My representations are mine in so far as they are linked in the unity of a consciousness in such a way that the 'I think' accompanies them" (*Kant's Critical Philosophy*, 15).

46: According to Deleuze, this notion that the *I think* is not attached to a determinate entity is at the heart of Kant's objection to Descartes. With the Cartesian *cogito*, writes Deleuze, "the I think is an act of instantaneous determination, which implies an undetermined existence (*I am*) and determines this existence as that of a thinking substance (I am *a thing that thinks*). But how can the determination apply to the undetermined if we cannot say under what form it is 'determinable'?" ("On Four Formulas," 29). With this objection Kant profoundly challenges the Cartesian formulation which equates the empty representation 'I think' to the determinate substance 'I am a thing which thinks.'

tween time as an abstract synthetic process and the concrete determination of that which exists in time, transcendental philosophy conceives of a self that is based on the absolute difference between the 'Transcendental I' and the empirical ego.

Critique demarcates this difference by a rigorous determination of the boundaries of knowledge. The Ego, as consciousness of inner sense, admits knowledge whereas the I, for Kant, can never be known (but is always presupposed in knowing). Existing in a realm outside all experience, transcendental apperception is never the object of direct awareness. Devoid of all logical characteristics, the I, writes Kant, is nothing other than a numerical identity. Empty of all content, stripped of its ties to substance or personality, the I becomes an empty slot. Necessary to explain the very possibility of experience, the 'Transcendental I' can be thought but never known. Transcendental apperception is thus philosophy's final answer to the Oracle at Delphi. For Kant, 'know thyself' has become a rigorous impossibility, an illegitimate use of reason.

There is then, in Kant, a radical difference between what we are, and what we know ourselves to be. For according to the 'paradox of inner sense' we are only conscious of ourselves after we have been worked over by that part of ourselves that we can never know. Kant thus posits a subject that is exterior in relation to itself.[47] An empty synthetic process that accompanies all your representations, the I in Kant is so named not because it exists inside you, but because wherever you are, it is. In Deleuze's reading of Kant, this finds its expression in Rimbaud's formula 'I is an *other*.'

What this section has sought to show is that this 'other' is time. Deduced from the temporal continuity that underlies experience, transcendental apperception is determined solely as the agent of the transcendental form of time. For Kant, as per Deleuze, "I is an act which constantly carries out the synthesis of time."[xix] Thus, while the ego marks the interiority of the subject, the I can only be defined as the exteriority of time. In introducing time into thought, Kant inserts an irreparable fissure into the core of the subject. To quote Deleuze: "the form of interiority means not only that time is internal to us but that our interiority constantly divides us from ourselves, splits us in two."[xx]

47: This notion of a subject in an exterior relation to itself has obvious resonance with the psychoanalytic distinction between the Ego and the Id. Freud himself recognized that his notion of the unconscious borrowed much from transcendental thought. "The psycho-analytic assumption of unconscious mental activity appears to us," he writes in his essay "The Unconscious," "as an extension of the corrections undertaken by Kant" (577).

According to Heinrich Heine, the name of Immanuel Kant "has the might of an exorcism." His thought, Heine writes "was a revolution, and one not wanting in horrors."[xxi] Even "night-wandering spirits are filled with terror" at the sight of Kant's *Critique of Pure Reason*.[xxii] Deleuze agrees: Kant's "thinking machine is absolutely frightening."[xxiii] This fright arises from the fact that Kant has transformed the nature of philosophical horror, replacing Cartesian fear with a sort of transcendental dread against which the certainty that guards us against the demon is powerless. For Kant, there is no security in self-consciousness, for it is nothing but a mask. By implanting uncertainty at the core of interiority, Kant riddles even the *cogito* with doubt. Like the replicants in the film *Blade Runner* (1982), transcendental philosophy thus torments the subject with the taunting refrain, 'you are not what you think you are.'[48] With Kant, then, "everything happens as if the 'enemy' of thought was within."[xxiv] This enemy—the transcendental outside—does not exist in another time or another space. Its exteriority consists only of the fact that it knows nothing of borders. Thus, unlike Descartes' demon, it can neither be locked out nor contained. One no longer needs to be afraid that the 'reality' of outer perceptions is a trick, for Kant's 'modern consciousness of time' plagued us with a much more intimate fear. Surrounding us in an inaccessible exteriority which infiltrates the inside at the very level of its production, the Kantian outside (or the syntheses of time) not only constitutes the experience of the external world, it generates the very experience of ourselves. As Deleuze writes, with Kant, "it is not time that is interior to us; it is we who are interior to time."[xxv]

1.3 — The Schematism: Time and Abstraction

In "Theatrum Philosophicum," Michel Foucault proposes that all philosophy can be defined according to its underlying antagonism towards the principal figure of classical thought. "What philosophy," he writes, "has not tried to overturn Platonism? [...] Are all philosophies individual species of the genus 'anti-Platonic'? Does each begin with a declaration of this fundamental rejection?"[i] These questions, when applied to Kant, will serve as the guiding thread in the final pages of this chapter. For to follow Kant in his exploration of transcendental time

---

48: In *Tarrying with the Negative*, Žižek writes of *Blade Runner* as a Kantian film: "In *Blade Runner*, Deckard, after learning that Rachel is a replicant who (mis)perceives herself as human, asks in astonishment: 'How can it not know what it is?' We can see, now, how more than two hundred years ago, Kant's philosophy outlined an answer to this enigma" (15).

demands, as Foucault suggests, a return to critique's initial declaration, a fundamental rejection of transcendence.

The *Critique of Pure Reason*, as has already been noted, overturns Platonism by discovering an abstract form of time that has been freed from its subordination to movement. It would be a mistake, however, to assume that this implies that Kant's argument with Plato can be restricted to any particular zone or dialogue, for the notion of abstract time does much more than transform the ancient conception of temporality.[49] As this section will make clear, abstract time subverts Plato at his core by revolutionising the notion of abstraction as such

It is important to note from the start, however, that these two moves, the redefinition of time and the reformulation of the abstract, are ultimately indistinguishable, as critical thought only makes time abstract by equating the abstract with time-production. This circuit, explicated in the chapter on 'The Schematism,' serves to distinguish abstraction from the transcendence of the philosophical idea. No longer distant and withdrawn from its concrete instantiations, abstraction, in Kant, becomes directly implementable. Operating as the general medium of exchange,[50] abstract time is not a transcendent form situated beyond the world of phenomena but becomes instead the immanent plane of the transcendental.

Thus, abandoning both the interiority of the subject and the transcendent, eternal idea, the *Critique of Pure Reason* subordinates thought to the abstract production of time. For this reason, the attempt to situate Kant in the 'anti-Platonic genus' that defines philosophy will inevitably prove inadequate. Foucault's questions, when applied to critique, are not definitive but strategic. Having discovered the abstract synthetic machine which constitutively underpins the philosophical idea, Kant becomes immersed in a revolution that extends far beyond the history of ideas. For, as we will see in the following chapter, the Kantian notion of transcendental time has at least as much to do with capitalism as it does with philosophy.

To begin to unravel these claims requires an examination of the role given to time in the chapter on 'The Schematism.' A notoriously difficult concept in Kant, 'The Schematism' is best understood by the cru-

---

49: Plato's most explicit discussion of time is found in the dialogue "Timaeus," but as we will see, the Kantian engagement with Plato has implications which extend far beyond this particular dialogue.

50: As the 'third thing' which functions to connect the two heterogeneous parts of the system, 'The Schematism' has certain similarities to the abstraction which Marx sees as necessary to the production of exchange-value. This will be discussed in further detail in chapter two.

cial function that it serves. Put simply, the schema is a 'monogram' or diagram which connects the faculty of sensation discussed in the 'Transcendental Aesthetic' with the faculty of understanding as discussed in the 'Transcendental Logic.' The difference between sensation and understanding, as has been previously stated, is one of the basic distinctions at work in the *Critique of Pure Reason*. The schematism, as the abstract plane that connects these two sides, is thus the necessary link which provides coherence to the underlying structure of the First *Critique*.

The 'Transcendental Aesthetic,' as was shown in the first section of this chapter, is dedicated to a discussion of time and space as the *a priori* forms of sensation. Though animated by the synthesis of intuition, these pure forms, according to Kant, are essentially receptive in nature. They act on what is given, ordering sense data into a transcendental grid. As Deleuze writes, they are the "means by which we pose the manifold as occupying a certain space and *a certain* time."[ii] Dedicated to the presentation of the manifold, the faculty of sensation synthesizes the diversity of intuition into an image capable of being perceived.

The understanding, on the other hand, is defined as the spontaneous production of *a priori* concepts. In the 'Transcendental Logic,' Kant outlines these concepts in what is known as the table of categories. Twelve in number, the categories are laid out in four groups of three, with specific principles which determine both their order and their relations. By making use of the table of categories, the understanding provides knowledge through the act of representation. Deleuze describes this as follows: "The important thing in representation is the prefix: *re*-presentation implies an active taking up of that which is presented; hence an activity and a unity distinct from the diversity which characterize sensibility as such."[iii]

Thus, by the time one reaches the chapter on the schematism, the realm of the transcendental has been divided, split between, on the one side, the production of the image, and, on the other, the production of concepts. Yet insofar as these processes remain separated, they work in vain, for neither thoughts nor perceptions are capable on their own of constituting experience. To quote Kant's famous formula: "Without sensibility no object would be given to us, without understanding no object would be thought. Thoughts without contents are empty, intuitions without concepts are blind."[iv] According to the First *Critique* therefore, there can be no account of knowledge which does not synthesize our *a priori* understanding of the concepts with our intuition of the objects of experience. Crucial here is the fact that for Kant, unlike for Plato, concepts only gain their legislative power through some ulterior

I: Quantity (Time Series)	Judgements	Category	Schematism
	Universal	Unity	Number
	Particular	Plurality	Number
	Singular	Totality	Number
II: Quality (Time Content)	Affirmative	Reality	Being in time
	Negative	Negation	Not being in time
	Infinite	Limitation	Intensive degree
III: Relation (Time Order)	Categorical	Of Inherence and Subsistence	Permanence in time
	Hypothetical	Of Causality and Dependence	Succession
	Disjunctive	Of Community (reciprocity between agent and patient)	Coexistence
IV: Modality (Scope of Time)	Problematic	Possibility-Impossibility	Determination at some time or another
	Assertoric	Existence-Nonexistence	Existence in some determinate time
	Apodeictic	Necessity-Contingency	Existence at all time

Table 2. The Categories

mechanism which makes them directly and immediately applicable to phenomena. "Concepts," writes Kant, "are altogether impossible, and can have no meaning, if no object is given for them."[v]

The discussion of 'The Schematism' thus inevitably begins with a question. "How, then," asks Kant, "is the *subsumption* of intuitions under pure concepts, the *application* of a category to appearances, possible?"[vi] Kant is here searching for a key. The task of 'The Schematism' is to provide a medium of communication—something that is at once intellectual and sensible—which can serve to fuse the two halves of his system together. "Obviously," writes Kant, "there must be some third thing, which is homogeneous on the one hand with the category, and on the other hand with appearance, and which thus makes the application of the former to the latter possible."[vii]

This 'third thing' is time. Thus, while it initially seemed as if the form of time was clearly situated alongside space in the 'Transcendental Aesthetic,' in his discussion of 'The Schematism,' Kant abstracts the form of time from this particular determination. As the previous section on 'The Deduction' showed, it is not only sensation, but thought as well, which occurs in time. Thus, for Kant, just as all appearances are subject to temporal form, so too are the categories. In order for the *a priori* concepts to connect with the appearance they must, according to Kant, "contain *a priori* certain formal conditions of sensibility, namely, those of inner sense."viii

Providing the categories with a temporal dimension is the task of 'the transcendental schema.' "This formal and pure condition of sensibility to which the employment of the concept of the understanding is restricted, we shall entitle the *schema* of the concept."ix By ensuring that they can be expressed as a determination of time, it is the schema of the concept which implements the categories, giving them an organizational function in relation to intuition.

Although both the concept and the image are conditioned by time, the production of the schema arises neither from the understanding nor from sensation. Submerged in a realm anterior to knowledge, the schema is produced by the operations of a third faculty, the transcendental imagination. "The schema is in itself always a product of the imagination," Kant writes, and "the two extremes, namely sensibility and understanding, must stand in necessary connection with each other through the meditation of the transcendental function of imagination."x Situated in the middle—on the diagonal line in between intuition and understanding—Kant describes the synthetic process of the transcendental imagination as a secret art. "This schematism of our understanding, in its application to appearances and their mere form, is an art concealed in the depths of the human soul, whose real modes of activity nature is hardly likely ever to allow us to discover, and to have open to our gaze."xi

In discovering the secret art of the productive imagination, the First *Critique* formulates time as a circuit of abstract production. In both sensibility and the understanding, production occurs in a linear flow, channelled into the production of a product (the concept or the image). With the imagination, on the other hand, production is taken to a higher power of abstraction in which the product (the schema) is itself nothing other than the process of abstract production.[51]

The schema is neither an image nor a concept, but a diagram. Like all true diagrams, it is not a static representation, but a functional ma-

---

51: It is this discovery, which will be explored in greater detail in the chapters which follow, which plugs transcendental thought directly into the technological and social machines of capitalism.

chinic component.[52] As an aspect of transcendental time, it operates, for Kant, as the abstract process through which experience is produced. With the chapter on 'The Schematism' then, Kant frees time from being locked into any particular determination—either on the side of the image or on the side of the concept—and makes of it instead the abstract plane of connectivity on which his whole system depends.

In Platonic philosophy, the abstract is equated with a realm that exists outside time. Universal and eternal, this realm is only accessed through the transcendence of ideas. The process of abstraction, then, was considered to be philosophy's privileged tool. As a method of extraction or generalization, it served to prompt a 'recollection' of all that is universal, eternal, and transcendent in the idea. By drawing away from temporally determined appearances, abstraction was thus used to connect one with a realm outside time.[53]

Defined in this way, the abstract is dialectically opposed to the concrete. The distinction between these two spheres corresponds to the difference between essence and appearance, the basic duality which, as we have seen, functions as the structure for the whole of classical thought. Within this duality, the concrete is associated with temporally determined appearances, while the abstract belongs to the eternal nature of essences. Separated in this way, the abstract and concrete exist on two separate levels. Bound by a rigid hierarchy, the relation between them is one of reflection. Thus, just as the appearance is conceived as a degraded image of the essence of the idea, for Plato, the concrete is conceived of as a shadow of the abstract.

For Kant, it is not a realm outside time, but time itself that is abstract, however. Conceived of in this way, the abstract ceases to be equated with the transcendence of the idea and is instead the process by which concepts (or ideas) are applied to the objects of sense perception. That is to say, for Kant, concepts are only implementable because they are given a temporal determination by the abstract production of time. It is this abstract production which constructs an immanent plane of connectivity, a sort of general medium of exchange on which the Kantian system of the transcendental is based.

As a process of production, the abstract ceases to be dialectically opposed to the concrete, and transcendent reflection gives way to an immanent connection. The relation between the abstract production of

---

52: This is why Deleuze speaks of the schematism as "rules of production" ("Kant: Synthesis and Time," 53). For a discussion of the diagram as it functions in Deleuze and Guattari, see *A Thousand Plateaus*, 143–146.

53: A good example of this is found in the discussion of the slave's knowledge of geometry found in the dialogue "Meno."

time and temporally determined appearances is no longer dichotomized, for in transcendental thought, abstraction operates within the concrete.[54] Abstraction is thus conceived not as a means through which one can escape from the illusion of appearances into the truth of the idea, but rather as the virtual synthetic processes through which the actuality of appearances are produced.

Despite the fact that he distinguishes between abstraction and ideas, Kant still seeks to maintain that at its most abstract, the production of time takes place inside the mind of the knowing subject. However, the fact that the schema is described as a hidden art whose secrets can never be revealed suggests that perhaps even he is aware that the transcendental philosophy of time is irreducible to an epistemological theory.[55] A process of construction that is neither perceived nor understood,[56] the production of abstract time (or schema) is not a product of interiority, but belongs instead to the unconscious plane which produces the inside.[57] Kant's contention that the schema is found "concealed in the depths of the human soul" is ultimately nothing but vague lyricism and must be considered illegitimate from the standpoint of critique. For as we have seen, according to the immanent criteria of transcendental thought, the production of time cannot be confined to the interiority of the subject, philosophical or otherwise.

It used to be the case that the ultimate agent of abstract production was found in the realm of metaphysics. It was believed that the transcendence of God created us and the world that we experience. We have seen, however, that the Kantian Revolution has demolished this belief. With his sustained attack on metaphysics, the "Queen of all the sciences," critique undermined the transcendence of God and, to use Heine's words, functioned as "the sword that slew deism" in philosophy.[xii]

54: In Deleuze and Guattari's transcendental materialism, abstract machines are defined as follows: "There is no abstract machine, or machines, in the sense of a Platonic Idea, transcendent, universal, eternal. Abstract machines operate within concrete assemblages: They are defined by the fourth aspect of assemblages, in other words, the cutting edges of decoding and deterritorialization" (*A Thousand Plateaus*, 510). Both transcendental materialism and abstract machines will be discussed in detail in chapters three and four.

55: It can, in fact, be argued that Kant is only inclined towards epistemology when he is not being transcendental enough.

56: Since it is neither a concept nor an image, the abstract production of transcendental time can be neither known nor perceived.

57: Defined as a 'secret and hidden art,' the schematism should be understood as an unconscious process.

The conventional tale is that Kant replaced God with man.[58] Developing a theory of production which does not pass-through God, Kant placed the transcendental subject in the role of the ultimate creator. To quote Alistair Welchman in his thesis, "'Wild above rule or art': Creation and Critique," the Kantian subject "operates a production fully theological in scope: it is nothing less than the production of the empirical world, of the universe as such."[xiii] In what follows, it is argued that it is the inhuman forces of time that surpass the power of the subject as the ultimate agent of transcendental production.

This chapter began by maintaining that the Kantian discovery of the transcendental required a revolution in the nature of time. The classical conception which conceived of time as equivalent to the phenomenal world of change and motion had to be overthrown. In its place, Kant constructed an account of a constant, formal time within which all variation takes place. He called this the "form of inner sense" due to the fact that it conditions all thoughts and perceptions from within. Yet, as we have seen, in locating time inside the subject, Kant radically altered the notion of interiority by subordinating it to the exteriority of time. In the chapter on 'The Schematism,' this exteriority of time overturns the transcendence of ideas (and of God) by replacing them with an immanent plane of abstract production which is nothing other than the transcendental production of time.

58: It is important to keep this term gendered. For as Irigaray points out in her writings on Kant, "any theory of the subject has always been appropriated by the masculine" (*Speculum of the Other Woman*, 133).

2 — Time in Modern Capitalism

To describe Kant and capital as two sides of a coin is as necessary as it is ridiculous. A strange coin indeed that can synthesize a humble citizen of Königsberg with the run-away reconstruction of a planet.

—Nick Land, *The Thirst for Annihilation*, 3

2.0 — Time in Kant and Capitalism

In the previous chapter it was argued that Kant's Copernican Revolution was not, as is traditionally contended, centrally concerned with a change in the role of the human subject but was instead about a transformation in the nature of time. Subordinating the human intellect to the abstract, synthetic, and productive operations of temporality, the *Critique of Pure Reason* demonstrates that it is not the subject that produces time, but rather time that produces the interiority of the subject. Transcendental philosophy, then, is not simply an epistemological theory, but must also be understood as the discovery of something fundamentally new in the nature of time.

In the following chapter, we will see that at the dawn of capitalism, centuries before the writing of the First *Critique*, history registers a change at the empirical level in the culture and technology of time.[59] Thus, we will find that the transformation of time in Kant's philosophical revolution is matched by an equally dramatic "revolution in time"[60] brought on by changes in technology, sociology, geography, and economics. By bringing together these two revolutions, this chapter seeks to investigate the links between the production of a capitalist time, and time as it is conceived of in transcendental philosophy.

In order to do this most effectively, the chapter is composed of three sections divided according to the following themes: 1) the technological development of the clock and the emergence of a new form of time, 2) the synthetic nature of the capitalist temporal regime (with particular emphasis on Greenwich Mean Time (GMT) and the equation 'time = money'), and 3) the problems and philosophical implications which inevitably arise when one attempts to connect historical change with transcendental philosophy.

59: This will be explored by examining the work of a variety of socio-historians of time including, amongst others, David S. Landes, Lewis Mumford, and Gerhard Dohrn-van Rossum.
60: This phrase is taken from David S. Landes' book, *Revolution in Time: Clocks and the Making of the Modern World.*

In his book *History of the Hour: Clocks and Modern Temporal Orders*, Gerhard Dohrn-van Rossum writes that it is now considered to be 'textbook wisdom' that in the late-Middle Ages, there occurred in the culture of the West a transformation in the apprehension of time. The most important instrument of this transformation was the invention and development of the mechanical clock. The impact of the clock—which Lewis Mumford has called the "key-machine of the modern industrial age"—is impossible to overestimate.[i] For as we will see, the rapid growth and overwhelming influence of this new device attests to the fact that the clock was not merely an advance in timekeeping technology but was also the expression of a more fundamental alteration in the nature of time itself. With the arrival of the mechanical clock there arose, for the first time in history, an abstract, secular, homogeneous, quantitative, and autonomous mode of time which was separate and distinct from the historical, astronomical, and qualitative time of the calendar.[61]

It should be immediately apparent that the distinctive features of clock time—its distinction from the movement of objects in the external world and its autonomy from the events which happen inside it—closely correspond to the Kantian form of time discussed in the 'Transcendental Aesthetic.' It would thus appear that the first great critical reversal which revolutionizes the classical conception of temporality by conceiving of a time independent of change is mirrored by transformations which occurred to the nature of time under capitalism.

The notion that Kantian thought is linked to developments in the technology of time should come as no surprise, for as we will see, the lore surrounding Kant's life and habits suggest that, as an empirical subject, Kant was obsessed with the temporality of the clock. What this chapter seeks to maintain is that the time which governed Kant's life seeped into his writings and made a crucial impact on his philosophy. In assuming a link between Kant's life and his writings, this chapter seeks to propose that Kant discovered a new form of time not by looking into the hidden recesses of the human soul, but through his sensitivity to the way time was functioning in the culture which surrounded him.[62]

61: The distinction between clocks and calendars will be discussed in detail in the following section.

62: This is not to say that Kantian philosophy can be reduced to socio-economics, for the connection between Kantian thought and clock time cannot be explained through a linear, causal relation. In fact, the precise relation between these two aspects of the "revolution in time" is extremely complex and is thus treated as one of the main themes addressed throughout this thesis.

It is not only the technology of the clock, however, which links Kantian thought to the production of capitalist time. For when seen through the perspective of transcendental philosophy, it becomes apparent that capitalist time establishes itself as a universal, synthetic regime. This perspective is importantly different—but nevertheless compatible with—the analyses of capitalist temporality that are traditionally maintained by the socio-historians of time. From Mumford to Marx, the story of the emergence of a modern industrial time is implicitly structured through the dynamics of dialectical struggle. In a tale riddled with nostalgia and warnings, these thinkers lament the fact that in the modern period, the concrete, organic, and natural time of the calendar has been overwhelmed and dominated by the artificial time of the clock.[63]

Seen through the lens of the Kantian system, however, clocks and calendars no longer appear as two separate sides of a battle. For, as we have seen, the *Critique of Pure Reason* operates with a tripartite structure which is capable of connecting apparent divisions through a process of abstract production. Replacing dialectics with the "synthesised or electronic way of handling philosophy," transcendental thought configures the time of capitalism not as the tyrannical rule of the clock, but rather as the establishment of a new regime of synthesis.[ii] Instead of subordinating the more 'natural' time of the past, it sees capitalism as constituting an abstract plane of connection which brings together the time of the clock with the temporality of the calendar. This abstract connection is instantiated by Greenwich Mean Time (GMT), an 'artificial' synthesis which acts as the universal standard of a globalized time.

The establishment of GMT—with its synthesis of clocks and calendars—is further combined under capitalism with another crucial synthesis, most succinctly captured by the phrase 'time = money.' This equation, which constitutes the basic formula of the capitalist system, involves, as we will see, not only a new and autonomous form of time, but also a transformation in the cultural and economic practices which serve to constitute a particular temporal regime.[64] It is precisely these transformations in the cultural-economics of time, and the practices which they make possible, which provide the primary conditions of existence for the capitalist social system.

63: To quote Mumford: "Abstract time became the new medium of existence. Organic functions were themselves regulated by it: one ate, not upon feeling hungry, but when prompted by the clock: one slept, not when one was tired, but when the clock sanctioned it" (*Technics and Civilization*, 17).

64: As we will see, these practices include such phenomena as wage labour, credit, and interest.

A certain confusion arises, however, with the recognition that the capitalist production of time could only have taken place within a particular historical context. The invention and development of the mechanical clock, the establishment of GMT, and the practices which equate time with money required that certain contingent socio-economic forces be in place. And yet, the paradoxical fact is that these forces were determined in large part by the temporality that they made possible. In short, capitalist time depends upon a particular historical formation, and yet this historical formation presupposes the production of capitalist time from the start.[65] The fact that the production of capitalist time introduces a new mode of temporality that is independent of change, that it operates through the establishment of universal synthesis, and that these syntheses are presupposed in the culture they produce suggest that, like transcendental philosophy, capitalism accesses a realm independent of empirical processes and is productive not of events that occur inside experience, but of the underlying conditions that make experience possible. Escaping the confines of interiority, it functions not only through that which happens in time, but as the abstract production of time itself.

The difficulty with this claim, however, is that the attempt to equate transcendental time with capitalist time runs into the familiar problem of how to connect philosophical concepts with material reality. Put simply, this problem can be stated as follows: capitalism is a historical event thought to be empirically produced and thus, by definition, falls outside the domain of Kantian thought. For, as we have seen, the first crucial step in identifying the realm of the transcendental is to differentiate it from the experiential world of the empirical. How then could capitalism, a socio-economic event which occurs in time, be associated with the transcendental? What is the relationship between the empirical change in time that occurred at the onset of capitalism, and the revolution in the theory of time that occurred in transcendental philosophy?

This is the problem which the final section of this chapter seeks to address. It does so first by turning to the work of Karl Marx. For it is in Marx where one finds one of the most consistent and well-known attempts to connect philosophical thought with the concrete socio-economic conditions of material practice. Marx concurs with Kant that

---

65: Capitalism, then, must be conceived of cybernetically—that is, as a system which operates with feedback loops, or non-linear circuits of production in which 'A causes B *and* B causes A.' In this way, culture and technology no longer need to be viewed through models of linear causation but can be seen instead as locked into non-linear circuits of reciprocal presuppositions. It is undoubtedly a circuit, or cybernetic loop such as this, that is responsible for generating both the time of the clock and the culture to which it belongs.

analyses should not be based on experience but should concentrate instead on the conditions which make experience possible. His work departs from Kant, however, in that it subordinates transcendental structures to the internal forces of history. According to the principles of historical materialism, production at all levels ultimately rests with the dialectical struggles of the past. For Marx, the *a priori* are not eternal, but subject to change and transformation. Transcendental time is thus determined by historical time.

Though Marx gives an account of how Kant's philosophy of time might relate to capitalism, the Marxist analysis will ultimately be seen as inadequate, for Marx's insistence on the productive forces of history leaves no room for a theory of transcendental production. Thinking dialectically rather than synthetically, his conception of material production risks folding the transcendental back into the empirical. Thus, though offering a bridge between philosophy and the empirical conditions of capitalism, Marx's writings manage to hide precisely the zone that Kant's work makes visible.

In order to bridge the gap opened between Kant and Marx, the chapter turns finally to the work of Michel Foucault. By taking on board the Marxist critique of idealism without falling back into a naïve empiricism, Foucault develops a theory that has the potential to link Kant with capitalism without sacrificing either the empirical or the transcendental.

For Foucault, just as for Marx, the *a priori* is historical. His books are famous for mapping the ways in which transcendental structures vary from age to age. Yet, unlike Marx, Foucault is deeply suspicious of accrediting these changes to the internal dynamics of history. According to Foucault, the rhythm of historical transformations "doesn't follow the smooth, continuist schemas of development which are normally accepted."[iii] Foucault's work thus leads us to the conclusion that although transcendental structures change in time, these changes are not themselves historically produced.

Foucault combines a Marxist historicism with transcendental thought in order to arrive at the notion of discontinuity. This often-controversial concept is meant to signal the breaks in history when, in the space of only a few years, an entire regime of power which governs all that can be said and seen is subject to a 'global modification.' In Foucault's work, the continual passage of time is interrupted by sudden eruptions. The interiority of history is opened to forces from the outside. Thus, for Foucault, it is not that the transcendental can be reduced to history, but rather that history is punctuated by transcendental events. It is thus the task of this thesis to explore capitalism's peculiar intimacy with these discontinuities.

2.1 — Clock Time

Throughout history, social revolutions have tended to be linked to calendric transformations. New leaders—whether religious or political—have often sought to inaugurate their reign through the introduction of a new calendar. For the calendar, as we will see, is closely tied to the specificity and individuation of a culture, and is therefore viewed—both by rulers and by revolutionary groups—as the means through which they can separate themselves both from their immediate past and from their existing surroundings. Thus, calendric change has been seen by cultures as the first and most crucial step in establishing their autonomy and solidifying their traditions.

The capitalist revolution, however, has ignored this tendency, for capitalism as a social system has a peculiar indifference—and therefore practical conservatism—to its calendric milieu. In its entire history there has been but one successful attempt at calendric reform.[66] This occurred in 1582, at the dawn of capitalism, when Pope Gregory XIII introduced modifications into the Julian calendar. The Gregorian reforms, however, were not intended as the installation of a new calendar, but rather as the modernization of an old one. Pope Gregory had no desire to challenge the culture of the existing calendar, he simply wanted an improvement in timekeeping accuracy, as the Julian calendar was slowly coming out of sync with the seasons. In order to stop this slide, Pope Gregory XIII initiated a number of fairly modest changes. He decreed that the 4th of October would skip to the 15th of October,[67] he moved the beginning of the year from March 25th to January 1st, and he made a slight adjustment to the Julian leap year axiom.[68] These reforms gave the Julian calendar an added degree of precision while leaving all the essen-

---

66: There was a serious attempt at calendric reform during the French Revolution that occurred through the introduction of a timekeeping system known as the 'Calendar of Reason.' "Launched in 1792—the revolutionary Year One—this new calendar had uniform months of 30 days each, taking on an extra 5 (or 6) days at the end. These were reserved for holidays called *Virtue, Genius, Labor, Opinion* and *Recompense*. Instead of gods and emperors it used names for the months: *Nivose* for snowing months, *Pluvoise* for Rainy Month, *Thermidor* for Heat Month, and *Brumaire* for Foggy Month. Weeks were 10 days long, with three weeks per month. Days were likewise divided in a decimal arrangement into 10 hours each of 100 minutes, with every minute containing 100 seconds" (Duncan, *Calendar*, 238). However, the 'Calendar of Reason' lasted only until 1806 when Napoleon quietly reintroduced the Gregorian system.

67: This particular reform prompted a series of riots in which "mobs collected in the streets and shouted, 'Give us back our 11 days'" (Duncan, *Calendar*, 228).

68: The Gregorian calendar, like the Julian calendar, treats every fourth year as a leap year. The only difference is that in the Gregorian calendar, no century year is a leap

tial elements—the eras, the numerals, the counting systems, and the festivities—unchanged.

Under capitalism, the Gregorian calendar has spread across the planet[69] and now appears as the dominant time-registry of the global oecumenon, overcoding local calendars without serious challenge.[70] This is a testament to an ultra-conservatism in capitalist time, for despite its globalized culture, capitalism operates with the calendar of the Holy Roman Empire.

This almost parodic stability in calendrics is starkly contrasted by the remarkable changes that have happened to the technology of the clock. Capitalism's "revolution in time" thus combines an extreme conservatism on the side of the calendar with an unprecedented social and technological run-away on the side of the clock.

Socio-historians agree that the crucial turning point in the history of capitalist time occurred with the development of the mechanical clock. Though it has so far proved impossible to pinpoint the precise place, time, and circumstance of this invention, most historians date the process, in Europe, to the late thirteenth or early fourteenth-century.[71] It is commonly agreed that the key to this technological breakthrough was a simple engineering device known as the verge and foliot escapement. By regulating the speed and flow of a spoked wheel, a small metallic lever was able to internally generate a standardized beat or pulse. This was undoubtedly a crucial step in making the clock a consistent and reliable device for keeping track of time. As Lewis Mumford writes, after the creation of the mechanical clock, "the clouds that could paralyse the sundial, the freezing that could stop the water clock on a winter night, were no longer obstacles to time-keeping; summer or winter, day or night, one was aware of the measured clank of the clock."[i] This first

---

year unless it is exactly divisible by 400 (*e.g.*, 1600, 2000). "A further proposed refinement, the designation of years evenly divisible by 4,000 as common (not leap) years, would keep the Gregorian calendar accurate to within one day in 20,000 years" (Encyclopaedia Britannica, "Gregorian calendar").

69: The Gregorian calendar was adopted by 'the Protestant German states in 1699, England and its colonies in 1752, Sweden in 1753, Japan in 1873, China in 1912, and the Soviet Union in 1918' (Encyclopaedia Britannica, "Gregorian calendar").

70: The first serious challenge to the global dominance of the Gregorian calendar occurred at the dawn of the third millennium and was brought on by a computer bug known as Y2K. This will be discussed in detail in chapter four.

71: Joseph Needham's work on Chinese science has shown that some type of mechanical clock was developed centuries earlier (perhaps as early as the eighth century). Nevertheless, by the time Jesuits came to China in the sixteenth century, there was no sign of these devices. For a good summary of this work and the issues that it raises; see Dohrn-van Rossum, *History of the Hour*, 86–88.

technological breakthrough unleashed a series of inventions and discoveries (from the pendulum to the metric beats of the caesium atom) which have combined to make the clock the most precise and accurate machine that has ever been built. As Mumford suggests, from the mechanism of early clockwork to the digital pulse of cybernetic computers, clocks and clock making have consistently been at the forefront of technological innovation.

> In its relationship to determinable quantities of energy, to standardization, to automatic action, and finally to its own special product, accurate timing, the clock has been the foremost machine in modern technics; and at each period it has remained in the lead: it marks a perfection towards which other machines aspire.[ii]

At first glance it would appear that the difference between clocks and calendars is ultimately nothing more than a difference in scale. While the calendar is used to count the days, months, and years, the clock divides the day into hours, minutes, seconds (and now, ever more intricately divided subseconds). Yet the seeming simplicity of this distinction is deceiving, for as we will eventually see, implicit in the distinction between these two types of timekeepers is a distinction between two very different types of time. Thus, in developing the technology of the clock, capitalism had discovered and unleashed something entirely new in the very nature of time.

In order to understand what is peculiar about clock time, it must be first distinguished from the temporality of the calendar. At its most abstract, this distinction rests on the different ways these two devices combine a beat and a count—the two elements that are necessary in calculating the time. The beat, a regular and repeating pulse or tick, is used as the basic unit of measure, while the count, on the other hand, provides the numerical sequence which places the units of measurement into an ordinal series. In order to tell the time, all timekeepers, whether calendars or clocks, require some kind of synthesis between these two elements.

Calendric time is based on astronomy. The calendar takes its beats from the revolutions of the planets. Its tick is determined by the earth's rotation around the sun. All calendars, from the ancient Egyptian to the modern Gregorian, use the day as their basic unit of measure. Defined most simply then, the calendar is a day count. Yet, as Thomas Crump writes in his book, *The Anthropology of Numbers*, "in practice no system ever confined itself to the counting of days."[iii] For calendric uniformity, the constraint on the side of the beat is made up for by the complicated web of differences which are added to the side of the count.

The calendar complicates the linear, numerical sequence that adds up the days by developing a system of counting that is based on a series of cycles. By combining a variety of astronomical movements with the rhythms of religious tradition (*i.e.*, the yearly cycle of earth around the sun, the monthly cycle of the moon, and the 7-day week of the Genesis story) the calendar envelops the day count into longer and more complicated cycles of time.[72]

The great problem for calendrics is that these cycles are inevitably incommensurable. The most striking example of this is the incompatibility of the lunar month with the solar year which results from the discrepancy that exists between the time it takes for the earth to travel around the sun (365 days, 5 hours, 59 minutes, and 16 seconds) and the 12 months (29.5 days each) which make up a lunar year. Since almost all calendars seek some mode of accounting for both these cycles, the different elements of the calendar invariably come out of sync. Thus, in all calendars, supplementary axioms of convergence—known as intercalations—are required in order to harmonize the cycles and reconcile the count.[73]

The incommensurability of the cycles and the necessity of intercalations ensure that the time of the calendar is intrinsically rhythmic. Produced through a variety of different but interconnected cycles, the calendar is made up of a multiplicity of systems all intertwined. Metric regularity gives way to cyclic discontinuity as the periodicity of the tick becomes governed by a polyrhythmic count.

The most common expression of calendric time is found in the practice of dating. Viewed as a numerical sequence or pattern, the date is the record of a rhythm. Using a combination of temporal units which are qualitatively distinct, the date is inherently synthetic. 8/29/00, for example, is a combination of day, month, and year. It is a string of numbers (lacking a common modulus) which expresses the heterogeneity intrinsic to calendric temporality.

The calendar's numerical complexity—its heterogeneity at the level of expression—speaks to the fact that the time of the calendar is itself composed of qualitative variations. Calendric time is directed towards the question 'when?' This temporal marker, which depends on the dif-

---

72: In the Gregorian calendar for example, the day count is subsumed under four cycles: the week, the month, the year, and the era (B.C./A.D.).

73: In the Gregorian calendar, this is known as the leap year axiom, the practice of inserting one day every four years.

ference between past, present, and future, presupposes qualitative distinctions in the nature of time itself. Thus, it is not only the internal variation at the abstract level of the count which makes the calendar fall on the qualitative side of the quantity/quality divide.

In the calendar, temporal units are not only determined numerically, but are also distinguished by intensive changes in temperature, light, climate, etc. Thus, the calendar not only dates events, but is also, as we will see, a timekeeping device which is ultimately structured according to the events which it is dating. For in the calendar, the separation between time and that which occurs in time is very difficult to make.

This merging of time with concrete phenomena occurs because of the calendar's close links with astronomy. Based on the revolutions of the planets, calendric temporality is determined by repetitive, natural events such as days, lunar cycles, seasons, etc. These astronomical occurrences act as a sort of macrocosm for organic life, further strengthening the qualitative nature of calendric time.

The discipline of chronobiology, for example, attests to the fact that the 24-hour day is connected to the internal rhythms of the human sleep/wake cycle. The lunar month, which governs the movement of the tides, is—in almost all cultures—closely linked with a woman's menstrual cycle.[74] The year is tied to the passage of the seasons which regulates everything from life cycles to migration patterns to the extremely influential rhythms of agriculture.

With a rhythmic, heterogeneous count tied to astronomy, organic life, and the cycles of civilization, the calendar has always had a close affinity to ritual and religion. Traditionally, the calendar was the sole responsibility of religious leaders (in Egyptian, the word for 'priest' means 'star watcher'). Almost all cultures give great attention to the maintenance of an accurate calendar, since it is this that structures the rhythms of religious life. Punctuated by ritual, holy festivals, and prayer, the passage of calendric time is a cultural celebration.

It is thus not an exaggeration to claim that one's culture is one's calendar. In a book entitled *Hidden Rhythms*, Eviatar Zerubavel uses the example of Judaism to illustrate this point. According to Zerubavel, the Jewish people distinguish themselves from Gentiles through the specificity of their calendar. He stresses, in particular, the importance given to the observance of the Sabbath, a weekly reminder of tradition which operates to structure and determine the rest of the week. "The Jewish

---

74: As Samuel Macey writes in his book, *The Dynamics of Progress: Time, Method and Measure*, "months, moons and menstruation are so closely related that we use the same root -word for all three of them" (26).

calendar," writes Zerubavel, "has been hailed as the single most important book of the people of Israel. It has been said to have preserved the Jews as a people, to have united all those who have been scattered around the world and made them one people."[iv]

It is perhaps this which explains the tendency for cultural revolutions to inaugurate calendric change. The adoption of a new calendar is amongst the most powerful means of separating a people from their social surroundings. By celebrating different holy days and not sharing in the same festivities, a new calendar works to entrench cultural difference. Thus, Christianity distinguished itself from Judaism through the adoption of a luni-solar calendar, and by switching the Sabbath from Saturday to Sunday. Mohammed, operating with the same principle, "replaced the luni-solar calendar that had prevailed in Arabia with an entirely lunar calendar."[v] He also made the Islamic day of rest fall on a Friday, thus distinguishing his followers from both the Christians and the Jews.

Clock time, as we will see, can be differentiated from the calendar on a point-by-point basis. First, clock time substitutes the calendric emphasis on the count by innovating on the side of ticks or beats. Using cardinal rather than ordinal numbers, the clock does not count time: it measures it. The clock is by its nature indifferent to astronomy. It can, as is the case with the sundial, use the rotations of the planets as its mode of measure, but its tendency has been to find the tick of time elsewhere. Following a line through metallurgy and on to geology, the clock extracts the beat away from astronomical movement. As David S. Landes writes in his book, *Revolution in Time: Clocks and the Making of the Modern World*, "to the physicist any stable oscillation is a clock."[vi] The clock, then is a machine which either engineers its own tick—as is the case with the mechanical clock—or incorporates one from the outside into its own internal mechanism—as is the case with clocks which run on the pulse of a quartz crystal. Thus, unlike the calendar in which a vast distance separates the count from the beat, clocks have assimilated natural time into the machine.[75]

Secondly, clock time is metric rather than rhythmic. There are no intertwining cycles or irregular beats in the constant ticking of a clock.

75: This tendency for clocks to develop a new form of time independent of astronomy reached its apex in the 1960's with the development of the atomic clock. This machine "which depends for its operation on the incredibly precise rate of decay of a caesium isotope," has now become the ultimate chronometric reference (Grant, *The Book of Time*, 71). "Atomic clocks, which operate at accuracies equivalent to an error of one second in 150,000 years enable us with ease to measure irregularities in the rotation period of the Earth itself the former standard of timekeeping" (161).

Unlike a calendar in which each date has a specificity of its own, clock time is homogeneous. 'August 21, 1998,' for example, is a sign attributed to a particular historical year (the year the presidency was rocked by scandal, two years away from the millennium, etc.), allied with a specific season (summer), allocated to a particular time in that season (towards the end), and linked to a designated day of the week (Friday). Yet, while calendric units are constrained by the qualitative aspects of the time which they are meant to designate, the units of clock time are based on arbitrary divisions which are purely conventional.[76] This results in a strong tendency of the clock to autonomize the time from any events outside its own mechanism.[77]

Unlike the calendar, clock time does not date events, but instead determines the length of time they take. It replaces the internal variation and complicated system of counting with a metric and homogeneous measure. Extracted from history and stripped of ceremony, ritual, and religion, the regular beat of the clock is allied with quantity rather than quality. It is an abstract and formalized time indifferent to the events which it measures.

For the majority of history, the clock has been subordinated to the calendar. Until the invention of the mechanical escapement, clocks, insofar as they existed as sundials, water clocks, and sand glasses, operated within the confines of the calendar. Using variable hours which were determined by the length of the day and fluctuated with the seasons, the time of the clock had little or no autonomy. Though it was used for certain civil functions,[78] in comparison to the calendar, the clock was a trivial device.

Thus, in focusing on the technological development of the clock, capitalism has actualized a distinction in time which had, until the capi-

---

76: Traditionally, clock time has been organized according to the Babylonian base 60 system (there are 60 minutes in an hour and 60 seconds in a minute). However, with the rise of digital technology, clocks have begun to split the second into gradations based on the decimal system (*e.g.*, the nanosecond, the picosecond, etc.).

77: This is most evident with cyberspace time which does not distinguish between the days of the week or even between night and day. This results in businesses having to develop new models in which they are 'open' 24 hours a day, 7 days a week, and is also an increasing factor in processes of globalization which make use of different time zones to increase productivity.

78: For example, in the fifth-century, water clocks were used in Athenian law courts to limit the time of speeches. "Since court proceedings usually had to be concluded within a day, the total speaking time in criminal trials was split three ways between the accuser, the accused, and the judges, using as a basis the approximate amount of water that flowed out of vessels on a short day (about nine hours)" (Dohrn-van Rossum, *History of the Hour*, 23).

talist regime, existed solely as a virtuality. In effecting a technological change that made clock time ever more independent from the calendar, capitalism not only invented a new type of timekeeping device, but it also discovered a new type of time.

"Academics' lives," Deleuze is quoted as saying, "are seldom interesting."[vii] Days are invariably filled with some mixture of reading, writing, and lecturing, and unless this routine is punctuated by some surprising or dramatic event, biographical details rarely hold much importance. In the case of Immanuel Kant, however, the situation is somewhat different. The legends surrounding Kant's life suggest that he performed the monotonous routine of his academic schedule with such extreme regularity and precision that one cannot fail to become absorbed in the meticulous, almost psychotic, timing of his day-to-day existence.

In an essay entitled *The Last Days of Immanuel Kant*, Thomas De Quincey combines historical fact with fictional flare to describe this existence in detail. Kant's day, according to De Quincey, began "precisely at five minutes before five o'clock, winter or summer, when Lampe, Kant's footman, who had formerly served in the army, marched into his master's room with the air of a sentinel on duty, and cried aloud in a military tone, 'Mr Professor, the time is come.'"[viii] Upon hearing this pronouncement, Kant rose immediately, and "as the clock struck five he was seated at the breakfast table."[ix] In accordance with his passion for order and "love for architectonic symmetry" Kant—so the story goes— adopted a routine reminiscent of the tables that structure the First *Critique*.[x] His daily schedule was divided into three parts of eight hours each, the first dedicated to work, the second to leisure, and the third to sleep. The first part, the working day, was brought to a close when at "precisely three-quarters before one he arose from his chair and called aloud to his cook, 'It has struck three-quarters.'"[xi] Kant then closed up his office and proceeded to lunch. After the meal at 3:30 pm, almost halfway into the section of the day reserved for leisure, Kant would go on his daily walk. He was greeted, according to legend, by the citizens of Königsberg who would look out their windows, wave to the professor, and set their watches by his movements. Thus, when Heine compares Kant to "the great cathedral clock," he is not speaking metaphorically, for if the stories are even partially true, the extremity of Kant's punctuality was such that his very activities functioned to tell the time.[xii]

As an empirical subject, then, Kant was deeply influenced by the clock. Historically, he was writing in a period in which these timekeepers had already achieved a certain amount of ubiquity and were well on their way to establishing themselves as the key device in timekeeping technology. A year before the publication of the First *Critique*, clocks made the first step in supplanting astronomy as the ultimate chronometric reference, when "in 1780 Geneva first started to use 'mean time' in preference to solar time."[xiii] Kant lived in a world in which clocks had long since been introduced to urban centres, and it is undoubtedly the case, as is clear from Heine's analogy, that central to the town of Königsberg was a public timepiece. Moreover, the lore which surrounds Kant's life suggests that some form of clock or watch adorned every room of his home and study.

Yet, while it is clear that clock time was a crucial factor in Kant's life, the impact it had on his writings remains uncertain. There is a strong tendency, especially in the discipline of philosophy, to separate a thinker's life from his work. This is reinforced in the case of Kant since at the very foundations of critique is an insistence on the split between empirical experience and transcendental thought. It is thus in accordance with his own principles that Kant's experiential existence be deemed irrelevant, for it is not through the empirical that one gains access to the transcendental.

One of the consequences of this line of thought is that it reinforces the commonly held assumption that Kant, like most other thinkers, made his philosophical discoveries by secluding himself from the outside world. According to this view, Kant explored the transcendental in the solitary confines of his office where, through a process of epistemological introspection, he developed his critique of reason by examining the operations of thinking itself.

The problem with this view is that it cannot help but ignore the uncanny resemblance which exists between the time of the clock which governed Kant's life, and the discussion of time found in the 'Transcendental Aesthetic.' This resemblance can be characterized according to the following features.

First, clocks converge with Kantian critique in that with both, time ceases to be under the control of an outside authority. Kant's relocation of time within the individual subject is paralleled in the history of timekeeping when, with the miniaturization of clocks and the mass production of cheap watches, time ceased to be in the hands of the priest or the ruler of the state and became instead the property of the individual. Thus, developments in timekeeping technology both echo and support the autonomy of the modern subject. To quote from David S. Landes:

> Where people had once depended on the cry of the night watch, the bell of the church, or the turret clock in the town square, now they had the time at home or on their person and could order their life and work in a manner once reserved to regulated

communities. In this way the privatisation (personalization) of time was a major stimulus to the individualism that was an ever more salient aspect of Western civilization.[xiv]

In both the history of the clock and in the First *Critique*, this personalisation of time corresponds to a process of interiorization. In Kant, as we have seen, time as the form of inner sense moves inside the subject to become both the limit and the defining feature of interiority. An analogous process can be said to have occurred with the technology of the clock. The clock, like the Kantian subject, is an internally articulated system which relates itself to the outside precisely through temporal autonomization.

Furthermore, clock time is similar to time as pure intuition in that the power of temporality becomes both the ultimate system of surreptitious capture and usurpation: the clock is a machine for producing time. Once developed, its products (hours, minutes, seconds) envelop everything, including its own internal processes. Even those objects and events of the external world that had once been used to mark the time (*i.e.*, the rotation of the planets) are now given precise and accurate measurement by the ticking of the clock.

The final and most important point of convergence, however, is that both clock time and time as a pure intuition revolutionizes the classical conception of time by liberating temporality from the events which happen inside it. In creating a purely quantitative time distinct from astronomy,[79] clocks developed a mode of temporality which ceased to be determined by the objects of the external world. In this way, the autonomy of clock technology parallels the Kantian distinction between a formalized structure of time, and the changes which occur inside it. Thus, in paying relatively little attention to the calendar as a timekeeping system in order to concentrate instead on the new technology of the clock, the production of capitalist time converges with the Kantian system, inaugurating a revolution—not in time but of time—which substitutes a transformation in time-marking conventions for a much more fundamental shift in the nature of time itself.

79: In 1967, the rate of caesium's pulse was calibrated to 9,192,631,770 oscillations per second. This is now the official measurement of world time, replacing the old standard based on the earth's rotation and orbit, which had used as its base number a second equal to 1/31556925.9747 of a year. This means that under this new regime of caesium, the year is no longer measured as 365.242199 days, but as 290,091,200,500,000,000 oscillations of caesium, give or take an oscillation or two (Duncan, *Calendar*, 234).

2.2 — The Synthetic Culture of Clock Time or: Time = Money

Joseph Conrad's novel *The Secret Agent* (1907) turns upon the idea that the most effective way of attacking capitalist culture is to target time itself. Set in London in 1886, *The Secret Agent* is a tale based on the historic attempt to bomb the observatory at Greenwich in 1894. In Conrad's tale, the rationale for this bizarre act is related through a conversation between the titular agent, Mr. Verloc, and his boss Vladimir, the Russian *agent provocateur*. Appearing on summons to Vladimir's office, Verloc is informed that in order to earn his keep he must use his links with the anarchist group 'Future of the Proletariat' to oversee a series of terrorist activities designed to arouse extremism amongst the British, discredit the revolutionaries, and provoke panic amongst the bourgeoisie. In order to accomplish these goals, Vladimir insists that all the traditional modes of terrorism must be abandoned. Attacks on either royalty or religion will not do. Assassinations are expected. Assaults on public buildings, while they undoubtedly cause some alarm, are easily dismissed as the act of a lone maniac. "A bomb in the National Gallery would," Vladimir concedes, "make some noise," but not amongst the right people.[i] To hit at the heart of the bourgeoisie, Verloc is instructed, one must strike against 'the true' "fetish of the hour": science and learning.[ii] "It would be really telling," says his boss, gloating in the persuasiveness of his own logic, "if one could throw a bomb into pure mathematics."[iii] Though this is unfortunately impossible, Vladimir contents himself with the next best thing: "What do you think," he asks, "of having a go at astronomy?"[iv] By the end of the meeting, it is clear that in order for Verloc to stay on the payroll, he must stage an attack on Greenwich. "Go for the first meridian," Vladimir demands as he pushes the disgruntled but acquiescent Verloc out of the room.[v]

Conrad's book sets out to ridicule the cruel and baseless inanity of this unsuccessful gesture. His is a story of the perversion of politics, the evil of ideology, emotional betrayal, and personal grief. And yet, the notion that Marxist revolutionaries should attack the prime meridian is not as absurd as it first appears. Though the bombing of Greenwich is perhaps ill advised, the thinking behind it is sound. For as we will see, there are few things as central to capitalism as Greenwich Mean Time.

The observatory at Greenwich made its initial impact in the mid eighteenth-century, when the clockmaker John Harrison devised a solution to what had come to be known as the longitude problem.[80] Up un-

---

80: The precise date for the development of H4, the clock that eventually won the Longitude prize, is 1759.

til the 1750s, ocean travellers had only one method with which to determine their location: latitude, judged by means that had been known for thousands of years (namely, an understanding of natural signs such as temperature and planetary positions). The much more arbitrary task of determining one's longitude, on the other hand, was, to quote from Dava Sobel's bestselling book on the subject, a dilemma "that stumped the wisest minds of the world for the better part of human history."[vi]

In 1714, the British Parliament sought to resolve this dilemma by offering a prize "equal to a king's ransom (several million dollars in today's currency) for a 'Practicable and Useful' means of determining longitude."[vii] What followed was a struggle that pitted the tradition of astronomy against the emerging technology of the clock. Since longitude is a fusion of space and time, the solution to the problem could come from one of two paths; either through the perfection of lunar charts, or through the development of a timekeeper that would handle the extreme conditions of ocean travel.[81] John Harrison defied the astronomers at Greenwich who favoured the lunar method and devoted his life to producing a clock which could keep the time at sea. In 1759, Harrison's work came to fruition with the completion of H4, the "timekeeper that ultimately won the longitude prize."[viii]

Harrison's marine chronometer was, undoubtedly, one of the most influential machines ever built. It played a critical role in securing control over the oceans, expanding trade routes, and stabilizing commercial networks. By offering a practicable solution to the longitude problem, Harrison's clock established Greenwich at the heart of the British empire and was thus crucial to the onset of global capitalism.

It was not until over a hundred years later, however, that the power of Greenwich was globally entrenched. By the late nineteenth-century, the rapid growth of communication and transportation—in particular the expansion of the railway system—meant that some kind of temporal coordination was essential. With each city, town, or village governed by its own local time, the scheduling of pickups, deliveries, arrivals, and departures was next to impossible. For industrialized culture to function, it became necessary to adopt a standard time frame.

The idea of dividing the world into 24 time-zones, 15 degrees of longitude wide, and one hour apart was initially devised to co-ordinate North American railway traffic. The installation of this plan, however, demanded that world time be synchronized on a zero point. This occurred in 1884 at the International Meridian Conference held in Wash-

---

81: This latter method rests on the fact that longitude can be inferred by knowing the time on board a ship and comparing it to the time at port.

ington, D.C. Here it was agreed that the prime meridian would be the one passing through the "centre of the transit Instrument at the Observatory at Greenwich."[82]/†

Mapped at 0° 00' 00.00," Greenwich thus became the official 'centre of time and space.' Still today, Greenwich is the "keeper of the stroke of midnight."[ix] It marks the beginning of the 'universal day' for all the world and defines the east/west position of everywhere else on the planet. "Greenwich time even extends into outer space: Astronomers use GMT to time predictions and observations, except that they call it Universal Time, or UT, in their celestial calendars."[x]

The history of Greenwich, then, is central to the emergence of capitalist production of globalized time. Beginning with a battle which pits astronomers against engineers, it tells the story of a transition into a new age in which the entrenched power of the 'star watchers' gave way to remarkable feats in engineering, technological innovation, and a continuous upward curve of industrial development. From the discovery of longitude to the standardization of time, Greenwich, as the centre of capitalist time, appears to neglect the calendar in order to celebrate instead the manifest triumph of the clock.

—History of the Clock—

It is common amongst sociologists and historians of time to trace the culture of the clock back to the monastic tradition of the Middle Ages. According to a number of accounts, it is in the monasteries of the West where one finds the first signs of a culture based on the quantifiable and abstract regularity of clock time.[83] Monks, in particular those of the Benedictine Order, divided their day into measurable units in order to develop a strict daily regime of work, rest, and prayer. "For centuries the religious orders had been the masters of discipline: they were the specialists of time, the great technicians of rhythm and regular activities."[xi] By scheduling time and "synchronizing the actions of men," reli-

---

82: There was opposition to this, primarily from the French, who "continued to recognize their own Paris Observatory meridian, a little more than two degrees east of Greenwich, as the starting line for another twenty-seven years, until 1911. (Even then, they hesitated to refer directly to Greenwich mean time, preferring the locution 'Paris Mean Time, retarded by nine minutes twenty-one seconds')" (Sobel, *Longitude*, 168).

83: In the opening pages of his book, *Technics and Civilization*, Lewis Mumford suggests that the clock, "the key-machine of the modern industrial age," arose out of the temporal culture which developed in the monasteries (14). "The monastery," he writes, "was the seat of a regular life, and an instrument for striking the hours at intervals or for reminding the bell-ringer that it was time to strike the bells was an almost inevitable product of this life" (13).

gious orders created a mode of existence based on discipline, rationality, and rule.[xii]

The temporal regularity and time scheduling of monastic life is said to have arisen initially in order to provide shelter against the unpredictability and confusion of everyday existence. Living in the isolation of the monasteries, monks created cloistered communities which offered seclusion and refuge from the chaos of ordinary life. To quote Lewis Mumford: "Within the walls of the monastery was sanctuary: under the rule of the order surprise and doubt and caprice were put at bay. Opposed to the erratic fluctuations and pulsations of the worldly life was the iron discipline of the rule."[xiii]

The force which imposed the timetable, however, should not be seen as a solely negative one. Time scheduling was more than a means of trying to keep the forces of chaos under control; it was also a positive religious injunction as the rhythms of prayer demanded an accurate account of the division of time. "The central element in monastic daily routine was divine worship. In keeping with Psalm 119, verses 164 ('A Seven times a day I praise thee') and 62 ('At midnight I rise to give thee thanks') it was performed seven times during the day and once during the night."[xiv] The fact that prayers occurred so often and that their scheduling did not adhere to calendric time (there are no calendric or astronomical means of determining midnight) meant that monks had to develop some other way of keeping track of the time. In order to accomplish this, the monasteries put the abbot in charge of maintaining a new temporal order, one which was no longer structured by the concrete rhythms of the planets but was determined instead in accordance with the dictates of monastic rule. Signalling the time by the ringing of a bell, the abbot would call the monks to prayer. Thus, unlike other religious practices in which the passage of time dictates when to pray, in monastic life prayer began to dictate the calculation of time.

This strict timetable of devotion was, as we will see, motivated by a theological necessity.[84] According to the monastic tradition, time scheduling was in itself a means of devoting oneself to God. "Idleness," wrote Benedict, "is the soul's enemy."[xv] His text, the *Benedictine Rule*, committed itself to fighting this enemy by developing a particular relation to time. Leisure was not permitted. For unless one adopted a disciplined structure which compartmentalized meditation, devotion, and work, idleness would seep into the soul and steal away time that was meant to be dedicated to God. Thus, if monks were to fulfil their religious duty and live according to the will of their creator, time had to be

---

84: This will be made clear in our discussion of Max Weber below.

strictly rationalized. According to this story, then, the clock was developed almost as a form of worship, necessary to uphold the beliefs of a certain strand in the Christian tradition.

This thesis, that clock time originated inside the walls of monasteries, has been challenged along a number of lines. In his book, *History of the Hour*, Gerhard Dohrn-van Rossum argues, for example, that while it is true that the monastic tradition rationalised time, it did not pay much attention to measuring it.[85] Time in the monasteries was regulated but it was not yet made regular. For the religious orders marked the division of the day not by the use of the clock but by the ringing of the bell. Still dependent on the temporality of the calendar, monastic time operated with hours that fluctuated with the seasons.[86] Temporal distinctions were made through divine office, not by the ticking of a mechanism.[87] Thus, discipline and scheduling were not by themselves sufficient to create the autonomy of clock time.

In a chapter entitled "Merchant's Time and Church's Time in the Middle Ages" in *Time, Work and Culture in the Middle Ages*, the historian Jacques Le Goff makes the claim that clock time arose not in the monasteries, but rather through the pragmatic culture of the merchants. He argues that in order for clocks to take hold, time had to be freed from the clutches of God. His essay begins with a discussion of usury. "Among the principal criticism levelled against the merchants," he writes, "was the charge that their profit implied a mortgage on time which was supposed to belong to God alone."[xvi] Both credit and interest, which are of course crucial to the merchant, demand that the prohibition on usury be lifted and that—as we will later see—money, not God, be equated with time.[88] Furthermore, in that they were operating

---

85: See Dohrn-van Rossum, *History of the Hour*, 33–40.

86: "Talk of 'iron discipline' or the machine-like or clockwork rhythm of monastic life, even in a purely metaphorical sense, is misleading, because it suggests a time giver (a machine or clock) external to natural rhythms and the daily round of human life. In actual fact, life according to the Rule was bound in a very high degree to natural time givers, daylight and the seasons, and was by no means marked by ascetic resistance to the natural environment" (Dohrn-van Rossum, *History of the Hour*, 38).

87: "Despite the density of activities, the ordering of the daily monastic routine got by with remarkably few indications of time. The beginning of the offices was linked not to a particular point in time but to a signal or short sequence of signals" (Dohrn-van Rossum, *History of the Hour*, 36).

88: Le Goff writes that once commercial networks were organized, time (and its relation to monetization) became an object of measurement. "The duration of a sea voyage or of a journey by land to one place or the other, the problem of prices which rose or fell in the course of a commercial transaction (the more so as the circuit became increasingly complex, affecting profits), the duration of the labor of craftsmen and workers (since the merchant was almost always an employer of labor), all made in-

in an environment of technological precision, navigational necessities, and complex financial dealings, merchants could no longer accept the unpredictability and variations of a time dominated by religion. To operate commercial networks, merchants needed a mode of time that could be explicitly measured and regulated.[89] Commercial capitalism thus requires a secularization of time which operates with constant rather than variable hours, one in which the science of technology rather than the authority of priests is in control.

Yet another factor, crucial to the development of clock time, was the process of urbanization.[90] Historically, rural life had been governed by the qualitative time of the calendar. The passage of the seasons, the natural cycle of the day, and the concrete rhythms of agriculture dictated how time was structured and filled. In the country, working time was task driven, and the duration and scheduling of each activity was determined by natural cues.

In the urban environment, on the other hand, time become unhinged from events. From a very early period, public clocks were installed in the city centres, and time in the towns became governed by these new machines. The time of the clock began to regulate when one was to eat, sleep, and especially when, and for how long, one was to work. As Mumford writes, "the bells of the clock tower almost defined urban existence."[xvii] With the migration from the country to the towns, then, there arose a regular, normal time associated with "daily life, a sort of chronological net in which urban life was caught."[xviii]

All three of these cultural forces crucial to the development of the clock—the discipline of monastic life, the secular world of merchant capital, and the growth of industrialized urban centres—have also been strongly linked to the development of capitalist culture.

---

creasing claims on [the merchant's] attention and became the object of evermore explicit regulation" (*Time, Work and Culture in the Middle Ages*, 35).

89: This was absolutely necessary due to the emphasis on facts, documentation, and double entry bookkeeping that were crucial components to the life of the merchant. To quote Le Goff: "The statuses of corporations, together with such commercial documents as account sheets, travel diaries, manuals of commercial practice and the letters of exchange then coming into common use in the fairs of Champagne (which in the twelfth and thirteenth centuries became the 'clearinghouse' of international commerce), all show how important the exact measurement of time was becoming to the orderly conduct of business" (*Time, Work and Culture in the Middle Ages*, 35).

90: Deleuze emphasizes this aspect in speaking of the relation between clock time and Kant. For Deleuze, it is "Kant's historical situation [which] allowed him to grasp the implications of the critical reversal [in the philosophy of time]. Time is no longer the cosmic time of an original celestial movement, nor is it the rural time of derived metereological movements. It has become the time of the city and nothing other, the pure order of time" ("On Four Formulas," 28).

It has been argued, most influentially by Weber and Mumford, that the structure and discipline of the monastic tradition was a crucial precursor to modern industrial society. Operating with the same model as modern factories, monasteries, writes Mumford, were crucial in "helping to give human enterprise the regular collective beat and rhythm of the machine."[xix] Having built a society based on order, rationalism, and rules, the influence of these religious communities was such that, according to Mumford, "the Benedictines, the great working order," can be seen as "the original founders of modern capitalism."[xx]

In much the same way, merchant capital is often viewed as the prototype of the capitalist system. There are, of course, crucial distinctions between merchant capital—which is restricted to circulation—and industrial capitalism—which extends capitalist relations into the sphere of production. Nevertheless, merchant capital laid down the grid of 'socially decoded' or commercially rationalized interchange within which industrial capitalism could develop.[91]

Finally, the ongoing process of urbanization, particularly because of its relation to the abstraction of labour, has also been seen as fundamental in the transition to the capitalist mode of production. The move away from the country stripped people of their concrete roles. No longer coded according to particular tasks or positions (the peasant, the farmer, the baker, etc.) vast portions of the population became defined purely as quantities of abstract labour power. Having lost access or ownership to the means of production, they became 'free labourers.' Thus, life in the city developed a socio-economic system in which labour could be traded with relative ease, a factor which many—from Smith to Marx and beyond—believe to be the key to capitalist production.

Thus, the proto-industrial discipline of monasticism, the rationalism of accountancy and credit practised by the merchants, and the large and fluid labour markets that arose through the process of urbanization are all considered key, both in the history of the clock and in the history of capitalism. Yet, one should not be surprised that the development of clock time is so intertwined with the production of capitalist culture, for as we will see, at the very foundations of capitalism is the synthetic operation which equates time with money.[92]

91: It has been argued, by Engels in particular, that merchant capital was the vehicle by which capitalism replaced feudal society.

92: As we will see, this relation between clock time and capitalist culture can neither be explained by the discourse of technological determinism (which presumes a one-way causal relationship which runs from technology to social systems) nor by social constructivism (which maintains a linear causality, but sees it as running in the opposite

—Time is Money—

Part 1: Weber and the Spirit of Capitalism

> Remember, that *time* is money. He that can earn ten shillings a day by his labour, and goes abroad, or sits idle, one half of that day, though he spends but sixpence during his diversion or idleness, ought not to reckon *that* the only expense; he really has spent, or rather thrown away, five shillings besides.[xxi]

According to Max Weber, when Benjamin Franklin spoke these words, words which warn against the dangers of idleness and wasting time, he was speaking as a mouthpiece for capitalist culture. His words are the embodiment of the Protestant ethic, an ethic which Weber has famously argued is the characteristic feature of 'the spirit of capitalism.'[93] For Weber, capitalist culture is a Christian culture since its 'spirit' corresponds to the beliefs, practices, and ethos of a particular strand in the Christian tradition. His work sets out to show that by cultivating an ethos of 'active asceticism,' this strand of Christianity became the first religion to have developed an economic ethic which is conducive to the capitalist way of life.[94]

This ethic depends, first of all, on what Weber has called the "disenchantment of the world."[xxii] Christianity, like its precursor Judaism, is founded on a grand exorcism which banishes magic, expels spirits, and strips objects of their animistic power. Outlawing the sorcerer, it

---

direction). As we will see in the following pages, the culture of capitalism and the technology of the clock are mutually involved in a circuit of reciprocal presuppositions such that it is impossible to say which precedes the other. It is clear both that the development of the clock could only have taken place within capitalist culture *and* that capitalist culture presumes, from its very beginning, the ubiquity of the clock.

93: The connections between critique and capitalism are no doubt due—at least in part—to Kant's obvious connections to Protestantism. This relation is stressed both by Heine, who argues that Kantianism is "nothing else than the last consequence of Protestantism" (*Religion and Philosophy in Germany*, 59), and by Weber who maintains that "being partly of Scotch ancestry and strongly influenced by Pietism in his bringing up [...] many of [Kant's] formulations are closely related to the ideas of ascetic Protestantism" (*The Protestant Ethic and the Spirit of Capitalism*, 243–244).

94: It would be a mistake, however, to assume that Weber's argument is that the Protestant religion is the cause of capitalism or the capitalist way of life. "No economic ethic," he writes, "has ever been determined solely by religion. In the face of man's attitudes towards the world—as determined by religious or other (in our sense) 'inner' factors—an economic ethic has, of course, a high measure of autonomy. Given factors of economic geography and history determine this measure of autonomy in the highest degree. The religious determination of life-conduct, however, is also one—note

puts the prophet in charge of a world that is "disenchanted of its gods and demons."[xxiii] The sacred, which is now captured by the monotheistic rule of transcendence, has retreated from the everyday. In place of a magical world, there arises a rational, intellectualized cosmos which is, for the first time, capable of being measured and quantified.

Seeking to distance itself from mysticism as well as from magic, the Judeo-Christian tradition shuns not only sorcery, but also what Weber calls the 'exemplary prophet,' a figure that is characterized by an ecstatic relation to the divine. Trance and possession are criticized since they attempt to flee from the world that God has created. What is required instead is the 'emissary prophet' who no longer functions as God's 'vessel,' but has become instead his 'tool.'[xxiv] With careful sobriety the emissary prophet encounters the divine as the giver of the law. Working as God's instrument, he teaches his population to mould life in accordance with the divine will.

The result is the ethos of active, "inner-worldly asceticism," Weber's name for an asceticism which has turned away from a "contemplative 'flight from the world' and dedicated itself instead to "'work in the world.'"[xxv] Placed in the role of custodian or guardian, the active ascetic seeks to "create the kingdom of heaven on earth,"† transforming the world through the activity of labour. With the active ascetic, then, economic activity ceases to be a hindrance to religious life and becomes instead a sacred duty.[95]

Weber maintains that the ethos of active asceticism reached its apex in Calvinism.[96] It is clear from his work, however, that the roots of the Protestant ethic predate the reformation. According to Weber, the first inklings of the religious spirit of capitalism can be found in the monasteries of the Middle Ages, for it is in these secluded environments where there first arose a culture based on order, discipline, and rule.

As we have seen, these qualities of monastic life arise from the fact that monks structured their existence according to a new regime of time—indeed, they developed a religious culture which deplored magical and mystical attempts to access realms that existed outside time. In place of this heretical 'escapism,' monasticism insisted on a 'this worldliness' in which spiritual fulfilment came from the management and

---

this—only one, of the determinants of the economic ethic" (*From Max Weber*, 268).

95: "In inner-worldly asceticism, the grace and the chosen state of the religiously qualified man prove themselves in everyday life. To be sure, they do so not in the everyday life as it is given, but in methodical and rationalized routine-activities of workaday life in the service of the Lord. Rationally raised into a vocation, everyday conduct becomes the locus for proving one's state of grace" (Weber, *From Max Weber*, 291).

96: For Weber's discussion of Calvinism as a religious foundation for worldly asceticism, see *The Protestant Ethic and the Spirit of Capitalism*, 56–80.

measure of time itself. Like the Puritans after them, they believed that "not leisure and enjoyment, but only activity serves to increase the glory of God."[xxvi] With their condemnation of idleness, they produced an ethos in which the "waste of time was the first and in principle the deadliest of sins."[xxvii] For according to the Christian ethic which Franklin would later expound, "every hour lost is lost to labour for the glory of God."[xxviii] Thus, writes Weber, "[i]t does not yet hold, with Franklin, that time is money, but the proposition is true in a certain spiritual sense."[xxix]

It is this which allowed these cloistered communities to engineer a culture which, by providing the kernel of the Protestant ethic,[97] managed to spread outside the monasteries' walls. By making time-bound labour a religious imperative, they provided the key to the development of active asceticism, a temporal ethos which, according to Weber, allowed the rationalized, divisible, and quantifiable world of capitalism to prosper.

Part 2: Karl Marx and the Labour Theory of Value

As is well known, Marx's work differs from Weber's in that his theory of capitalism rests not on an analysis of religion, but on a theory of material production. Nevertheless, as we will see, the synthetic statement 'time = money' plays as central a role for Marx as it does for Weber. Regardless of their differences, these two thinkers share the fact that they have developed theories of capitalism which are founded on a particular regime of time.

The key to the Marxist understanding of capitalism is the labour theory of value (which he inherited and modified from the prior history of political economy). As the economist Joseph Schumpeter writes: "The fundamental explanatory principle of any system of economics is always a theory of value. Economic theory concerns facts that are expressed in terms of value, and value is not only the prime mover of the economic cosmos, but also the form in which its phenomena are made comparable and measurable."[xxx] Thus, it is no accident that *Capital, Volume One* opens with a discussion of how commodities obtain their value.

According to Marx, commodities—or 'external objects'—can be "looked at from two points of view of quality and quantity."[xxxi] Qualitatively, commodities are defined by their use-value, that is, their value is

---

97: As Weber writes, "active self-control, which formed the end of the *exercitia* of St. Ignatius and of rational monastic virtues everywhere was also the most important practical ideal of Puritanism" (*The Protestant Ethic and the Spirit of Capitalism*, 72–73).

derived from the fact that they fulfil some 'human need.' Thus, a coat for example, viewed according to its use-value, is something someone wears to keep out the cold. As quantities, however, commodities cease to be determined by the uses they fulfil and become instead "the material bearers of ... exchange-value" (ellipses in original).xxxii The coat is no longer a garment to be worn, but rather an object that can be traded in the marketplace.

This switch from use-value to exchange-value occurs, according to Marx, through a process of abstraction. That is to say that the transformation from quality to quantity requires that commodities be stripped of their concrete use-value and be determined instead by something more abstract. According to Marx, the exchange relation necessarily takes the form of the equation x = y (*i.e.*, 100 loaves of bread is equal to 1 coat). What this equation signifies, he writes, "is that a common element of identical magnitude exists in two different things [...] Both are therefore equal to a third thing, which is in itself neither the one nor the other. Each of them, in so far as it is exchange-value, must therefore be reducible to some third thing."xxxiii

Thus, economic transactions in the form of exchange require the production of an abstract plane in which qualitatively distinct items can be compared. For in order to operate as a medium of exchange, commodities must be capable of being appraised according to some standard measure. This 'standard measure,' writes Marx, cannot "be a geometrical, physical, chemical or other natural property of commodities" since these concrete, qualitative characteristics belong to the commodity as use-value and, as we have seen, commercial exchange occurs through a process of abstraction in which commodities are extracted from their particular use or function.xxxiv

What the exchange relation necessitates, then, is a value determined by a common property that all commodities share. For Marx, this common factor is the fact that all commodities are a product of human labour. Everything from corn to clothes to cars has been created by the hands of the worker. It is important to note that labour is here understood not according to its concrete manifestation (the labourer as farmer, baker, smith, etc.), but is seen instead as "human labour in the abstract."xxxv Thus, Marx concurs with the conclusion of modern political economy (from Adam Smith) that the value of commodities are determined by the quantity of abstract labour which their production requires.

Posing the question as to how this abstract quantity—that is, the amount of labour contained in each item of exchange—is to be determined, the labour theory of value answered thus: through aggregate labour time. "The quantity of labour," writes Marx, "is measured by its duration," or even more emphatically, "[t]he measure of labour is time."xxxvi Time, then, is the means through which abstract labour is quantified. It is the form or standard which serves to calculate exchange -value and is thus the means through which objects are transformed into commodities. To quote Marx: "As exchange-values, all commodities are merely definite quantities of *congealed labour-time*."xxxvii

In the Marxist theory, labour time not only determines exchange-value, but is also the crucial use-value for industrial capitalism and is thus the principal of surplus value. It is this recognition which has been seen—by Lenin amongst others—as the corner stone of Marx's economic theory.[98] For it is surplus value which, according to Marx, accounts both for the (rigorously quantifiable) exploitation of the worker and for the (exactly equivalent) generation of profit and wealth for the capitalist class.

According to the analysis in *Capital*, surplus value is generated by the fact that the capitalist makes the labourer work for more time than is necessary for the reproduction of labour itself. The economist Eugene von Böhm-Bawerk describes the theory as follows. Under capitalism, the working day is divided into two parts:

> In the first part—the "necessary working time"—the worker produces the means necessary for his own support, or the value of those means; and for this part of his labour he receives an equivalent in wages. During the second part—the "surplus working time"—he is exploited, he produces "surplus value" without receiving any equivalent for it.xxxviii

To quote Marx, "the fact that half a day's labour is necessary to keep the labourer alive for 24 hours does not in any way prevent him from working a whole day."xxxix In short, "surplus value is produced by the fact that the capitalist makes the labourer work for him a part of the day without paying him for it."xl The bourgeois mode of production, then, extracts surplus from the 'extra' time that the labourer is forced to work.

Thus, the two key features in Marx's analysis of the capitalist system—exchange-value and surplus value—are constituted through the operations of time. This shows that though Marx is known for his commitment to historicism, the mode of temporality that he sees at work in capitalism is not at all historical. In his analyses of capitalist time, Marx ignores the qualitative time of the calendar in order to concentrate in-

---

98: See Lenin, *Marx, Engels, Marxism*, 54.

stead on the homogeneous, uniform, and purely quantitative time of the clock. For according to Marx, it is the constant ticking of the clock which, as an instrument of labour discipline, underlies the industrial capitalist system by equating time with money in the form of hourly wage-rates, thus providing the universal measure of abstract labour.

Part 3: Böhm-Bawerk and the Positive Theory of Capital

The notion that the capitalist synthesis, 'time = money,' rests solely on the time of the clock is brought into question by the Austrian econo- mist Eugen von Böhm-Bawerk. Böhm-Bawerk's 'positive theory of cap- ital' challenges the implicit bias of both Marx and Weber by focusing, as we will see, on the crucial importance of the variations of qualitative— and ultimately intensive—time in the constitution of capitalist produc- tion.

For our purposes, Böhm-Bawerk's theory is best approached through his book, *Karl Marx and the Close of His System*, a work which, according to Joseph Schumpeter, "will never cease to be *the* critique of Marx in so far as the theoretical content of Marx's system is con- cerned."[xli] The importance of this book in economic theory stems from the fact that it provides a succinct account of why the labour theory of value should be replaced by the theory of marginal utility.[99] Böhm- Bawerk's stated aim is to show that the labour theory of value is, even within Marx's own writings, confused and unworkable.[100] It's success in this regard is such that it, as Paul Sweezy writes in the introduction to the text, "might almost be called the official answer of the economics profession to Marx and the Marxian school."[xlii]

The crucial factor for us here is that Böhm-Bawerk's argument with Marx centres on the question of time. It deals, as Schumpeter says, with "the treatment of the time factor, which is the origin of nine-tenths of

---

99: Schumpeter summarizes the problem with Marx's theory as follows: "The essential point is not whether labour is the true 'source' or 'cause' of economic value. This question may be of primary interest to social philosophers who want to deduce from it ethical claims to the product, and Marx himself was of course not indifferent to this aspect of the problem. For economics as a positive science, however, which has to describe or explain actual processes, it is much more important to ask how the labour theory of value works as a tool of analysis, and the real trouble with it is that it does this very badly" (*Ten Great Economists*, 28).

100: Böhm-Bawerk's main contention is that the labour theory of value as laid out in *Capital, Volume One* cannot be reconciled with the average rate of profit discussed in *Capital, Volume Three*. To quote Böhm-Bawerk: "Marx's third volume contradicts the first. The theory of the average rate of profit and of the prices of production cannot be reconciled with the theory of value" (*Karl Marx and the Close of His System*, 30).

the fundamental difficulties that beset the analytic construction of the economic process."[xliii] For, according to Böhm-Bawerk the problem with Marx, and more generally with the labour theory of value, is that it misses the overall workings of capitalism by not paying adequate attention to the primary role of credit (and interest rates) in the system of capitalist production.

Capitalism, according to Böhm-Bawerk, is characterized by a switch away from direct production in which "the existence of the good *immediately* follows the expenditure of labour," to what he calls 'roundabout production' in which the means of production are themselves produced.[xliv] Böhm-Bawerk explains this distinction through a variety of illustrations, the simplest of which is the example of collecting water. In a society based on direct production, water is collected by going to the river each day. In a system based on roundabout production, however, a pipe is built that can carry the water directly into one's home.

In Marxist terms, this can be stated by saying that the technological developments intrinsic to constant capital are a necessary feature of capitalist production. Yet, though this can be phrased through Marxist terminology, it is not a statement of Marx's own position, for Marx's concentration on labour power—coupled with his insistence that surplus value can only be generated through variable capital (employed labour)—meant that he could only view constant capital as a mass of dead labour—a necessary but sterile weight. Böhm-Bawerk thus departs from Marx in developing a theory in which change in constant capital has a fundamental role both for the creation of profit and for the circulation of capital.

For Böhm-Bawerk, then, the time of technological innovation, research, and development is inserted as a positive force in the economy. For the crucial fact about roundabout production is that while it obtains a greater result and yields a larger final product than direct production (it is obviously ultimately more efficient to get your water from a tap than to have to go to the river each day to collect it) it does so by sacrificing time. Roundabout production is 'time consuming.' "The roundabout ways of capital," writes Böhm-Bawerk, "are fruitful but long; they procure us more or better consumption of goods, but only at a later period of time. This is one of the ground pillars of the theory of capital."[xlv] "In this loss of time which is, as a rule, bound up with the capitalist process," he continues, "lies the sole ground of that much-talked-of and much-deplored dependence of labourer on capitalist."[xlvi] The capitalist, as bearer of risk, mobilizes labour, through credit, on the prospects of future production potentials (not merely that of immediate extraction of surplus value).[101] Joseph Schumpeter explains the theory as follows:

> Workers and landlords live on what their means of production produce. They do *not*, however, live on what they are at any given time engaged in producing—their current output is of course not yet ripe for consumption—but on products that have been produced at *some previous time*. To furnish this store of means of subsistence is the function of the capitalists—workers and landlords can be said then to live, always and everywhere, on advances made to them by the capitalists.[102/xlvii]

This, however, is only one side of the equation. Böhm-Bawerk's analysis insists that credit is always coupled with interest, for it is by means of interest that capitalism is able to profit on the sacrifice of time inherent in its mode of production. Böhm-Bawerk's "positive theory of capital" then rests on twin forces of time in which the temporal delay of roundabout production is compensated by the phenomenon of interest. "The great synthesis of these two elements, this disengagement and combination of time and added returns, alone makes possible a consistent theory of the role of time in production."[xlviii]

Interest, the practice of charging money for time, is founded, according to Böhm-Bawerk, on the qualitative difference between present and future. It rests on the fact that present goods are more highly valued than those which become available in the future.[xlix] That is, one is generally willing to pay more for something which is available now than for the same product which will only be available at some future date. There is then, in short, a difference in value between present and future commodities: "interest is simply the price expression of this difference."[l]

Thus, whereas the labour theory of value shows how time works as a force in the construction of the labourer and constitution of the working day, for Böhm-Bawerk, time is itself a positive economic force. Rather than the relation between time and money being mediated by labour time, the situation is closer to the reverse, since industrial capitalism itself develops within the context of prospective production— 'industrial revolutions' or technological innovations—which are antici-

101: To attempt, as Marx does, to calculate a 'rate of exploitation' without reference to this prospective production radically diminishes the importance of the time element in the system.

102: The labour theory of value is necessarily blind to this fundamental aspect of the capitalist mode of production. For in determining value through duration of labour time, it fails to take into account the effects of when this labour takes place.

pated by interest rates (the cost of credit). For Böhm-Bawerk, then, it is the intensive difference between present and future (a difference which is irreducible to the time measured by clock) which ultimately accounts for the capitalist equation of time with money.

In the previous section it was argued that the split between calendars and clocks corresponds to an abstract distinction in the nature of time itself. It sought to show that in the period since the Middle Ages, a process of abstraction occurred—not in human thought, but through technical invention and engineering—which made this distinction manifest. The development of the mechanical clock and its subsequent innovations freed time from its sole representation in the calendar and, like the time of the 'Transcendental Aesthetic,' established a new mode of temporality which is capable of acting as an autonomous force.

This section followed on from this distinction and showed how the invention of clock time was crucial to the development of a capitalist culture. In this sense, our discussion would appear to concur with the analyses of capitalist time made by the historians and sociologists that are mentioned above, for the majority of these thinkers adopt the view that capitalist time is defined by "the dominance of clock time over space and society."[li] Writing with a deep nostalgia, they warn of the triumph of an abstract and artificial time that has supplanted the 'natural,' organic, and concrete time of the calendar. Capitalism is conceived as a historical event which inaugurated the tyrannical rule of an "empty" time, "divisible into equal, constant, and nonqualitive units."[lii] With the clock, claims Mumford, "abstract time became the new medium of existence."[liii] Alienating people from the qualitative time of the past, it established a world in which a uniform, continuous, and homogeneous time was disassociated from the intrinsic variation of human events.

Our investigation into the theories of Böhm-Bawerk, however, have shown that the capitalist emphasis on clock time must be combined with an account of how the capitalist economy relates to the qualitative time of calendrics.[103] For in equating time with money, capitalism not only functions to extract discipline, work, and efficiency from the abstract time of the clock, but also converts the variations of calendric time into direct economic activity.

103: In the capitalist production of time, calendric temporality operates less as a marker of astronomical cycles than it does as a dating system which distinguishes between past, present, and future. Astronomy, as we have seen, has taken on a secondary role, since the planetary revolutions are now measured by the ticking of the clock. Nevertheless, the calendar is still used to index qualitative distinctions, (year, month, and day of the week), that are inaccessible to clock time and yet crucial to capitalist processes of production.

Thus, in the connection between Kant and capitalism, the analogies between time in the 'Transcendental Aesthetic' and the formal temporality of the clock must be seen as only one side of the story. This is important since, as our discussion of the First *Critique* made clear, the 'Transcendental Aesthetic' is only a single piece of the Kantian system. Intrinsic to the very structure of the *Critique of Pure Reason* is the notion that intuition is blind unless it is combined with the operations of the understanding.

In the same way, without the calendar, the clock is incapable of telling the time, for as has already been noted, the ticking which marks the passage of hours, minutes, and seconds can never, no matter how accurate it becomes, calculate the day, month, or year when something occurs. Thus, clocks are 'blind' without the dates and a.m./p.m. markers which the calendar provides. Telling the time is thus itself a synthetic operation which combines the hour, minute, and second with the calendric anchors of day, month, and year.

In the Kantian system, the two distinct parts of critique are joined together through the schema. Hidden in the recesses of the imagination, the secret of the schema takes the synthetic production of time to its highest power of abstraction. It is thus able to construct a plane which can connect the 'Aesthetic' with the 'Logic,' joining the intuition of time together with the temporal concepts of the understanding.

A transcendental reading of the sociology, economics, and technology of time reveals that the production of capitalist time operates, like the diagram of the schema, to construct an abstract plane which can connect the two sides of timekeeping with each other. Thus, rather than assuming that the transformation to capitalist time occurred by replacing the calendar with the clock, it recognizes that the development of a standardized chronometric could only take place in conjunction with the adoption a globalized calendar.[104] Furthermore, it sees in the universal equation of time with money an abstract process of production which mobilizes both the time of the clock and the time of the calendar into a particular synthetic regime and thus views this equation, or synthesis, as operating on the same plane as the transcendental production of time.

104: The fact that 'the day for all the world begins at Greenwich' shows that GMT is not, as it may first appear, a standardized time based entirely on the clock. In fact, Greenwich time is a synthesis between clock time and the calendric count.

2.3 — History and the Transcendental

This chapter has sought to demonstrate how elements in the transcendental structure of time can be mapped on to the temporal regime of capitalism. The aim in concentrating on this correspondence was not to reduce the transcendental to the status of the empirical, but rather to uncover evidence of transcendental synthesis in the sociological, economic, and technical formations of the empirical world. The claim, then, is not that Kant's writings are the result of the historical experience of capitalist time, for Kant's critical work and his discovery of the transcendental production of time, depends, as we have seen, not on an exploration of experience but on the underlying conditions which make experience possible. What this chapter seeks to maintain, however, is that these abstract, synthetic conditions which underlie experience are not restricted, as Kant believed, to the eternal inner workings of the human subject, but are also found in the technical and cultural machines that have developed within the history of capitalism.

In an attempt to unravel this assertion, the following section turns to the work of Karl Marx and Michel Foucault, two thinkers who maintain that what appear as the universal structures of the transcendental are, in fact, subject to change and transformation. That is, according to both Marx and Foucault, the *a priori* is itself historical. Thus, both provide an account, however implicit, of how it is that the empirical history of capitalism can coincide so closely with the *a priori* domain of the transcendental.

It soon becomes apparent, however, that Marx and Foucault differ radically in their accounts of the relationship between history and the transcendental. Their theoretical positions follow along two very different lines. At stake in this divergence is, as we will see, two drastically distinct ways of understanding history, interiority, and the agency of change.

For Marx, historical time operates as a closed system. The ultimate force in the generation of change, time creates the *a priori* through the power of its own internal dynamics. Foucault's work, on the other hand, reveals that there are certain empirical transformations that are so dramatic and sudden that they can only be explained through the gaps and holes that break open in what otherwise appears as the sealed interiority of history. Foucault thus maintains that rather than being produced inside history, the transformation of the *a priori* impacts history as a force of the outside.

In examining both these theories, the following pages explore the line between experience and that which is independent of experience. It does so in order to ascertain how it is that the transcendental circuits of production manage to affect the empirical domain of history, and vice versa. The underlying aim, once again, is to reveal the interconnections between the Kantian Revolution in the philosophy of time, and the capitalist revolution in the production of time. These interconnections, as we will eventually see, lead ultimately to the conclusion that there are certain events in the history of capitalism which have accessed the *a priori* plane of the transcendental.

Though Marx's take up of Kant is rarely made explicit in his writings, the Marxist critique of Kant is well known, for throughout his texts, Marx implicitly challenges the Kantian position for its ahistoricity.[105] This argument is found in one of its most succinct forms in the opening pages of the *Grundrisse*. Though Marx focuses here on eighteenth-century economists rather than on philosophers, the attack he makes can be easily applied to Kant, as the crux of Marx's contention is that by basing their analyses of production on the individual rather than on the forces of history, these economists presuppose what they should be explaining. For "the eighteenth-century individual," writes Marx, with "the product on one side of the dissolution of the feudal forms of society, on the other side of the new forces of production developed since the sixteenth century [there] appears as an ideal, whose existence they project into the past."[i] By taking the individual "[n]ot as a historic result but as history's point of departure," these economists miss the real forces at work in capitalism, for they fail to see that the bourgeois individual is a product of capitalist production which is itself ultimately a product of the socio-economic forces of history.[ii] To begin with, the individual is, for Marx, "among the unimaginative conceits of the eight-

---

105: "For Marx, Engels and Lenin, Kant's theory of knowledge was defective in three related ways. First, it was held to be ahistorical in its account of the *a priori* contributions made by the mind in the constitution of knowledge: for Kant these fundamental concepts were universal properties of the mind whereas Marxists have tended to understand human cognitive powers as subject to historical transformation and development. Connectedly, whereas Kantianism locates the *a priori* conditions of objective knowledge in the faculties of the mind, Marxism characteristically locates them in indispensable human social practices which have bodily as well as mental aspects. Finally, Engels and Lenin argued that the boundary between the world of knowable 'phenomena' and the unknowable 'things-in-themselves' was not, as Kantianism required, fixed and absolute but was historically relative. The potential knowability of the world as it is, independent and prior to the human subject, was seen as essential to the empirical world-view of Marxism" (Benton, "Kantianism and Neo-Kantianism," 279).

eenth-century" since it takes a contingent product of a particular time and place and treats it as an *a priori* condition of experience.[iii]

Insofar as it is targeted against the economists' presuppositions rather than their conclusions, Marx's argument recalls the structure of transcendental critique. Speaking as a true Kantian, Marx contends that theoretical knowledge should begin not with experience, but with the constitutive forces that produce that experience. However, the content of Marx's assertions can also be read as an example of critique 'turned on its head.' Thus, Marx's historical materialism attempts to do to Kant what it is so famous for doing to Hegel.

Formulated in this way, Marx's attack on the "unimaginative conceits of the eighteenth-century" can be reread as follows: Kant is said to have asked what are the necessary conditions that produce experience. His answer depended on a revolutionary new role for the transcendental subject. Marx turns this question around and asks, 'what are the necessary conditions which produce the transcendental subject.' His answer, of course, is capitalism.

Marx's contention, then, is that Kant mistakes a particular and contingent product of capitalism—the bourgeois individual—for the universal and eternal subject of philosophy. Implicit in this contention, as we will see, is the notion that transcendental structures are ultimately produced through the internal dynamics of history. For, according to historical materialism, capitalism is a particular socio-economic arrangement that "is itself the product of a long course of development, of a series of revolutions in the modes of production and exchange."[iv]

Marxist history, as is well known, generally divides into three phases, or modes of production, the ancient, the feudal, and the bourgeois.[106] These three phases are related dialectally such that each successive mode of production develops out of the internal contradictions of the previous one. Joseph Schumpeter summarized this point as follows: "The forms of production themselves have a logic of their own; that is to say, they change according to necessities inherent in them so as to produce their own workings."[v] Thus, according to Marxist philosophy,

---

106: Actually, Marxism usually singles out four stages of development. Note the following from Marx's *Contribution to the Critique of Political Economy*: "In broad outlines we can designate the Asiatic, the ancient, the feudal, and the modern bourgeois methods of production as so many epochs in the progress of the economic formation of society" (13). Marx believed, however, that the first of these, the Asiatic mode, existed outside the progressive development of history; see *Karl Marx on Colonialism and Modernization*. The over-simplification of a history characterized by these three rigid stages was questioned and complicated, even by Marx himself, in later writings. Nevertheless, it is still considered to be the basic structure of historical materialism.

the ancient necessarily gave way to the feudal, and the feudal necessarily gave way to the bourgeois. Each stage is both historically and dialectically related to the previous one such that "higher relations of production never appear before the material conditions of their existence have matured in the womb of the old society."[vi] It is this logical unfolding of history which is, for Marx, the ultimate force of production and the real agency of change: it generates both the capitalist system and its corresponding structures of knowledge.[107]

Thus, for Marx, it is no great surprise that Kant's account of the philosophy of time should converge with changes in the technology and socio-economics of time which have emerged under capitalism for both, regardless of the fact that they occur in radically different spheres, are a product and expression of the same stage of historical development. Transcendental and capitalist time coincide since both are the result of the inevitable changes in modes of production which constitute the internal dynamics of historical time.

In likening his philosophy to the Copernican Revolution, Kant seems to anticipate the Marxist contention that the discovery of the transcendental was a fundamentally historical event. Indeed, it is only as a historical event that it makes any sense to speak of his thought as a revolution. Nevertheless, Kant is insistent that the discovery of the transcendental could not have been derived from historical causes.

In the 'Transcendental Doctrine of Method,' the last section of the First *Critique*, Kant describes how his philosophical method relies on the architectonic, or the "art of constructing systems."[vii] This requires the extraction of an *a priori* schema or outline which "lies hidden in reason, like a germ."[viii] Once uncovered, this *a priori* schema, writes Kant, is capable of making "a system out of a mere aggregate of knowledge."[ix]

The *Critique of Pure Reason*—a text so complex it could only have been written with such a monogram or outline in mind—is Kant's demonstration that the art of the architectonic exists. Yet, Kant is adamant that this is an art which can never be learnt, for learning according to Kant, is based on the successive accumulation of facts. As such it can only add one thing after the other, destined to remain at the level of the aggregate; endlessly piecing parts together, it is caught by the successive temporality of history.

> Anyone, therefore, who has *learnt* (in the strict sense of that term) a system of philosophy [...] although he may have all its principles, explanations, and proofs, together with the formal

---

107: See in particular Karl Marx, *The German Ideology*.

divisions of the whole body of doctrine, in his head, and, so to speak, at his fingers' ends, has no more than a complete *historical* knowledge of [that] philosophy.[x]

Although Kant contends that "philosophy can never be learned, save only in a historical fashion," he nevertheless maintains that the art of the transcendental necessarily eludes all such historical knowledge.[xi] For according to Kant, to be in history is to be trapped inside experience, stuck at the level of an empirical succession. The "cosmical concept" of the transcendental (which is inherently systemic and involves the production of time itself) cannot be accessed through the interiority of successive temporality.[xii] Thus, though Kant's Copernican Revolution is dated and thus appears as if from history, its genesis is necessarily exterior to historical time. For, as we have seen, Kant's is a revolution that does not occur *in* time but *to* time.

Thus, in seeking to reduce the transcendental to historical forces, Marx deliberately suppresses the radicality of the Kantian philosophy of time. By enveloping everything within the closed system of historical development and asserting that the *a priori* are ultimately a product of the *a posteriori*, he leaves no room for a theory of transcendental production. Moreover, in maintaining that transcendental time is determined by historical time, it can be argued—in a Spinozistic sense—that Marx fails to take heed of his own materialism. Though he seeks to reformulate Hegelian idealism by sticking to the 'real ground of history,' his commitment to dialectics requires that temporal transformations be overcoded with the transcendent logic of historical time, whose own production can never be explained. That is to say that Marx's historical, evolutionary, or developmental philosophy which focuses on the processes of production as they occur in time cannot also account for the production of time itself.

For an analysis that is at once more transcendental and more materialist, we turn now to the work of Michel Foucault. Foucault's works concentrate on the workings of power in order to map shifts in historical regimes. Power, in Foucault, serves as a diagram for the underlying forces governing everything from what people believe, to how bodies move, to the way in which objects are produced.[108] Thus, by investigating the transformations in different regimes of power—he focuses especially on the shift from the classical to the disciplinary regime—Foucault arrives at a theory of discontinuities which itself underlies the rigidity of *a priori* structures.

108: For a discussion of Foucault's work on power as a diagrammatics, see Deleuze, *Foucault*, 33–36.

According to Foucault, in the disciplinary regime, power has ceased to be in the hands of the despot. Rather than a "privilege that one might possess," power begins to operate as a "network of relations," its "dispositions, manoeuvres, tactics, techniques and functionings" circulating everywhere within the social field.[xiii] No longer the type of force which lashes out from above, the micro-physics of disciplinary power inserts itself directly into the body, subtly articulating its motions, posture, and rhythms. In this new 'economy,' power is productive rather than repressive. It must be "conceived not as a property, but as a strategy."[xiv] Such a power, writes Foucault, "has to qualify, measure, appraise, and hierarchize rather than display itself in its murderous splendour."[xv]

Foucault introduces this new regime in the first few pages of *Discipline and Punish* through an examination of a prisoner's timetable. Thus we find amongst the first signs of the transformation of power, a rationalization, scheduling, and control of time. Foucault's work traces this new form of control as it spreads from prisons to factories to schools.[109] To quote from an exemplary passage:

> In the elementary schools, the division of time became increasingly minute; [...] In the early nineteenth century, the following time-table was suggested for the *Écoles mutuelles*, or 'mutual improvement of schools': 8.45 entrance of the monitor, 8.52 the monitor's summons, 8.56 entrance of the children and prayer, 9.00 the children go to their benches, 9.04 the first slate, 9.08 end of dictation, 9.12 second slate, etc.[xvi]

Foucault insists, however, that this maniacal ordering of time was only the first step in the new 'economy' of power. As the disciplinary regime unfolded, monastic asceticism was replaced by a more constructive force.

> The principle that underlay the time-table in its traditional form was essentially negative; it was the principle of non-idleness: it was forbidden to waste time, which was counted by God and paid for by men [...] Discipline, on the other hand, arranges a positive economy; it poses the principle of a theoretically ever-growing use of time: exhaustion rather than use.[xvii]

109: Disciplinary power "cannot be identified with any one institution or apparatus precisely because it is a type of power, a technology, that traverses every kind of apparatus or institution [...] making them converge and function in a new way" (Deleuze, *Foucault*, 26).

Thus, the role of time became crucial not only for scheduling the days' activities, but also for a sort of internal articulation of the body. "In the correct use of the body, which makes possible a correct use of time, nothing must remain idle or useless: everything must be called upon to form the support of the act required."xviii In the disciplinary regime, writes Foucault, "time penetrates the body and with it all the meticulous controls of power."xix

This is the world of Taylorism: chronometric efficiency, and time and motion studies; a world in which the bodies of soldiers, schoolchildren, and most especially workers are subject to "[a] sort of anatomo-chronological schema of behaviour [...] The act is broken down into its elements; the position of the body, limbs, articulations is defined; to each movement are assigned a direction, an aptitude, a duration; their order of succession is prescribed."xx

The goal is to maintain "maximum speed and maximum efficiency" by "extracting, from time, ever more available moments, and from each moment, ever more useful forces."xxi In a regime in which time is equated with money, power must develop "a new technique for making profit out of the movement of passing time."xxii The question of the disciplinary regime, writes Foucault, is "[h]ow can one capitalize the time of individuals, accumulate it in each of them, in their bodies, in their forces or in their abilities, in a way that is susceptible of use and control? How can one organize profitable durations? The disciplines [...] must be understood as machinery for adding up and capitalizing time."xxiii

In *Discipline and Punish*, the shift from the classical to the disciplinary regime is introduced through the contrast between two modes of punishment. In a famous passage, Foucault opposes a graphic depiction of torture with a meticulous description of the rigid time-scheduling of prison life. "We have, then," writes Foucault in the opening section of the book, "a public execution and a timetable [...] Less than a century separates them."xxiv

This swift passage from one form of punishment to another is often taken to be exemplary of what Foucault called discontinuities. This concept is introduced by Foucault in order to explain how and why, at certain moments, a particular regime of power undergoes "a global modification."110/xxv Foucault makes use of the concept by repeatedly showing how, over the course of history, there have been moments when, "in

---

110: "My problem," Foucault is quoted as saying, was "to pose the question, 'How is it that at certain moments and in certain orders of knowledge, there are these sudden take-offs, these hastenings of evolution, these transformations which fail to correspond to the calm, continuist image that is normally accredited?'" (*Power/Knowledge*, 112).

the space of a few years," an entirely "new 'regime' in discourse and forms of knowledge" emerged.[xxvi]

Discontinuities thus mark a sort of irruption that crashes into history as "the intrusion of an outside."[xxvii] Operating in an exterior relation to the developmental forces of history, they appear as if from nowhere, introducing an entirely new regime of power and reconditioning the *a priori* structures on which our experience depends. Thus, for Foucault, as Deleuze writes, "[t]hings are not joined together by a process of continuity or interiorization [...] but instead they rejoin above and beyond the breaks and discontinuous (mutation)."[xxviii]

The term discontinuity, however, not only designates transformations in the operations of power, but also marks a heterogeneity intrinsic to the nature time itself. Contained within the sentence from *Discipline and Punish* that is quoted above, for example, is a distinction between various modes of temporality, from the festive time of the torturous spectacle, through the metric and quantitative time of the prisoners' timetable, to the time which marks the passing of the century. These different time systems are radically—even transcendentally—incommensurable. Even the supposed consistency of historical time fails to tie them together: there is nothing in the continuity of time (the century) that can account, for example, for the introduction of a new mode of time as evidenced in the timetable. Thus, the concept of discontinuity is not only used empirically to show the breaks or ruptures in history but is also used transcendentally to designate the lack of consistency or continuity between radically different structures of time.[111] In this way, Foucault begins the process of constructing the conceptual tools necessary to connect the exteriority of the transcendental production of time with the interiority of historical variation, or the changes which happen in time.

111: This notion of discontinuity connects with what Deleuze sees as Foucault's transcendentalism. Deleuze depicts Foucault as a neo-Kantian by running his work through the machinery of the First *Critique*. He sees the Kantian division between 'The Logic' and 'The Aesthetic' as transformed by Foucault into the distinction between visibilities and statements, and views Foucault's diagrammaticism as the "analogue of the Kantian schematicism" (*Foucault*, 82). The legitimacy of these mappings, according to Deleuze, stems from the fact that Foucault, like Kant, is interested in the *a priori* conditions of experience, and like Kant, sees in these conditions a distinction between receptivity (intuition, or visibilities) and spontaneity (understanding, or statements) (60). This analysis by Deleuze strengthens the notion that the concept of discontinuity is introduced by Foucault in order to construct a transcendental view of historical change.

3 — The Materialist Revolution: Time in *Capitalism and Schizophrenia*

3.0 — Aeon or: The Plane of Consistency

In the classical Western tradition, time was considered to be synonymous with change. Manifest in the celestial revolutions, it was measured by the cyclical processes of astronomy and felt in the patterns of seasonal variation and the passage of day into night. What the preceding chapters have sought to show is that—in what can loosely be called 'modernity'—developments in both philosophy and in the socio-economic milieu have revolutionized this classical conception of time. More specifically, they have focused on the fact that in both the philosophy of Immanuel Kant and in the timekeeping practices that have emerged under capitalism, time ceased to be identified with change. What these revolutions have produced instead, is a distinction between time as an abstract grid or structure, and the changes and movement which occur within it.

The question of this thesis is how an innovation such as this can occur to the abstract nature of time. Or, to put it another way, how are we to explain events which happen not only in time, but to time? Our response, as we will see, requires that time be understood as an abstract process of production which is itself open to transformative events. This necessitates a further reformulation of the relation between time and change such that these concepts are no longer equated—as in the classical tradition—nor subordinated to a hierarchical relation—as in the modern conception—but rather coexist together on an immanent plane.

Both the writings of Immanuel Kant and the history of capitalism's timekeeping systems provide some suggestions as to how such an account might be formulated. First, we find in Kant a theory of time which ceases to be the result of a single act of transcendent creation. No longer tied to the realm of metaphysical speculation, transcendental time—the invention or discovery of the First *Critique*—is defined as a process of *a priori* synthesis. This is of crucial importance since an immanent theory of temporal innovation requires, first of all, a conception of time that is not transcendently fixed.

Secondly, as we have seen, the Kantian discovery of time as a process of production comes during a period of great historical change in the culture and technics of timekeeping practices. The history of time under capitalism is a story of continuous innovation, mutation, and change. These changes, which include the development of the mechanical clock and the establishment of global time-zones, have been so profound that it is not uncommon for theorists to argue that at the core of capitalism as a socio-economic system lies its unique ability to have transformed the nature of time.[112]

It is far from clear, however, how material innovations in the culture and technics of time can be linked to time as it is conceived of by transcendental philosophy. The problem this thesis encounters then, is how to synthesize these two sides and thereby establish a connection between the transcendental conception of time and the technical machines (clocks and calendars), socio-economic institutions (GMT), and cultural imperatives ('time = money') that constitute time in the capitalist world. Implicit in this problem—as should be clear from the preceding chapters—lies a more general question which concerns the relationship between abstract thought and material practice. This thesis has formulated this question in the terms set out by the transcendental philosophy of time. In doing so, it sees the link between the philosophical and the cultural (conceived of as a particular technological and socio-economic regime) as dependent on an immanent relation between the transcendental production of time and empirical innovations in timekeeping technologies, and the cultural practices which surround them. As such, the previous chapter sought to explore the complexity inherent in trying to establish this relation by way of a debate between the writings of Kant and works of Marxist philosophy.

According to Kant, as has already been shown, the schism between the transcendental and the empirical creates a disjunction between historical change and the philosophical structure of time. This is because Kant associates change with the experience of the empirical world. The transcendental, on the other hand, is absolutely detached from the realm of continuous movement. Transcendental time is thus conceived of as a 'pure intuition' which Kant names 'the form of inner sense.' It functions, in this role, as a numerical synthesizer, ordering and sequencing anything which happens to fill it. A one-dimensional linear succession which provides the underlying format to every thought and perception, time is a constant structure or matrix that is indifferent—and exterior—to the empirical attributes through which it is experienced. Thus, Kant maintains that while all appearances necessarily occur in time, "we can

---

112: We have seen in the previous chapter that the works of the key theorists of modern capitalism—for example Mumford, Marx, and Weber—can all be formulated in this way.

quite well think time as void of appearances."[i] This distinction between time and the changes which occur within it is—as has already been noted—what makes Kantian thought revolutionary. It also, however, serves to separate the transcendental philosophy of time from its cultural, technological, and socio-economic surroundings.

It is precisely on this point that Marx(ism) criticizes Kant. For according to Marx(ism), in ignoring thought's socio-economic context, idealist philosophy mistakes consequence for cause, and remains blind to the primary processes of production. Historical materialism attacks the *Critique* through its famous contention that philosophy is dependent upon its material conditions and that reason's *a priori* structures are determined by the empirical forces of history.[113] Thus, for Marx, the changes which occur in time are ultimately responsible for the production of an abstract conception of time.

However sympathetic one might be to Marx's underlying intention, the notion that the nature of time is a product of history is paradoxical at best. It is unacceptable here because it rules out the possibility of transcendental production and thus cannot account for innovation in the abstract construction of time. It is the strength of transcendental philosophy to show that there is a realm, independent of experience, which is itself productive. It is this realm of abstract production which constitutes the underlying conditions of the empirical world. Every historical mode of production happens in time and therefore necessarily presumes a process of production which it itself cannot—at least straightforwardly—produce. As Kant writes in the 'Transcendental Aesthetic,' since time "underlies all intuitions," the "actuality of appearances is possible at all" only inside the representation of time.[ii] In failing to see time as a presupposition of the changes which occur within it, Marx suppresses the exteriority of the transcendental. Slipping into Hegelian idealism, he betrays his materialist inclinations by positing the logic of dialectical history as the everlasting structure of time.

113: Note the following from Marx's *The German Ideology*: "In direct contrast to German philosophy, which descends from heaven to earth, here it is a matter of ascending from earth to heaven. That is to say, not of setting out from what men say, imagine, conceive, nor from men as narrated, thought of, imagined, conceived, in order to arrive at men in the flesh; but setting out from real, active men, and on the basis of their real life-process demonstrating the development of the ideological reflexes and echoes of this life process. The phantoms formed in the brains of men are also, necessarily, sublimates of their material life-process, which is empirically verifiable and bound to material premises [...] It is not consciousness that determines life, but life that determines consciousness" (42).

The problem, then, remains, for neither Kant nor Marx can account for how an event which occurs in time (and is thus empirical) can effectuate innovation in the transcendental nature of time. Michel Foucault attempts to address this problem with his concept of discontinuities, a concept which is meant to designate the "rifts and instabilities" that operate to disrupt the apparent continuity of historical time.[iii] There is then in Foucault, as Deleuze writes, *"an emergence of forces which doubles history,* or rather envelops it, according to the Nietzschean conception."[iv] These forces are undoubtedly linked to the Kantian synthesis of the transcendental in that the rifts or cracks they break open mark, above all, the incommensurability of transcendental structures. Yet the actual process through which this doubling of history takes place is left unclear. Foucault thus shows us the fact that the transcendental is at work in the generation of history, but he neither gives an account of the ways in which these transcendental disruptions operate in themselves, nor how they are able to connect with or act upon the empirical matter of history.[114] It is this problem which must be surpassed if we are to succeed in projecting a line that can connect the temporal machines of capitalism with the transcendental production of time.

In the classical tradition, time was defined in relation to the concept of eternity. Its identity as a process of never-ending change was conceived of negatively, in opposition to the wholeness, unity, and stasis of the eternal. Plato, as we have seen, described time as the image of eternity, a description which ensured that temporal change be regarded as belonging to the realm of appearance and illusion. Despite its all-encompassing nature, time was a mirage, a shadowy mirror of the eternal nature of forms.

From the beginning, this thesis has viewed the Kantian and capitalist revolutions in relation to this classical tradition. We have seen how, when taken together, they provide us with a modern conception of time. However, though they are successful in transforming the nature of time, both leave the concept of eternity basically unaltered. It is the con-

114: In his book, *The Order of Things*, Foucault himself admits that he focused on outlining discontinuous change without examining either the causes of these changes or the mechanisms through which they occur. To quote Foucault: "It seemed to me it would not be prudent for the moment to force a solution I felt incapable, I admit, of offering: the traditional explanations – spirit of the time, technological or social changes, influences of various kinds – struck me for the most part of being more magical than effective. In this work, then, I left the problem of causes to one side; I chose instead to confining myself to the transformations themselves, thinking that this would be an indispensable step if, one day, a theory of scientific change and epistemological causality was to be constructed" (xiii).

tention of this thesis that to make the connection between Kant and capitalism—and thus develop a materialist account of the transcendental production of time—requires a reformulation not only of our conception of time, but also of that which constitutes its outside (that which is conventionally thought of as eternity).

The following chapter seeks to accomplish this by drawing on the work of Deleuze and Guattari. In particular, it focuses on two main elements of their work which, taken together, enable them to explain how cultural and technological innovations in timekeeping practices can effectuate changes in the abstract production of time. These two elements are:

1. A revolution that frees transcendental production from the interiority of idealist thought.

Towards the beginning of their two-volume work, *Capitalism and Schizophrenia*, Deleuze and Guattari evoke the name of transcendental philosophy to call for a revolution, "this time materialist," which is aimed at transforming critical thought.[115] This 'second' revolution follows Kant in making use of the practice of critique to replace the transcendence of creation with the synthetic processes of the transcendental. This time, however, the revolution proceeds by way of a critique of the Kantian system itself. Subtracting the illusion of transcendence (which remains as a relic in Kant's writing) in favour of a philosophy based on immanence, Deleuze and Guattari unshackle transcendental production from the organized unity of the subject, liberating it from the realm of epistemology and representation. According to Deleuze and Guattari's 'transcendental materialism,' abstract production is a material process, not an epistemological one. Deeply influenced by Spinoza, their work dissolves the rigid distinction between matter and thought and is thus able to flatten

---

115: In *Anti-Oedipus*, Deleuze and Guattari present this revolution as a critique of psychoanalysis. "In what he termed the critical revolution, Kant intended to discover criteria immanent to understanding so as to distinguish between the legitimate and the illegitimate uses of the syntheses of consciousness. In the name of *transcendental* philosophy (immanence of criteria), he therefore denounced the transcendent use of syntheses such as appeared in metaphysics. In like fashion we are compelled to say that psychoanalysis has its metaphysics—its name is Oedipus. And that a revolution—this time materialist—can proceed only by way of a critique of Oedipus, by denouncing the illegitimate use of the synthesis of the unconscious as found in Oedipal psychoanalysis, so as to rediscover a transcendental unconscious defined by the immanence of its

cultural, technological, socio-economic, and philosophical events on to a single plane.[116]

2. A philosophy of time that replaces the notion of eternity with the concept of Aeon.

We have seen from the start that central to Kant's Copernican Revolution is a redefinition of time. This section will show that *Capitalism and Schizophrenia's* materialist revolution also involves a reinvention in the philosophy of time, though it diverges from Kant by concentrating not so much on the interiority of time, but on the exteriority of the eternal.

In the Kantian system, eternity appears in a variety of different ways. In the 'Transcendental Aesthetic,' it is constituted as the infinity of an extensive series; in 'The Deduction,' it is produced as the whole of time conceived of as one; and in the doctrine of the thing-in-itself, it mirrors the classical conception of a quasi-divine transcendence. Deleuze and Guattari overturn all of these conceptions of eternity, replacing them with their own unique reformulation of the Gnostic notion of Aeon. Thus, in Deleuze and Guattari, everlasting extension gives way to an intensive continuum. This is held together not by a unified identity, but by the singularity of a plane populated by machinic multiplicities whose continuous processes of variation make no distinction between what occurs in time and the production of time itself. These singularities—or Aeonic occurrences—are not above, beyond, or segregated over and against time, but are rather flat with the production of time and constitute its immanent outside.

It is with this notion of Aeon as an immanent outside that Deleuze and Guattari's transcendental materialism manages to close the gap between an abstract production of time and the socio-history of timekeeping practices. Through the concept of Aeon, they uncover the possibility of events that do not break into time from a transcendent beyond—as is the case with eternity—but rather constitute a plane of virtuality whose intensive variation is ultimately responsible for the production of our experience of time.

---

criteria, and a corresponding practice that we shall call schizoanalysis" (75).
116: It is for this reason that Deleuze and Guattari are able to speak in a single breath of vegetation and linguistic analyses, geological formations and the Gothic literature of H.P. Lovecraft, packs of wolves and Kantian theory, tics, and the philosophy of Spinoza.

3.1 — Transcendental Materialism: *Capitalism and Schizophrenia's* Critique of Kant

For Deleuze and Guattari, the world is composed of two planes—or rather, there is a single plane which composes itself in two ways.[117] The most familiar of these—the one that seems most common or easy to perceive—they name the plane of organization and development. On this plane, the world is governed by structure and genesis, and things are determined according to their substance and form. This is why the plane of organization has more in common with an overall plan—the plan of divine creation—than it does with the flat geometry of a plane.[118] Functioning with a tree-like logic of evolutionary growth, the plane of organization treats everything as a kind of organism. Bound by arborescence and hierarchy, it operates through a process of stratification, always placing one level on top of the other in accordance with a strict code.[119] Unable to account for its own immanent production, this stratified plane necessarily appeals to the interiority of a higher dimension as ultimate cause. The plane of development is thus invariably hidden or elusive, existing "only in a supplementary dimension to that to which it gives rise ($n + 1$)."[i] This is why, for Deleuze and Guattari, the strata are 'judgments of God,' and also why the plane of organization is otherwise known as the plane of transcendence.[ii]

"Then, there is an altogether different plane, or an altogether different conception of the plane."[iii] Here, things escape the form, substance, and hierarchy of the organism by partaking in intensive voyages and by drawing lines of flight. On this plane—the plane of immanence or consistency—there is no distinction between nature and artifice, matter and thought, people and things. Populated by singularities, not subjects, this is a Spinozistic conception of the plane[120] in which bodies are defined

---

117: These two planes are not dialectically opposed as thesis is to antithesis, both because the two planes are simultaneously and continuously under production, and also because there is always a series of complex passages between them. As Deleuze and Guattari write, "why does the opposition between two kinds of planes lead to a still more abstract hypothesis? Because one continuously passes from one to the other, by unnoticeable degrees and without being aware of it, or one becomes aware of it only afterwards" (*A Thousand Plateaus*, 269).

118: As Brian Massumi, the translator of *A Thousand Plateaus* points out, in French "the word *plan* designates both a 'plane' in the geometrical sense and a 'plan'" (xvii).

119: Stratification as a process of production characterized by split intensities, double articulation, and relations of hierarchy is described in detail in the plateau entitled "10,000 B.C.: The Geology of Morals," in *A Thousand Plateaus*, 39–74.

120: The plane of consistency or immanence is exactly equivalent to Spinoza's understanding of Substance or Nature as defined in the *Ethics*, and this is why Deleuze and

by the power of their relations. Consisting solely of collective assemblages or intensive multiplicities, the plane of consistency is constituted by its immanent lines of communication and connectivity. In this way, it has more in common with the heterogeneous multiplicity of the rhizome than with the organized unity of the tree.[121] Like a rhizome, it is flat insofar as it spreads horizontally rather than through the addition of stratified layers: it is a plane, not a plan, in that it requires nothing above or beyond itself to act as the agent of its own production. As Deleuze and Guattari write, "however many dimensions it may have, [the plane of immanence] never has a supplementary dimension to that which transpires upon it."[iv] It is thus necessarily a force of destratification. As the plane where "form is constantly being dissolved," it dismantles the authority and structures of development, escapes from organization, and overturns or eludes the judgements of God.[122/v]

Deleuze and Guattari's engagement with Kant is, in large part, determined by their relation to these two different planes. This is attested to by the fact that without this as a reference point, their take up of Kant can often appear contradictory and confused, for it is never quite certain whether Kant should be considered as an ally or an enemy. Is his thought central or can it be ignored? This confusion is partly due to the general method of *Capitalism and Schizophrenia*, which seems to have more in common with the sample-based creations of digital technology than with traditional modes of philosophical analysis. Treating texts as a DJ would tracks, Deleuze and Guattari emphasize rhythm and style[123] just as much as logical argumentation, and work by extracting refrains they can use rather than through the adoption of a totalizing or overarching theory.[124]

Guattari call the *Ethics* the "great book of the BwO [Body without Organs]" (*A Thousand Plateaus*, 153).

121: This distinction—between tree and rhizome—is explicated in the introduction to *A Thousand Plateaus*, 3–25.

122: It is in a text entitled "To Have Done with the Judgment of God" where Antonin Artaud first creates the concept of a 'body without organs.' "Man is sick because he is badly constructed. We must make up our minds to strip him bare in order to scrape off this animalcule that itches him mortally, god, and with god his organs. For tie me up if you wish, but there is nothing more useless than an organ. When you will have given him a body without organs, then you will have delivered him from his automatic reactions and restored him to his true freedom" (570–571).

123: For example, lecturing on Kant, Deleuze advises his students not to follow every line of what "is really a very difficult book," but rather to just "follow the rhythm" ("Kant: Synthesis and Time," 34).

124: As Foucault writes in the introduction to *Anti-Oedipus*, "it would be a mistake to read *Anti-Oedipus* as the new theoretical reference (you know that much-heralded theory that finally encompasses everything, that finally totalizes and reassures)" (xii).

Yet, as with all good synthetic creations, Deleuze and Guattari's sampling of Kant is subject to the most rigorous criteria. Their aim—as stated at the outset—is to embark on a revolution that will transform transcendental idealism into a materialism. This they accomplish by discarding all those elements of the Kantian system which serve to bind it to the plane of organization and development, not so as to deny the importance of his system, but rather so as to remain true to the method of critique. For, as we will see, it is this method itself which insists that the realm of the transcendental be liberated from the structure and plan of the organism and flattened on to an immanent plane.

In order to follow this critical revolution, we will begin in the strata, as Deleuze and Guattari advise,[125] and attempt to enumerate the various features which organize and develop Kantian thought into an overall plan.

The preface to the *Critique of Pure Reason* presents the work as a comprehensive system that is intended as the exhaustive inventory of all the possessions of pure reason. It is meant to provide 'the science of transcendental philosophy' with a "complete architectonic plan."[vi] "In this enquiry," writes Kant, "I have made completeness my chief aim, and I venture to assert that there is not a single metaphysical problem which has not been solved, or for the solution of which the key at least has not been supplied."[vii] So certain is he that nothing has escaped his all-inclusive structure, that Kant maintains that the *Critique* "leaves no task [for its] successors save that of adapting it in a *didactic* manner according to their own preferences, without being able add anything whatsoever to its content."[viii]

Kant's confidence in the exhaustiveness of his work stems from his belief in the systematic unity of critique. For Kant, the art of constructing systems consists in the ability to unite the manifold of knowledge under one idea. Ordered by this single identity, the system is likened to an animal body, which even as an embryo contains all its parts within the whole. Conceived of in this manner, transcendental philosophy is complete from its very inception and should evolve like any other organism, "grow[ing] from within (*per intus-susceptionem*), and not by any external addition (*per appositionem*)."[ix]

As an organism, the transcendental system originates out of the mind of the human subject. Known alternatively as the transcendental unity of apperception, the transcendental subject, or the 'I think'— this "pure original unchangable consciousness"—is the seed or embryo of

---

125: "It is through a meticulous relation to the strata that one succeeds in freeing lines of flight" (Deleuze and Guattari, *A Thousand Plateaus*, 161).

the architectonic.[x] Functioning in the *Critique* to unite the synthetic multiplicity under a single idea, it serves to provide uniformity to the manifold, synthesize concepts with intuition, and ensure that all our experiences are our own. It is, in short, both the cause and creator of *a priori* synthesis, and as such forms the structuring principle of the plan.

The ability to treat the transcendental as a systematic unity is ultimately a result of the epistemological nature of Kantian thought, for it is only when thought of as an epistemological representation that the synthetic manifold can be organized under a single idea. It is no coincidence then, that in Kant, *a priori* synthesis (or the abstract conditions of experience) conforms to the principles of reason; rather, it is because the transcendental is a mental structure imposed on the world through the interiority of the knowing mind that this isomorphy necessarily exists. As Kant writes, "the order and regularity in the appearances [...] we ourselves introduce," for "such synthetic unity could not be established *a priori* if there were not subjective grounds of such unity contained *a priori* in the original cognitive powers of our mind."[xi] Composed on the plane of organization then, Kantian philosophy is less concerned with what the world is really like than with how we are destined to know it.

It is through this attempt to limit the ambitions of philosophy, however, that the Kantian system makes way for the judgments of God. Critique had sought to restrict the domain of reason to an island, yet in conceiving of the transcendental as an epistemological representation, it invariably sees that beyond this "land of truth" is a "wide and stormy ocean."[xii] Restricted to an interiorized world of phenomenal representations, critical thought cannot help but point to a realm beyond its borders. Kant names this the thing-in-itself and seeks to banish it from his system by insisting that because it transcends all knowledge, it must remain exterior to the scope of philosophy.[126]

Yet, with the distinction between what we know and the thing-in-itself, Kant aligns himself with his classical predecessors. "Limit[ing] all that we can theoretically *know* to mere appearances," he divides the world according to the traditional disjunction which opposes the reality of essence to the shadowy illusion of appearances.[xiii] It is this which is ultimately responsible for the idealism of Kantian thought and is also what allows for an element of transcendence to permeate the entirety of his system. According to the doctrine of the thing-in-itself, the synthetic structures of the 'I think' are haunted by a transcendent or higher di-

---

126: "The true correlate to sensibility, the thing in it itself is not known and cannot be known" (Kant, *Critique of Pure Reason*, 74 [A30/B45]).

mension which the subject cannot know. In this way, Kant guides thought precisely towards those metaphysical questions he claims he is trying to avoid. Supposedly confined to epistemology, critique seeks to limit reason, but only in order to leave room for faith.

With its systematic unity, its strengthening of the subject, and its faith in epistemology and the transcendence which this implies, it may seem as though one finds in Kant a philosopher who conforms with absolute exactitude to the stratified conception of the plan. Surely even God could not ask for a more uncompromising mode of development, a stricter organizing structure, or a more stringent desire for unity. Yet, nonetheless, the Kantian system too is composed of lines of flight. For despite the apparent rigidity of the architectonic, there is a path in critical philosophy which leads away from the form of the organism and the hierarchical structure of the plan. On this line, transcendental philosophy appears less as a totalizing system and more as a systematic method. From this point of view, the critical project turns away from its organization and development and aims instead to demolish hidden transcendence in order to discover an immanent plane.

As every student of Kant is aware, transcendental philosophy is based on the practice of critique. "Our age," writes Kant "is, in especial degree, the age of criticism, and to criticism everything must submit."[xiv] What is meant here by criticism is a philosophical method or tool which bases thought on criteria immanent to the understanding. Targeting metaphysics, "the Queen of all the sciences," critique denounces transcendence as an illegitimate synthesis in order to remain on an immanent plane.[xv] Aimed at ensuring that nothing be granted that cannot "sustain the test of free and open examination," it insists on abandoning any principles that demand unquestioning belief.[xvi] In this way, critique is inherently anti-authoritarian.[127] Refusing "to be any longer put off by illusory knowledge," it "dismisses all groundless pretensions" and refuses to seek recourse in "despotic decrees."[xvii]

Transcendental materialism draws on Kant's Copernican Revolution in that it is based on the practice of critique. Like Kant, Deleuze and Guattari adopt the critical method in order to rid thought of the illusion of transcendence and develop a philosophical system which adheres to immanent criteria. In this way—though it is far from the didactic analyses Kant expected from his successors—*Capitalism and Schizophrenia* is a strictly Kantian text. It soon becomes clear, however, that to follow

---

127: This is why the French Revolution is often seen as the political equivalent to Kant's philosophical revolution. See, for example, Heine, *Religion and Philosophy in Germany*, 108.

through with the critical method so that the thought of the transcendental can reach the plane of consistency, there is much in Kant's own work which must be overturned. The time has come for the Kantian system itself to submit to critique.

In the hands of Deleuze and Guattari, then, Kantian thought undergoes a radical transmutation. This is done in accordance with Kant's own principles, not by adding anything new to the system, but rather through a process of subtraction. Though they use nothing but this simple arithmetic procedure, Deleuze and Guattari's critique nevertheless has a devastating effect, for what they subtract is the identity and unity of the system—that is, the one thing essential to the completeness of the architectonic plan.

From the point of view of transcendental materialism, it is the critical project itself which requires that the system be dismantled in this way. For the notion that the transcendental plane can be united under one idea is, according to Deleuze and Guattari, an attempt—however surreptitious—to "re-establish a kind of transcendence" and thus cannot be reconciled with the immanence demanded by critique.[xviii] As Deleuze and Guattari write, "unity always operates in an empty dimension supplementary to that of the system considered."[xix] Thus, unity must be subtracted from the system ($n - 1$) if the syntheses of the transcendental are to be flattened on to an immanent plane.

Deleuze and Guattari's assault on systematic unity thus necessarily involves a critique of the transcendental subject. For in maintaining that the synthetic *a priori* are processes which occur inside the mind, Kant positions the subject, as we have seen, as the system's single, organizing idea. It is in this context that the 'critique of Oedipus' found in *Capitalism and Schizophrenia* must be seen, for according to Deleuze and Guattari, the subject is "the locus of an illusion."[xx] Though it is merely a peripheral side effect of more primary processes, it operates by falling back on the agents of its own production "which now seem to emanate from it as a quasi-cause."[xxi] The subject is thus a residuum which presents itself as an original foundation, the product of a 'miraculating machine.'[128] Thus, according to *Capitalism and Schizophrenia*, to follow Kant in presuming the interiority of the human intellect is a betrayal of the critical project, for the Kantian contention that we only have access to a

---

128: In *Anti-Oedipus*, Deleuze and Guattari speak of the body of capital in the same way: "It falls back on all production, constituting a surface over which the forces and agents of production are distributed, thereby appropriating for itself all surplus production and arrogating to itself both the whole and the parts of the process, which now seem to emanate from it as a quasi-cause. Forces and agents come to represent a miraculous form of its own power: they appear to be 'miraculated' by it" (10).

world that we ourselves have constructed is an illegitimate synthesis of reason. In this way, Deleuze and Guattari's critique of the subject is strictly equivalent to Kant's attack on metaphysics, since both are dismissed for their reliance on transcendence, authority, and faith.

Replacing the illusionary transcendence of the subject with a Spinozistic lens, Deleuze and Guattari release transcendental production from its confines in representation through the development of a non-epistemological critique. Seeking "to determine an impersonal and pre-individual transcendental field," they strip from the Kantian system the 'error of idealism' and detach the synthetic *a priori* from its containment inside the mind.[xxii] *Capitalism and Schizophrenia* thus treats the synthesis of the First *Critique* not as the operations of conscious reasoning, but as the machinic functions of a purely materialist unconscious[129] which does not represent the real, but operates instead as the abstract force which constructs it.[130]

Finally, as we will see in greater detail in the following section, Deleuze and Guattari revolutionize Kant by ultimately dismantling the distinction between essence and appearance. Acting as Spinozists, they flatten the Kantian division between what we know and the thing-in-itself on to a continuum or immanent plane, as Kant's attempt to restrict his philosophy to epistemology sacrifices the immanence of criteria to a faith in transcendence. For Deleuze and Guattari, then, Kant's claim that his work is derived from the *a priori* development and organization of the architectonic plan is an attempt to 'reterritorialize' the immanence of the transcendental field. What Kant discovered when he gained access to the realm of the transcendental was not the unity and identity of an organism, but the disorganized multiplicity of a common plane; what Deleuze and Guattari, following Artaud, will call the Body without Organs (BwO).

It should be clear by now that in order to engage with transcendental philosophy, the *Critique of Pure Reason* must be treated not as a representational text but as a conceptual key. An approach from this perspective requires that we view Kant less as an Enlightenment thinker and more, to quote Deleuze, as "the analogue of a great explorer."[xxiii] Seen from this perspective, the Kantian texts cease to be the colorless ac-

---

129: In *Anti-Oedipus*, Deleuze and Guattari describe the unconscious as a factory, a workshop (55). "For the unconscious itself is no more structural than personal, it does not symbolize any more than it imagines or represents; it engineers, it is machinic. Neither imaginary nor symbolic, it is the Real in itself, the 'impossible real' and its production" (53).

130: This is why the question posed by *Capitalism and Schizophrenia* is not, 'What does it mean?' but rather, 'How does it work?'

counts from the law courts of reason and become instead the record of a 'stationary voyage' which unlocks realms beneath and between the empirical world. Underneath the rigid boundaries of appearances, transcendental philosophy discovers the seething processes of the synthetic *a priori*—a plane of production which, though it functions independently of experience, is no less real for being abstract. In the Kantian system, it is this transcendental plane, with its continuous processes of connection and combination, which replaces the transcendence of God and metaphysics.

That Deleuze and Guattari have followed Kant on this voyage, and are committed to a philosophy driven by synthesis, is made clear from the very first lines of *Capitalism and Schizophrenia*: "Everywhere *it* is machines—real ones not figurative ones: machines driving other machines, machines being driven by other machines."[xiv]

To see the world in terms of a machinic production is not—as it may first appear—to be caught in an industrialized or mechanistic vision. Operating with post-cybernetic principles, Deleuze and Guattari define machines neither by the form of technical integration nor the molar-manufactured substances of transcendent technology, but rather by disintegrated molecular production which combines (amongst others) biological, chemical, geological, and cultural components. The machines of Deleuze and Guattari operate as intensive multiplicities—flat or rhizomic assemblages—functioning immanently rather than as mechanisms controlled by a transcendent, supplementary, or preprogrammed plan.

In equating transcendental synthesis with machines, Deleuze and Guattari replace the Kantian emphasis on the unity of the subject and its epistemological representations with non-human agents defined solely by their ability to connect things together or drive things apart. They thus push Kantian thought on to its most destratifying line and develop a philosophy—true to a radically transcendental critique—which dismantles the architectonic by transforming the Kantian plan on to a flat, intensive, and immanent plane.

3.2 — From Eternity to Aeon

From the point of view of the philosophy of time, Deleuze and Guattari depart from Kant not so much by questioning his account of time, but rather through a critique of his notion of eternity. This critique, as we will see, involves a radical mutation in the philosophical understanding of the eternal, for despite the revolutionary nature of Kantian thought, his notion of eternity varies little from the view of the eternal developed in the classical Western tradition. With Deleuze and Guattari, however, eternity becomes something altogether different. Rather than an idealist construction—which it is for both Kant and Plato—Deleuze and Guattari develop an account of the eternal which is fully materialist but nevertheless exterior to time. In this way, transcendental materialism discovers a notion of the eternal properly belonging to the immanence of critique. This discovery is of such importance that just as it has been said of Kant that "all the creations and novelties which he brings to philosophy rest on the creation or discovery of an entirely new conception of time," so too can it be said of Deleuze and Guattari that all of their creations and novelties rest on an entirely new conception of eternity.[i]

In the *Critique of Pure Reason*, eternity is produced in at least three different ways. It first appears in the 'Transcendental Aesthetic' as a formal property of the intuition of time. According to Kant, time as intuition (or the form of inner sense) is best thought of as an extensive arithmetic sequence whose closest analogy is a one-dimensional number line.[131] Like a number line, the transcendental form of time is an everlasting, homogeneous series, infinite in both directions. Thus, in this first instance, it is the infinitude of time which constitutes eternity.

The second place in which eternity is produced is in the 'Transcendental Deduction.' Here, the eternal is considered to be an aspect of the transcendental unity of apperception, as it is the unity of the subject which ensures that the everlasting series of time be brought under a single identity. United in this way, the eternal, in this second case, is constructed as the whole of time conceived of as one.

The third zone in Kant's writings in which the eternal is consolidated is in the doctrine of the thing-in-itself. There, the eternal is evoked in opposition to the phenomenal appearance of time. Conceived of as a divine essence, eternity, in this doctrine, is considered to be the timelessness of a transcendent outside.

The conception of eternity developed by Deleuze and Guattari differs fundamentally from all three of these instantiations within the Kantian system for three reasons. First, because the kind of infinity which is aligned with the transcendental materialist notion of eternity is not the extensive infinity of an everlasting series, but rather the intensive infinity of continuum. Secondly, though the eternal as an intensive

---

131: To quote from Kant's First *Critique*: "We represent the time-sequence by a line progressing to infinity [...] and we reason from the properties of this line to all the properties of time" (77 [A33/B50]).

continuum involves the whole of time, this is not because it is united under a single subject. Instead, for Deleuze and Guattari, the eternal is the mode of time proper to the plane of consistency. This single plane is characterized by the continuous variation of machinic multiplicities and not by the stasis of an unchanging identity. Finally, though the intensive time of the plane of consistency is exterior to time, it is not conceived of as a transcendent beyond. Rather, as we will see, eternity, for Deleuze and Guattari, is a body which constructs an immanent outside.

—1: Extensive versus Intensive Time—

> What is this time which need not be infinite but
> only "infinitely subdivisible?" It is the Aion.
>
> —Gilles Deleuze, *The Logic of Sense*, 61

According to Kant, our intuition of appearances is comprised of extensive magnitudes. "Appearances," he writes, "are all without exception *magnitudes*, indeed *extensive magnitudes*."[ii] What Kant means by an extensive magnitude is one whose parts are apprehended successively—that is to say, the pure intuitions (space and time) are extensive in that they order the manifold of appearance into a succession. This successive synthesis operates by organizing things into parts, and then gathering those parts into a whole. Thus, according to transcendental philosophy, to perceive something in space and time is to apprehend it as an aggregate. To quote from the First *Critique*, "every appearance is as intuition an extensive magnitude; only in the successive synthesis of part to part in [the process of] its apprehension can it come to be known" (brackets in original).[iii]

In the work of Deleuze and Guattari, the Greek God Chronos provides the name for extensive time. Constructed as an infinite series of extensive magnitudes, Chronos is characterized by the "successive advance from one moment to another," marking the linear order of a purely metric time.[iv] Composed entirely of "interlocking presents" which follow one another forever, it is a time made up of homogeneous units, measured instants, or cardinal beats which serve to enclose the multiplicity of the world in between its limits.[v] In Kantian terms, Chronos is the temporality of experience, the form of time in which the empirical ego is caught.

Yet, as even Kant himself is aware, our perception of the world is not altogether captured by the temporality of Chronos. In a somewhat obscure section of the First *Critique* entitled the 'Anticipation of Perception,' Kant makes clear that there is something other than intuition at work in the construction of appearances. Since space and time are never perceived directly, there must be something in addition to intuition that constitutes perception. This Kant calls the "matter for some object in general," the "real of sensation," or "*realitas phaenomenon*," and insists that instead of extensive magnitudes, it is comprised of intensive degrees.[vi] "In all appearances," he writes, "the real, that is an object of sensation, has an intensive magnitude, that is, a degree."[vii]

The difference between extensive magnitudes and intensive degrees is perhaps most obvious in our perception of space, since the same extensive space can be filled with varying degrees of intensities. To quote Deleuze: "the same space can be filled by a more or less intense red, the same room can be filled with a more or less intense heat, the same volume can be filled with a more or less dense matter."[viii]

Yet the distinction between the intuition of extension and the apprehension of intensities is just as much a temporal one, for there is a time of intensities that differs fundamentally from the extensive temporality of Chronos. Deleuze and Guattari name this intensive time Aeon, and throughout their work, systematically oppose it to the workings of Chronos. It is these two readings of time—time as Chronos and time as Aeon—which transcendental materialism uses to replace the classical disjunction between the appearance of time and the essence of eternity.

Aeon can be distinguished from Chronos, first of all, because unlike extensive magnitudes, the apprehension of intensities does not take place through successive syntheses. Rather than "proceeding from parts to the whole," intensities are instead apprehended in a single instant.[ix] To quote Deleuze:

> The apprehension of an intensive quantity is instantaneous, which is to say its unity no longer comes from the sum of its successive parts. The unity of a given intensive quantity is apprehended in an instant. Which amounts to saying that when I say "it's 30 degrees," the 30-degree heat is not the sum of three times ten degrees [...] thirty degrees is not three 10-degree heats.[x]

Thus, unlike extensive magnitudes, intensive degrees are not made up of homogeneous units. Rather than a temporal succession which unites the manifold of sensation into aggregates or organized wholes, Aeon is comprised solely of intensive quantities, each of which is itself a multiplicity. According to Deleuze and Guattari, these intensive multiplicities "cannot increase or diminish without their elements changing in nature."[xi] They thus create a diagonal line which bypasses the stratic distinctions between constant and variable, quantity and quality, and produce a time of continuous variation whose elements cannot change in size without changing in nature.

> One of the essential characteristics of the dream of multiplicity is that each element ceaselessly varies and alters its distance in relation to the others [...] These variable distances are not extensive quantities divisible by each other; rather, each is indivisible, or "relatively indivisible," in other words, they are not divisible below or above a certain threshold, they cannot increase or diminish *without their elements changing in nature* [...] What is the significance of these indivisible distances that are ceaselessly transformed, and cannot be divided or transformed without their elements changing in nature each time? Is it not the intensive character of this kind of multiplicity's elements and their relation between them? Exactly like a speed or a temperature, which is not composed of other speeds or temperatures but rather is enveloped in or envelops others, each of which marks a change in nature.[xii]

Since it is not composed of an everlasting series of homogeneous units, Aeon does not share the infinity of Chronos. Yet, nonetheless, there is an Aeonic infinity that is greater than the whole of Chronic time. This is because the instant in which intensities are perceived necessarily opens itself on to a continuum. For, as we have seen, to say that intensities are apprehended instantaneously does not mean that they occur inside a unit of extensive time.

Like extensive aggregates, intensive quantities are multiplicities, but they are composed of intensive rather than extensive parts. They divide (but only into themselves) in accordance with an order of envelopment whose ultimate term is absolute continuum '0.' In Kant's words, the apprehension of intensities "can diminish to nothing (the void) through infinite gradations."[xiii] Thus, the continuous variations of intensive multiplicities provide the matter for a potentially "infinite subdivision of the abstract moment."[xiv] This occurs through a process of intensive numbering that is based on ordinal sequencing—of greater and lesser—rather than cardinal units. Thus, while extensive magnitudes are counted as the aggregation of parts, intensive degrees can only be quantified as more or less, as intrinsically determined by their distance from absolute cessation ('0') towards which each "can diminish in its degree *in infinitum*."[xv] Though they are comprised of magnitudes, intensive quantities do not measure the successive units of an aggregate but mark an order of differences—or irreducible distances—from degree-zero. It is this virtual continuum, immanent within each instant, that constitutes the infinity of Aeon.[132]

—2: The Unity of Eternity versus the Multiplicity of Aeon—

As has already been noted, the infinity of extensive time is not the only way in which the concept of eternity operates in the Kantian system. In fact, from the point of view of the classical tradition, the infinitude of the 'Transcendental Aesthetic' has more in common with the everlasting than it does with the eternal. In the 'Transcendental Deduction,' however, Kant comes closer to his classical predecessors by presenting unity as an essential property of the eternal. In insisting that the intuition of time be united by the transcendental subject,[133] Kant produces a notion of eternity which can be defined as the whole of time conceived of as one.

According to the Kantian system, it is a necessary and universal principle that the everlasting series of time belongs under the transcendental unity of apperception. This is a result of the fact that for Kant, time is ultimately nothing more than an epistemological representation. Denied "all claim to absolute reality" time, in Kantian language, is 'empirically real but transcendentally ideal.' That it is to say, "if we abstract from the subjective conditions of sensible intuition, time is nothing."[xvi]

Yet in a somewhat complicated twist, the transcendental subject is defined as nothing other than the constant synthesis of time. For despite the fact that it is almost theological in scope, the Kantian subject is remarkably barren. Devoid of all logical or qualitative characteristics, its identity is a purely numerical one. For Kant then, the I is an empty slot,

---

132: This difference between the infinite series of Chronos and the infinitely subdivisible Aeon can perhaps best be understood through the work of Georg Cantor, a nineteenth-century mathematician who specialized in the problem of infinity. Cantor's work shows that there are different types of infinity. The first—and smallest kind—corresponds to Chronos in that it is characterized by any number line extending infinitely in both directions. Cantor called this a 'countable infinity,' or Aleph null ($\aleph_0$). Cantor realized, however, that there are infinitely more numbers in between two points on a number line, if one includes the irrationals, then the infinite set of whole numbers. In other words, there is an infinity greater than Aleph null which exists between any two points on the number line. Cantor called this greater infinity c for continuum. It is continuum that corresponds to the intensive infinity of Aeon.

133: "There can be in us no modes of knowledge, no connection or unity of one mode of knowledge with another, without that unity of consciousness which precedes all data of intuitions, and by relation to which representation of objects is alone possible" (Kant, *Critique of Pure Reason*, 136 [A107]).

defined as nothing other than its ability to remain the same. Conceived of in this manner, the subject—as has already been noted—becomes inextricably bound to the production of time, first, because it is only time (which functions both as the form of inner sense and as the secret of the schematism) which is abstract enough to organize and unite the heterogeneous elements of the system, and second, because as the system's numerical synthesizer, time is essential to the subject's identity. This bind is, in fact, so strong that the transcendental unity of apperception can be seen as synonymous with the operations of transcendental time. To repeat a quotation from Deleuze, "I is an act which constantly carries out the synthesis of time."[xvii]

Thus, in Kantian thought, the infinity of temporal succession is encompassed under a single identity whose unity is conceived of as the whole of time. It is this unity of time which ensures that the multiplicity of the transcendental be formed into an organized totality, while also serving to guarantee the eternal nature—or transcendental completeness—of the Kantian system itself.

As we have seen, transcendental materialism breaks from Kant by viewing unity as a mode of organization produced on the plane of development. Constructed in accordance with the hierarchical structures and tree-like logic of this stratified plane, unity always involves a supplementary dimension. Deleuze and Guattari thus consider it to be a transcendent synthesis, illegitimate from the point of view of critical thought. This is not to say that the production of unity is not materially instantiated; the power of the strata is real. Rather, it is to claim that the unity of the transcendental subject, which Kant considers a necessary presupposition, is itself the product of a contingent structuring principle which happens to be manifested in the architectonic plan. For Deleuze and Guattari, then, the unified subject is a stratified mode of individuation which does not belong to the immanent plane of transcendental thought.

Deleuze and Guattari's critique of unity has important implications for the Kantian theory of eternity developed in the 'Transcendental Deduction.' According to Deleuze and Guattari, the notion of a subject that unites the whole of time under a single identity is not eternally given but is rather produced on the extensive plane of Chronic time. "Chronos," they write, is "the time of measure that situates things and persons, develops a form, and determines a subject."[xviii] Thus, rather than emanating from a presupposed identity, the extensive units of Chronos organize subjects and structure their formations. Always at work dividing things into parts and arranging those parts into wholes,

Chronos, as the time proper to the plane of organization, constitutes the eternal unity of time as a transcendent illusion.

The eternal time of Aeon, on the other hand, constitutes an immanent, intensive plane that is systematically opposed to the experiential world of extensive organization. Since this immanent, undivided plane is not segmented into parts, it cannot be unified into wholes. Thus, as the time of immanence or consistency, Aeon knows nothing of unity.

Unable to be captured under the identity of the transcendental subject, Aeon operates with a mode of individuation that has nothing to do with unified subjects or entities. "There is a mode of individuation," write Deleuze and Guattari, "very different from that of a person, subject, thing or substance [...] A season, a winter, a summer, an hour, a date have a perfect individuality lacking nothing, even though this individuality is different from that of a thing or a subject."[xix]

Instead of being determined by the higher unity of subjects or things, Aeon is populated by "machinic assemblages" (or "intensive multiplicities") whose singularity has more in common with the destratified nature of Spinozistic Modes than it does with the structure and form of identity. In Aeon, write Deleuze and Guattari, individuation is "a question not of organization but of composition."[xx] Dedicated to exploring this non-unified individuality, *Capitalism and Schizophrenia* develops a cartography which maps out the two dimensions (or axes) of this composition: the longitude and latitude of the plane. Drawing on Spinoza, Deleuze and Guattari discover that these two axes can be characterized first by relations of speed and slowness between unformed elements (longitude), and second, by the corresponding capacity for affecting and being affected (latitude).[xxi] According to the Spinozistic materialism of Deleuze and Guattari, these two axes define the individuality of a body on the immanent plane of Aeon.[134]

These intensive singularities, machinic multiplicities, or bodies in the Spinozistic sense, are not individuals that remain consistent throughout time; rather, they are events or Aeonic occurrences that are themselves immanent to the very nature of time. They are becomings, not beings. Comprised of "continuums of intensities" whose elements cannot change in size without changing in nature, these events are in a process

---

134: "In short, if we are Spinozists, we will not define a thing by its form, nor by its organs and its functions, nor as a substance or a subject. Borrowing terms from the Middle Ages, or from geography we will define it as a longitude or latitude [...] The longitudes and latitudes together constitute Nature, the plane of immanence or consistency, which is always variable and is constantly being altered, composed or recomposed, by individuals and collectivities" (Deleuze, *Spinoza*, 127–128).

of "continuous variations, which go beyond constants and variables"; they are "*becomings* which have neither culmination nor subject."[xxii]

These becomings, or intensive events, are eternal in the sense that they involve the whole of time not by uniting it under a single identity, but rather by constituting a mode of distribution in which time is not segmented into parts. As flat multiplicities composed on a single, undivided plane, intensities fill the whole of time to a greater or lesser degree.

For these reasons, Aeonic occurrences break down the distinction between the constant structure of time, and the changes which occur inside it. For as we have seen, the plane of consistency has no supplementary dimension from that which it gives rise. Aeonic events do not occur in time not because they belong to a transcendent outside, but because they are flat with the single plane of immanence which collapses the distinction between time and that which populates it. Equally immanent within any given moment of Chronos, in Aeon "everything happens at once."[xxiii] Operating with a mode of distribution that is incommensurable with the order of Chronos, Aeonic events cannot help but scramble the linear sequence of extensive time.[135]

The identity of Chronos knows the world as a perpetual present, for though the plane of organization segments time into past, present, and future "in accordance with Chronos, only the present exists in time."[xxiv] Past, present, and future are known only as the present that has been, the present that is, and the present that will be. As Schopenhauer says, "[n]o man has lived in the past and none will ever live in the future, the present alone is the form of all life."[xxv]

"Endlessly decompos[ing] itself in both directions at once," Aeon, on the other hand, "forever sidesteps the present."[xxvi] Enveloping the whole of time without unifying it, Aeon is "already past and yet in the future, at once more and less, always the day before and the day after."[136/xxvii] As the "indefinite time of the event," it exhibits a power of virtuality irreducible to the actuality of Chronic time.[xxviii]

135: For a good pulp fiction account of Aeon, see Stephen King's book, *The Shining* (1977), which centres on Jack Torrance's encounters with the Aeonic singularities that haunt the Overlook Hotel.

136: "Aeon: the indefinite time of the event, the floating line that knows only speeds and continually divides that which transpires into an already-there that is at the same time not-yet-here, a simultaneous too-late and too-early, a something that is both going to happen and has just happened" (Deleuze and Guattari, *A Thousand Plateaus*, 262).

—3: Aeon, or Time as Thing-in-Itself—

According to Schopenhauer, Kant's great doctrine "is the doctrine that space, time, and causality belong not to the thing-in-itself but only to the phenomenon, that they are only the forms of our knowledge, not qualities of the thing-in-itself."[xxix] As we have already noted, it is this notion of the thing-in-itself which constitutes the idealism of Kantian thought. It is also, for this reason, the element of the Kantian system which comes closest to the notion of the eternal conceived of by classical philosophy. For in distinguishing between the world that we know and the thing-in-itself, Kant reproduces the classical disjunction which opposes the temporality of appearances to the essence of eternity. For implied in the doctrine of the thing-in-itself is that beyond the structures of the knowing subject—outside the representation of the mind and exterior to the world of phenomena—is another hidden plane of which time is not a part.[137]

In this doctrine, then, eternity is constituted as the timelessness of the thing-in-itself. Evoked as a divine essence, Kant considers it to exceed the limits of critique. It thus operates in the Kantian system as the relic of an older tradition in which knowledge was based not on the immanent principles of the understanding, but on the transcendent authority of faith. Aware that this contradicts the explicit aims of the critical project, Kant attempts to banish all questions pertaining to the thing -in-itself by insisting that they are beyond the scope of transcendental thought. Yet, from the point of view of the philosophy of time, it is already too late. Kantianism has collapsed into a Platonic vision in which time is seen as a trap or enclosure, and eternity, its transcendent outside.

It is here that transcendental materialism's revolt against Kant is most starkly apparent. For, as should now be clear, Deleuze and Guattari replace the opposition between our capture in the phenomenon of time and the exterior essence of the eternal with two different planes of production governed by two different times. In Deleuze and Guattari, it is the transcendent plane of Chronos which produces the interiority of time, and the immanence of Aeon which is its outside.[138]

137: To quote Schopenhauer: "Whatever the thing-in-itself may be, Kant rightly concluded that time, space, and causality [...] could not be its properties, but could come to it only after, and in so far as, it has become representation" (*The World as Will and Representation*, 120).

138: In this sense, the difference between Aeon and Chronos corresponds to the Kantian distinction between the transcendental production of time and the empirical changes in time. Aeon, however, can only be equated with transcendental time if the transcendental is conceived in the terms set out by Deleuze and Guattari's materialist revolution. For Aeon, as we will see, corresponds to the transcendental production of

This notion of an immanent outside requires that Kant's 'great doctrine' be radically transformed. It demands that the idealism which severs what we know from the thing-in-itself be replaced with a materialist plane of consistency which no longer segments or divides.

Deleuze and Guattari conduct this transformation through the adoption of the Kantian theory of intensities. The reason they give so much weight to this particular aspect of transcendental thought is because it is here that the Kantian system becomes fully machinic rather than epistemological. As the 'real of sensation,' intensive quantities are directly affective, not representational. As even Kant himself writes, they have a direct "degree of influence on the sense[s]."[xxx] A production of the real that stems neither from concepts nor the forms of our perception, intensities are what are left when intuition and the understanding are stripped away.

In that it is exterior to the transcendental structures of representation, degree-zero intensity—a state which is immanent to every perception but is nonetheless never perceived—is neither a cessation of thought nor a negation of sensation but is matter as an immanent abstraction.[139] Thus, at degree-zero, intensity—the 'matter of sensation' or 'realitas phaenomenas'—constitutes abstraction as a body which substitutes for any transcendent notion of the absolute reality of the thing-in-itself. Deleuze and Guattari call this abstraction the "uninterrupted continuum of the BwO."[xxxi]

> The BwO causes intensities to pass; it produces them and distributes them in a spatium that is itself intensive, lacking extension. It is not space, nor is it in space; it is matter that occupies space to a given degree—to the degree corresponding to the intensities produced. It is nonstratified, unformed, intense matter, the matrix of intensity, intensity '0'; but there is nothing negative about that zero, there are no negative or opposite intensities. Matter equals energy. Production of the real as an intensive magnitude starting at zero.[xxxii]

Since an intensity is nothing but a virtual descent to zero—which instantiates the distance, difference, or degree which it is—the zero-degree body of intensities functions as an 'immobile motor,' reciprocally produced alongside the intensive sequence itself (for which it provides an immanent limit).[140] It is this circuit of production which accounts for

time only as a body at zero-degree intensity.
139: As Deleuze and Guattari write: "You never reach the Body without Organs, you can't reach it, you are forever attaining it, it is a limit" (*A Thousand Plateaus*, 150).
140: See *Anti-Oedipus*, especially 8–9.

both the exteriority and immanence of the BwO. Intensities make their own plane—which nevertheless intrinsically exceeds them—and since this plane is untranscended, it can be subject to a time beyond that which it itself is.

Thus, Deleuze and Guattari's intensive mutation of critique invokes a temporality—Aeon—which is at once the ultimate real abstraction of both time and the thing-in-itself: matter-time at degree-zero.

The preceding pages have sought to show that despite the revolutionary impact that it had on the philosophy of time, Kant's transcendental idealism retains the classical notion of eternity. For with Kant, just as with Plato, unity, identity, being, and transcendence are all aligned with a conception of the eternal which is opposed to the phenomenon of time.

With the concept of Aeon, Deleuze and Guattari overturn this classical understanding of the eternal. It would be wrong, however, to assume that in ridding the transcendental of its classical ties to eternity, Deleuze and Guattari make of it a secular philosophy. Far from offering a crass materialism or a naïve empiricism, *Capitalism and Schizophrenia* is a Gothic text filled with demons, sorcerers, and werewolves, a text that traffics with the other side. Rather than a sad and disillusioned atheism which would discard the eternal archetype in order to insist that only time exists, and there is no outside, Deleuze and Guattari replace the classical disjunction of time versus eternity with 'two readings of time'—time as Aeon and time as Chronos. In substituting Aeon for eternity, however, they discard the traditional associations of unity, being, and identity which belong to a transcendent realm exterior to time, and replace it with the multiplicity, becoming, and the continuous variation of an immanent outside.

Though these two notions—Aeon and eternity—are in many ways diametrically opposed, they can nevertheless be seen, from a certain perspective, as functionally equivalent.

We have seen in the introduction that Western thought has traditionally lamented our birth into the phenomenal world of restless matter and temporal change. Entangled in the multiplicity of becoming, the human soul is seen to have been separated from its real, eternal essence by the illusory movement of time. Thus, the philosophical and religious quest is aimed at transcending the body and matter, escaping the ever-changing illusion of time, and reaching the truth of eternity.

It is clear from their continuous refrain to treat theory as creation, concepts as tools, philosophy as invention, writing as diagrammatics, and books as assemblages, that the work of Deleuze and Guattari is to be used and not interpreted. In the preface to *Anti-Oedipus*, Michel Foucault, recognizing this, warns the reader that they will find neither a theory nor a philosophy in the pages which follow. Instead, he writes, "I would say that *Anti-Oedipus* (may its authors forgive me) is a book of ethics."[xxxiii] Like Spinoza's *Ethics*[141] then, *Capitalism and Schizophrenia* is best thought of as a 'How To,' or, as Foucault says, as "a manual or guide to everyday life."[142/xxxiv] The aim of this guide is to develop a set of practices which construct lines of flight that can escape sequential order and the interiority of Chronos and make contact with the outside,[143] not so as to transcend matter into the world of spirit, but rather to access the destratified, unformed "Matter of the Plane," the body without organs, and the "singular, nonsegmented multiplicities, or the intensive continuums" that populate it.[xxxv]

141: Spinoza's *Ethics* is a purely practical text in that its aim is to lay down concrete rules for freeing oneself from 'sad passions' and to thereby map a path to an increase in power (or joyful encounters). It is for this reason that Deleuze and Guattari's writings on Spinoza concentrate not so much on the philosophical arguments, but rather on how one can "live in a Spinozist manner" (Deleuze, *Spinoza*, 123).

142: On the same theme, Foucault writes: "I think *Anti-Oedipus* can best be read as an 'art,' in the sense that is conveyed by the term 'erotic art'" (*Anti-Oedipus*, xii).

143: It is this that accounts for the strong Gothic component that runs through *Capitalism and Schizophrenia*, a text that is teeming with references to secrets, sorcery, animal becomings, werewolves, vampires, blind doubles, and Things from the 'Other Side.'

4 — The Aeonic Occurrence

Any event is a fog of a million droplets.

—Gilles Deleuze & Claire Parnet,
"On the Superiority of Anglo-American Literature," 65

And just believe me, friend Infernal Racket!
The greatest events – these are not our loudest, but our stillest hours.

—Friedrich Nietzsche, *Thus Spoke Zarathustra*, 104

4.0 — Anticlimax

In the Biblical tradition, eternity comes at the beginning and the end of history. The ongoing passage of time is thus framed, on one side, by the unformed void which pre-existed creation, and, on the other, by messianic redemption which acts as history's teleological termination point. To quote from the Book of Revelation: "I am Alpha and Omega, the beginning and the ending, the first and the last" (Rev. 22:13). Between these twin limits of time, the eternal impacts history only as punctuating moments in which a transcendent God interrupts the order of time through miracles and divine revelation. In the popular religious understanding of the West, these punctual moments have long since ceased. The world now waits for the eternal in the form of the apocalypse which will bring about the end of time.[144] Though most people leave the anticipation of such a moment to fanatic cults and fiction, at the end of the second millennium a temporal event, an event brought on by a computer bug known as Y2K, brought the promise or threat of the eternal envelopment of history to the fore.

As is now well known, when understood technically, Y2K stems from the fact that until only recently, computers were programmed to read only the last two digits of the year, assuming the prefix '19.' This programming convention dates back to the early days of the computer industry when memory was scarce and expensive, and each line of code was a precious resource.[145] At that time, a space saving protocol called

---

144: End of time apocalyptic scenarios which feed the current cultural imagination include nuclear war, ecological collapse, an asteroid impact, an alien invasion, and a nanotechnologically or genetically engineered virus or mutation.
145: Before technological advances in the early 1990s made high-capacity disk storage and memory chips affordable, memory was a key limitation in computer system design.

for dates to be recorded with 6 digits (YY/MM/DD) instead of 8 (YYYY/MM/DD). More than half a century later, this seemingly banal convention proved to have staggering consequences since it soon become clear that as a result of their two-digit dating system, many of the world's computers were incapable of making the magnitude jump necessary to register the year 2000. Instead of treating the stroke of midnight, December 31st, 1999 as the end of a unit in a linear succession, cyberspace took it to be the completion of a hundred-year count, the pre-programmed signal for computer clocks to return to year zero (99 + 1 = '00). Incapable of recognizing the difference between the year 1900 and the year 2000,[146] cyberspace needed to be 'fixed' if it was to smoothly process the impending millennium.

Though no one could predict the exact consequences if this 'glitch' was not dealt with in time, the fact that it was deeply embedded in a globalized system of date-sensitive information flows meant that, in the pre-millennial years, Y2K was the cause of widespread concern and even panic. The ubiquity of network computing coupled with the hierarchized nature of technological development (which has tended to add new applications on top of already existing code) resulted in the fact that the impact area of Y2K was practically unlimited. As the zero hour approached, it became clear that the vulnerable areas included worldwide finance (especially 'time sensitive' transactions such as payrolls, pensions, insurance policies, stock options, interest, and credit), transportation networks (including air traffic control), weapons systems (nuclear as well as conventional), hospitals, power plants, and most obviously, communication lines.[147] At its most extreme, this two digit error in programming code threatened to shut down planetary networks, erase large chunks of data, and severely disrupt the technological systems on which contemporary civilization depended.[148]

The fact that this threat coincided with the dawn of a new millennium led to a massive cultural investment in Y2K. What appeared from one side to be a simple, technical glitch coincidentally collided with a much older faith in eschatological history. In America, at the cutting edge of capitalism, science fiction scenarios fused with Christian proph-

---

146: Since 19 is the system's cipher, the year 00 is treated as 1900 and not 2000.

147: In the final stage of panic, concern extended to embedded chips which control everything from microwaves to elevators.

148: Note the following 1997 quotation from *The Economist*: "Care for a thrill? Consider what might happen if the 'Millennium Bug,' that tendency for many of the world's computers to mistake the year 2000 for 1900, is not eradicated in time [...] The cover of one news magazine asked recently 'Could two measly digits really halt civilization?' and answered 'Yes, yes—2000 times yes!'" (25).

ecy, producing a contemporary myth in which Y2K ceased to be a mere programming error and became instead the technical mechanism which would bring about the Biblical Armageddon. Thus, rather than a simple glitch which would occur within the evolutionary structure of history, Y2K came to be associated with catastrophic, empirical events that would signal history's very end.[149] On the Internet, Y2K was designated by another acronym that would capture this apocalyptic aspect of the millennium: the end of the twentieth-century was renamed TEOT-WAWKI (or 'The End of The World as We Know It').

On December 31st, 1999, the world watched, tense with anticipation, as Y2K made its way across the time-zones. Yet no matter where, when the clock struck midnight at the dateline, next to nothing occurred. There were no nuclear disasters, no airplane crashes, no market collapses, no power outages, no rioting, not even a terrorist attack. Thus, though it was perhaps sufficiently masked by theatrical gestures and elaborate firework displays, celebrations heralding the arrival of the twenty-first century were overshadowed by a pervasive sense of anticlimax. The most anticipated date in history was a non-event. In the days and weeks that followed, a sense of almost euphoric relief[150] was mixed with a strange anger, even contempt. Y2K, (or 'apocalypse not') is now believed to have been nothing but a hoax, a conspiracy, a myth.

Yet it is precisely the inability to associate Y2K with any actual or empirical incident (especially one of apocalyptic or messianic proportions) that serves to connect this singular, temporal event with the philosophy of Deleuze and Guattari. The fact that Y2K disappointed those awaiting an inauguration of eternity does not mean it was not flat with Aeon.

A Thousand Plateaus, the second volume of *Capitalism and Schizophrenia*, is composed of fifteen sections, thirteen of which are marked by dates. Though these dates correspond to singular events (*e.g.*, the origin of the state, the death of Genghis Khan, etc.) they are not to be mistaken for punctual moments. For Deleuze and Guattari, dates do not speci-

---

149: Everyone is by now familiar with the most apocalyptic scenarios which included nuclear accidents, plane crashes, major disturbances in communication and transportation lines, as well as shortages of food and other basic resources. These various disasters—so the story went—would result in spirals of panic which would feed on themselves, leading to riots, martial law, and general societal collapse. However farfetched, this basic narrative incited an expansion of survivalist movements (especially in America) where many people sold their homes in the cities and moved to the hills with a stockpile of food, firewood, and weapons.

150: Some maintain that the immediate post-millennium market drop was a result not of scepticism, but of increasing faith—the idea being that with nothing to stop it, the economy would grow too fast resulting in an increase in interest rates.

fy points in time, but rather tag plateaus. "A plateau," they write, "is always in the middle, not at the beginning or the end."[i] Defined as a "self-vibrating region of intensities whose development avoids any orientation toward a culmination point," a plateau substitutes the climactic instant for continuums of intensity,[151] and thus operates in an exterior relation to the linear sequence of Chronic time.[ii]

Like the plateaus singled out by Deleuze and Guattari, Y2K is dated—in its case precisely so—and yet, as the pervasive sense of anticlimax made clear, it nevertheless cannot be located at any particular point in time.[152] Thus the question, 'When did Y2K occur?' is inevitably met with a certain degree of mystification. A non-event at the time of its arrival, it is further confused by its unconscious origins and by the fact that it is unclear whether it ever existed as anything other than hype. The question, 'when did it happen?' thus slides into more nebulous questions such as, 'what happened?'[153] or 'did it actually occur?'

This ambivalence, or open-ended nature of the event, is a result of the fact that—as we will later see—Y2K is the name for a machinic multiplicity. As such, it envelops everything from the revolutions of the

---

151: "Bateson cites Balinese culture as an example [of plateaus]: mother-child sexual games, and even quarrels among men, undergo this bizarre intensive stabilization. 'Some sort of continuing plateau of intensity is substituted for [sexual] climax,' war, or a culmination point. It is a regrettable characteristic of the Western mind to relate expressions and actions to exterior or transcendent ends, instead of evaluating them on a plane of consistency on the basis of their intrinsic valuation" (Deleuze and Guattari, *A Thousand Plateaus*, 22).

152: The attempt to locate Y2K in time leads to a series of contradictory impulses. On the one hand, it is tempting to argue that Y2K, as an event, took place long before anyone was conscious of it in the early days of computing when the two-digit dating convention was first introduced. At the time, of course, no one was aware that this mundane bit of programming code would result in an end of the millennium catastrophe. If given any thought at all, it was assumed—in accordance with the science fiction visions of the 1950s—that the computer systems that were then being programmed would no longer be in use by the year 2000. It is just as plausible, however, to date Y2K to the more recent past—around the early 1990s—when the world began to awaken to the problem this dating convention would pose for the millennium, and financial institutions, military, security, traffic control, and other companies of various kinds began to realize that the problem had to be fixed. Yet another possibility, however, is to claim that Y2K—as an event—took place in 1999 when the media coverage, panic, intensity, and apocalyptic hype was at its strongest. Finally, it may be the case that Y2K will only make sense as a significant occurrence in the future when twenty-first-century historians use it as an index for changes that are still unclear.

153: Deleuze and Guattari write of the question 'what happened' in relation to the peculiar temporality of the novella, suggesting that the question itself is an index of Aeonic events. See "1874: Three Novellas, or 'What Happened?'" in *A Thousand Plateaus*, 192–207.

planets, to messianic prophecy, to the history of calendrics, to technological invention, to the cycles or waves of the capitalist economy. At the most extreme, one could view Y2K as spreading throughout the entire span of history. It thus implies an intensive temporality which exists outside the successive instants that constitute Chronic time. Like every intensive singularity, Y2K occupies the whole of time, to a greater or lesser degree.

Y2K will never be anything other than a virtual catastrophe. Though it has had enormous effects inside empirical history, it impacted Chronos only as a pure potentiality; as an immanent machinic accident,[154] Y2K is intensive rather than actual. As such, it must be considered not as a moment extended or unfolded in Chronos, but rather as a plateau or, in other words, a virtual occurrence composed on the immanent and intensive plane which constitutes the exteriority of Aeon.

4.1 — Time-Mutations

Throughout this thesis it has been argued that the modern conception of time—a conception produced in both transcendental philosophy and by the culture and technics of capitalism—involves a distinction between time as a formal structure and the historical variations which occur inside it. In previous social regimes when calendars were dominant and temporality was inseparable from the movements of the stars, this distinction did not exist, and time was itself inherently connected with the qualitative changes now associated with history.

However, both the Copernican Revolution in philosophy and the capitalist revolution in timekeeping systems have overturned this tradition by liberating time from its age-old subordination to movement. Unhinged from the cardinal points which it had been so long destined to measure, time became autonomous from the cyclical patterns of astronomy and there thus emerged a formal time conceived of as a purely

---

154: Y2K has obvious connections with Paul Virilio's theory of the accident. To quote Virilio: "For the Philosopher, substance is absolute and necessary, whereas the accident is relative and contingent. So the accident is what happens unexpectedly to the substance, the product of the recently invented technical object [...] In fact, if no substance can exist in the absence of an accident, then no technical object can be developed without in turn generating 'its' specific accident: ship=ship wreck, train=train wreck, plane=plane crash. The accident is thus the hidden face of technical and scientific progress" (*Politics of the Very Worst*, 92). The argument of this chapter, namely that Y2K corresponds to the virtual time of Aeon rather than the transcendence of eternity, is also in some ways convergent with Virilio's notion of the accident "as an inverted miracle, a secular miracle, a revelation" (90).

quantitative framework that was considered to be separate and distinct from the historical content which happened to fill it.

As we have seen, the culture and technics of modern capitalism emerged in conjunction with a synthetic, temporal regime which served to instantiate this new form of time. This temporal regime—or the capitalist production of time—can be characterized by the following features:

1. The invention and development of the mechanical clock

Though sundials, water clocks, and hour glasses have been in use throughout the long history of timekeeping,[155] it was not until the modern period that these devices gained any degree of technical or social autonomy. Prior to the modern period, the practice of timekeeping, like the philosophy of time, had been inextricably linked to the technical and cultural traditions of a temporality based on the calendar. Starting as early as the fourteenth century with the invention of mechanical escapement, growth in the precision, influence, and ubiquity of the clock ensured that clock time achieved a certain independence or autonomy from the qualitative time of calendar.

2. The synthesis of clock time with the calendar

Formal time, however, cannot be solely equated with clock time. For in order to tell the time, the division of the day into hours, minutes, and seconds must be synthesized with the days of the week and the months of the year. In order to function, timekeeping systems require both a beat and a count. Thus, the ticking of the clock must be combined with the counting system prescribed by the calendar.

3. The global standardization of time

Given tolerable accuracy, the decision of which calendar to use is a purely arbitrary one; capitalism requires only that the world agree on a standardized convention. As a global system from the start,[156] capitalism operates by drawing lines of com-

---

155: See chapter two, "The Division of the Day and Time-Keeping in Antiquity" in Dohrn-van Rossum, *History of the Hour*, 17–28.

156: This claim is supported by the work of Fernand Braudel and world-system theory. See Braudel's *Civilization and Capitalism*, and the works of Immanuel Wallerstein.

munication, trade routes, and transportation networks that criss-cross the globe. The development of a worldwide economy, however, necessitates that the planet be unified under a universal temporal regime. As we have seen, this regime was initially created through an international agreement which divided the planet into a series of standardized time-zones, placing the zero meridian at Greenwich. It also required the worldwide adoption of the Gregorian calendar. With these two things in place, capitalism was able to synthesize the ever-increasing precision of clocks with a unified dating system which could operate as a virtual standard across the globe.

4. The convergence of time with money

Disassociated from the world of empirical change and standardized across the planet, formal time is capable of being rigorously quantified. This allows time (and in particular, duration) to be directly converted into money. The equation 'time = money' is perhaps the most important synthesis in the capitalist regime and is found at the heart of modern analyses of capitalism, including, most famously, Weber's notion of the Protestant ethic and the labour theory of value. It is also, as we have seen through our examination of Böhm-Bawerk, crucial to phenomena such as interest and credit, two features that are essential to the capitalist economy and its mode of production.

These characteristic features of formal time are not static but are rather the result of an ongoing machinic process that produces the formalization of time. In the capitalist regime, it appears that this process—the machinic production of time—converges with the path of technological development. Thus, in contemporary (or postmodern) capitalism, formal time is considered to be instantiated by the digitization of both time and money that takes place in cyberspace.

In keeping with the capitalist trajectory, cyberspace time synthesizes clocks and calendars in such a way that the length of calendric intervals are no longer determined by the revolutions of the planets, but are governed instead by the ticking of the clock. Cut off from astronomical movements, calendars are a pure counting convention that can be programmed into a digital system from the start. With the digitization of time, clocks and calendars became part of the same technical machine. In cyberspace, the beat and the count—the two aspects of timekeeping systems—have become so intermeshed that it is impossible to say, for example, whether Y2K was a glitch in computer clocks, or an error in computer calendars.

The universal nature of Y2K—no country, however 'undeveloped' was thought to be spared—is evidence of the ever-increasing importance of the global standardization of time. Cyberspace, as the technological system of global capitalism in its contemporary phase, supplements—and in part even replaces—the previous dependence on physical trade routes and transportation networks with a virtual web in which geographical boundaries have become redundant. Dependent on instantaneous communications irrespective of place, this virtual web makes the demand for a standardized time that accompanied previous technological grids even more urgent. Cyberspace, like the capitalist system itself, is a distributed network which can only be united by a precisely synchronized and globalized time.

Cyberspace's emphasis on temporal precision and accuracy is primarily due to the intimate interactive dynamics which have developed between technology and economic systems. In cyberspace, flows of capital—which are never anything other than digital code—are continuously subjected to virtual transactions that are sensitive to minute variations in time. As digital code, time and money have converged on a single numerical and technical plane, making the conversion between the two ever more immediate and immanent.

All this is to say that the constitution of formal time is a continuing process constructed in conjunction with its own historical development which it itself 'falls back upon.' This history, however, involves only a very limited conception of change, for it is determined by an empirical advance that follows the smooth, upward curve of technological progress. The history of the clock, for example, tells the story of an evolutionary growth that progresses from mechanical escapement, to the pendulum, to the quartz crystal, to the atomic clock.[157] As a result of this growth curve, there appears to be an underlying constancy to change. Transformations, however, are subordinated to development such that change only occurs to heighten the accuracy and efficiency of the same basic devices.[158]

157: The atomic clock (which measures time by way of the metric beats of a caesium atom) is timekeeping's most current manifestation.

158: This progressive history of technology has reached unprecedented heights with the development of Information Technology. As everyone is all too aware, the cycles of obsolescence maintained by the computer industry happen at an ever-increasing speed. The trajectory of smaller and smaller machines capable of processing more and more data for increasingly diminishing costs seems itself to be continuously intensifying. For example, Moore's Law (which states that processing speeds will double every eighteen months) is itself now outdated.

116

Capitalism's construction of historical progress is much more than a convenient ideology,[159] for the notion that an underlying constancy to change produces a predictable trajectory is a necessary part of the capitalist machine. This is primarily due to the time-lag that is inherent in capitalist production. This time-lag, as we have seen, manifests itself in such phenomena as the investment in constant capital for future gains (roundabout production), credit, interest, and debt. Absolutely reliant on phenomena such as these, it is essential that capitalism treat history as a smooth upward curve,[160] for it is only with a story such as this that the difference between the present and the future can remain open to rigorous quantification.

The problem with this particular construction of the passage of time, however, is that it hides the fact that capitalist history is discontinuous, based more on "[r]uptures and [l]imits" than on the smooth continuity of empirical advance.[i] Underneath the mask of evolutionary development lies a series of radical innovations. As Fernand Braudel writes, "[i]s it not in the nature of capitalism, a sort of rule of the game, that it thrives on change, drawing strength from it?"[ii] Capitalism, then, produces the appearance of a continuous history while simultaneously feeding off unplanned, uncontrolled, unconscious mutations.[161]

For Deleuze and Guattari, social formations are defined not by modes of production, but by 'machinic processes,' and machines work, they write, "only by breaking down."[iii] Crises, ruptures, accidents, and anxieties are misunderstood when one regards them as threats. In order for a machine to function, "it must not function well."[iv] Abandoning the rigid form of the finely tuned, well-oiled mechanisms of a previous age, Deleuze and Guattari define machines through the principles of a post-cybernetic abstraction. No longer dependent on the smooth func-

---

159: That is to say that the 'myth' of historical progress is not constructed in order to fool the masses or as a mystification of underlying real value.

160: The most absurd examples of the prevalent notion that as time passes, things remain basically the same were evident around the time of the millennium when newspapers and magazines were filled with predictions of how our lives would be improved by a series of technical inventions—intelligent clothes, robotic vacuum cleaners, etc.—that would undoubtedly be in place for the year 3000. Surely Bill Joy, the CEO of Sun Microsystems, is much closer to the mark when he warns of the inevitability of unpredictable mutations arising from a convergence of Artificial Intelligence, nanotechnology, and genetic engineering.

161: As Deleuze writes: "Those who continue to have recourse to History and protest against the indetermination of a concept such as 'mutation' should bear in mind the perplexity of real historians when they have to explain why capitalism arose at such a time and such a place when so many factors could have made it equally possible at another time and place" (*Foucault*, 21).

tioning of clearly distinguished parts, cybernetic machines learn and adapt through their mistakes. Feeding on their own misfirings, they "operate only by fits and starts, by grinding and breaking down, in spasms of minor explosions."[v] Capitalism, an intelligent social machine, has learnt this rule. As Deleuze and Guattari write, "[t]he more it breaks down, the more it schizophrenizes, the better it works, the American way."[vi]

Yet these accidents, ruptures, and mutations are more than just breaks in the linear order of developmental history. For, as we have seen in our discussion of Foucault, real discontinuities are mutations not only in time, but to time. "Evolutionism," write Deleuze and Guattari, "has been challenged in many different ways (zigzag movements, stages skipped here or there, irreducible overall breaks)."[vii] *Capitalism and Schizophrenia*'s anti-evolutionism, however, relies on none of these challenges. Instead, it presents a "contingent, singular, ironic, and critical" version of "universal history" in which the great social formations—the primitive machine, the state, and capitalism itself—do not evolve in time, but coexist together as Aeonic virtualities.[viii] Each formation is thus haunted by the others; each 'stage' mutually entangled by strategies of anticipation and deflection.[162] The linear narrative that bases itself on the building blocks of history—successive instants or moments—is thus replaced with a story of flows and their blockages, convergent waves and cybernetic processes that defy linear causation. To quote from *A Thousand Plateaus*:

> Physics and biology present us with reverse causalities that are without finality but testify nonetheless to an action of the future on the present, or the present on the past, for example the convergent wave and the anticipated potential, which imply an inversion of time. More than breaks and zigzags, it is these reverse causalities that shatter evolution.[ix]

For Deleuze and Guattari, history is constituted by the extensive time of Chronos. Its tendency towards evolutionism, teleology, and an internal dynamic advance is a result of the fact that it is necessarily subordinated to a one-dimensional timeline—whose subjectivity is the state[163]—that progresses successively from one moment to the next. Yet

---

162: "In a sense," write Deleuze and Guattari, "capitalism has haunted all forms of society, but it haunts them as their terrifying nightmare, it is the dread they feel of a flow that would elude their codes" (*Anti-Oedipus*, 140).

163: According to Deleuze and Guattari, "history is always written from the sedentary point of view and in the name of a unitary State apparatus" (*A Thousand Plateaus*, 23). In *A Thousand Plateaus*, they oppose this state centred narrative to a "Nomadology, the

this successive, extensive temporality belongs, as we have seen, solely to the plane of organization and development, which—though it presents itself as transcendent cause—operates through the stratification of an immanent plane of consistency. The developmental structure of history, then, like the plane to which it belongs, masks its reliance on an underlying temporality that is intensive in nature. "The system in extension is born of the intensive conditions that make it possible, but it reacts on them, cancels them, represses them, and allows them no more than a mythical expression."[x]

For Deleuze and Guattari, then, the production of Chronic time is generated through the capture of Aeon. "All history does," they write, "is to translate a coexistence of becomings into a succession."[xi] In *Capitalism and Schizophrenia*'s anti-evolutionism, lines of flight, flows, and thresholds of intensity and the continuous process of Aeonic becomings "have replaced history, individual or general."[xii]

> The great geographical adventures of history are lines of flight [...] it is always on a line of flight that we create [...] This primacy of lines of flight must not be understood chronologically, or in the sense of an eternal generality. It is rather the fact and the right of the untimely: a time which is not pulsed, a hecceity [sic] like a wind which blows up, a midnight, a midday.[xiii]

The 'unexpected line' or 'imperceptible rupture' of the untimely—what Nietzsche called "that vaporous region of the unhistorical"—constitute, in Deleuze and Guattari's terms, singularities, machinic multiplicities, or Aeonic events that populate and mutually draw the plane of consistency.[xiv] It is on this plane—however suppressed—that histories take place and extend themselves.

> History is made only by those who oppose history (not by those who insert themselves into it, or even reshape it) [...] The dividing line passes not between history and memory but between punctual "history-memory" systems and diagonal or multilinear assemblages, which are in no way eternal: they have to do with becoming; they are a bit of becoming in the pure state; they are transhistorical. There is no act of creation that is not transhistorical and does not come up from behind or proceed by way of a

---

opposite of a history" (23). Though this topic relates to many of the themes of this thesis, it is far too complex to be dealt with in detail here. For a complete discussion, see "1227: Treatise on Nomadology—The War Machine" and "7000 B.C.: Apparatus of Capture," in *A Thousand Plateaus*, 351–423 and 424–473 respectively.

liberated line. Nietzsche opposes history not to the eternal but to the subhistorical or superhistorical: the Untimely, which is another word for haecceity, becoming, the innocence of becoming (in other words, forgetting as opposed to memory, geography as opposed to history, the map as opposed to the tracing, the rhizome as opposed to arborescence). "The unhistorical is like an atmosphere within which alone life can germinate and with the destruction of which it must vanish... What deed would man be capable of if he had not first that vaporous region of the unhistorical?" Creations are like mutant abstract lines that have detached themselves from the task of representing the world, precisely because they assemble a new type of reality that history can only recontain or relocate in punctual systems.[xv]

History seeks to dismiss Y2K as an accidental incident, for in accordance with the capitalist investment in the production of developmental time, it was necessary to present Y2K not as a mutation, but rather as a glitch, an error, an accident, a bug. In the post-millennial period, even this has been questioned. Yet, while history may remember Y2K as nothing but an overhyped mistake, on the plane that underlies history, Y2K has always been much more. Imperceptibly interrupting developmental time with a singular mutation, it introduced a break in the predictable trajectory of technological advance. This break was itself a temporal event made even more powerful by the fact that it existed primarily as a virtual catastrophe. Like the reverse causalities that Deleuze and Guattari evoke, it operated on the virtual plane that haunts history, empirically realized as a future that acts on the present, and a present that acts on the past.

Insofar as it was ever present, Y2K manifested itself most strongly in the years and months leading up to the millennium. Yet even at that time, Y2K was—at least when understood abstractly—primarily a challenge to the past. An act of calendric insurgency, Y2K threatened the authority of the Gregorian calendar by replacing it with cyberspace's own cyclical count.[164] Operating in this manner, it constructed itself as a

164: Put most simply, the problem with Y2K was that it threatened to replace the year 2000 A.D. with the year 00. This threat, though ultimately unrealized, was an unprecedented challenge to the authority of the Gregorian calendar. For, as year 00, Y2K indexes the fact that cyberspace, rather than reinforcing the temporal regime of modern capitalism, had surreptitiously installed a calendar of its own. Thus, while human culture and nation states had all agreed on the Gregorian calendar as a secular convention, until it was 'fixed,' cyberspace had not. It is the discrepancy between cyberspace's own calendar and the calendar developed by Pope Gregory XIII's reforms that is signaled by the sign Y2K. From the point of view of a radical calendrics, then, the at-time-bomb that permeated the distributed network of contemporary technology by directly targeting the pre-existing unity of capitalist time. Yet, though it contested the past, it functioned most effectively when it was thought to be in the future, incurring massive costs even as a pure potentiality.

As has already been noted, capitalism is a distributed network united not by the dominance of a particular region, culture, or ideology, but rather by the fact that the world is enveloped under a single, standardized time. This global temporal standard is, as we have seen, a synthesis between clock time and the worldwide adoption of the Gregorian calendar.[165] The fact that computers were operating—however imperceptibly—with a calendar which challenged this standard resulted in a virtual time-bomb that threatened the entire global temporal order. Thus, Y2K—at least as a potentiality—achieved the dream parodied in Conrad's *Secret Agent*. A timer so perfected that the timer is the bomb, it operates as if aware that the vulnerability of the system comes from its underlying unity and constructs itself as a sort of retrochronic bomb aimed directly at capitalism by targeting the pre-established order of time.

As a temporal mutation—or reverse causality that 'shatters evolutionism'—Y2K not only exemplified an effect of the present upon the past, but also—and even more starkly—an operation of the future on the present. This is most evident in the instability it introduced into the equation of time and money, an instability generated by the exposition of the pseudo-transcendence of Chronos. In modern capitalism, whether it be in Marx's labour theory of value, Weber's Protestant ethic, or Böhm-Bawerk's analysis of roundabout production, the equation 'time = money' is inevitably associated with duration. The cost of Y2K, however, was only indirectly determined by how long it would take to fix, for the amount spent on labour time and upgrading technology was continuously measured against the potential cost which would result from an error or discrepancy in the semiotic system which marks the

---

tempt to achieve 'millennium compliance' was not merely the reversal of a technical glitch, but a geo-political strategy aimed at the imposition of the Gregorian calendar on cyberspace. 'Fixing' Y2K required the abandonment of an existing calendar, one that had worked successfully around the globe for half a century.

165: Having achieved this standard, the regime of capitalist time insists that it is universally imposed. Thus, by the turn of the millennium there was not a single act(or) or location that could escape this all-encompassing envelopment. No matter how obscure, all local, religious, and culturally specific timekeeping practices are regularly converted into the Gregorian count. In this way, the production of capitalist time concretely implements the Kantian assertion that "[d]ifferent times are but parts of one and the same time" (*Critique of Pure Reason*, 75 [A32/B47]).

date. By revealing that a date—even as a virtuality—has immense economic consequences, Y2K indexed something that was apparently new in the economy of formal time. For what is crucial in the convergence of time and money on the digital plane is not only the immanence and speed of quantitative conversion, but also the increasing importance of systems and transactions that are hypersensitive to the date.

Thus, far from operating as a transcendent grid, Y2K makes clear that the dating system—or formal expression—of capitalist time is a component of the socio-technical apparatus that is itself in need of constant construction. It thus interrupts the apparent stability and continuity of Chronos by conflating the history of time (as technological development) with the variations intrinsic to time's own production.

As early as 1997, it was clear that Y2K was going to be "the single most expensive accident of all time," irrespective of what did or did not occur at midnight, December 31, 1999.†/xvi What makes this so critical for the abstract production of capitalist time is not only how much money was spent, but the fact that it was spent on 'fixing' the date, for in introducing the date as an accident—or positive force—in the capitalist production of time, Y2K constituted itself not only as a historical, but also a temporal mutation.

4.2 — Dates and the Semiotic of Aeon

We have already noted in chapter two that there exists an extremely tight mesh between calendric convention and cultural tradition. Far from a neutral device in the technology of timekeeping systems, calendars have consistently been aligned with a particular type of centralized control, and this is why they have been traditionally managed by the priests or the guardians of the state. For unlike clock time, all the elements of calendrics—the type of numeracy involved, the length and structure of the cyclical patterns, the astronomical revolutions which are chosen to be emphasized, the dates which are ritualized, and the determination of when to start the count—inevitably upholds and consolidates a particular cultural tradition.

It is no surprise, then, that there was an attempt by the Christian religion to claim the date 2000 A.D. as their own. Yet, though this attempt was only somewhat successful,[166] it nonetheless led to a series of

---

166: This is evident, for example, in the case of the religious section in London's 'millennium dome' which, though it was primarily funded by a Hindu family, nevertheless took pains to emphasize the Christian religion.

revealing confusions. For though it is true that Pope Gregory's reforms emerged from within the Christian tradition, according to the calendar he developed, midnight of December 31st, 1999 does not coincide with any particular festival, has no specific commemorative relevance, and does not (as Gregorian year) even mark the beginning of a new millennium.

The most radical, but nevertheless extremely pervasive, attempt to fuse the end of the twentieth century with Christianity involved—as we have seen—treating Y2K as the mechanism through which the prophecies foretold in the Book of Revelation would be realized. This required the creation of a contemporary myth in which the coming of the second millennium as a moment in a calendric count was consistently confused or interchanged with the notion of the millennium as found in Christian theology, where the latter signifies an eternal battle at the end of time when Satan is chained and sealed in the Abyss, and Christ is able to rule on earth for a period of one thousand years (Rev. 20). Needless to say, the idea that Y2K is the sign of the programmatic fulfilment of these prophecies has no doctrinal basis, nor is there anything in the Book of Revelation that is even remotely suggestive of the year 2000 A.D.

Less fervent—or imaginative—believers sought to claim the connection between religion and the date by insisting that the millennium was a commemorative sign for Jesus' 2000-year birthday. Though many people the world over seemed to accept this as a valid assertion, it has no historical, calendric, or religious legitimacy. For even if one accepts the dubious claim that Jesus' birth coincides with the starting point of the Gregorian calendar,[167] the only defensible date for the two-thousandth anniversary of Christ's birth is Christmas day, 2001.

The tendency to conflate New Years with Christmas seems to occur because they follow each other so closely in time. The Christian religion, however, attributes no particular significance to this temporal proximity. The move to place January 1st as the first day of the year was amongst the amendments introduced by Pope Gregory XIII in his attempt to improve the accuracy and precision of the Julian calendar. Yet these gains in accuracy were made at the expense of religious significance, as it is in the Julian calendar that New Years is a much more commemorative date since it falls on March 25th, 'Annunciation day,' which celebrates God's revelation to Mary that she would give birth to Jesus.

More serious, however, than the confusion between New Years and Christmas, is that to celebrate the year 2000 A.D. as the dawn of the

---

167: There is a great deal of debate over the exact year of Jesus' birth. The dates that are most commonly accepted, however, are either 04 B.C. or 12 B.C.

second millennium depends upon the arbitrary conversion of Roman numerals into Hindu-Arab ones. The Gregorian calendar was originally based on a system of alphabetical numerals developed by the Romans and derived from archaic tallying systems.[168] The most crucial feature of this system, from a contemporary point of view, is that—since it was developed before the European acceptance of the decimal system—it does not have zero sign or function. Lacking a year zero, the Gregorian calendar moves directly from 1 B.C. to 1 A.D., and thus marks the passage of two thousand years on January 1st, 2001. The current system of dating which synthesizes the Gregorian count with elements of decimal numeracy[169] is relatively recent.[170] European culture, and in particular the Church, was extremely resistant to Hindu-Arab numeracy, and it was only due to their obvious superiority in precision, accuracy, and efficiency that they were finally (reluctantly) absorbed by the Western world.[171] More than anything else, it is this adoption of the Hindu-Arab numerals that is celebrated in the date 2000.

These systematic confusions—confusions between the calendric millennium and millennialist beliefs, between New Year's Day and Christmas, and between the Roman and Hindu-Arab number systems—suggest that the massive investment in the millennium was more about the date as such than it was about anything that the date was purportedly meant to represent. As Y2K starkly dramatized, the sign 2000 A.D. had much more to do with the techno-social apparatus involved in the global standardization of time than it did with upholding any particular religious, cultural, or calendric tradition.[172]

168: See Georges Ifrah, *The Universal History of Numbers*, 196.

169: The decimal aspects of the contemporary use of the Gregorian calendar include the adoption of the Hindu-Arab numerals, and the emphasis on decades, centuries, and millennia.

170: The Arabs had introduced decimal numeracy to Europe as early as the ninth century. The development of the Gregorian calendar, however, makes clear that up until as late as the sixteenth century, the Church still preferred to use the much less efficient numeracy of Rome (Ifrah, *The Universal History of Numbers*, 537–543).

171: Ifrah writes how resistance to Hindu-Arab numeracy was based on a class dynamic. The "infinitely complicated use of the classical (Roman) counter-abacus" allowed knowledge of arithmetic to be confined to a privileged class who could afford the long and intricate training necessary to master such a baroque numerical system (*The Universal History of Numbers*, 577). Faced with a numerical system that could not fail to make arithmetic more democratic, the ruling classes derided it as a diabolical heresy and refused to engage with it for centuries (571–581).

172: The threat of Y2K was completely indifferent to any specific cultural belief or timekeeping practice. Any given nation or state could insist on their distance from the Gregorian calendar, but this had no impact on their immunity to the danger of Y2K. Cyberspace thus ensured that the millennium was, unquestioningly, a worldwide event.

All this is to say that what many believed to be a celebration of the date as representative sign—in this case, one that signals the apocalyptic end of history—served to mask an unconscious cultural investment in the date as number.

As the illegitimacy of any particular cultural claim to the year 2000 made clear, the libidinal energy that accompanied the millennium was inspired primarily by the decimal neatness of the numeral 2000 and by the substantial—if unconscious—cultural sensitivity to the zero sign. Millennial excitement, then, had less to do with the Gregorian calendar or the religious events prescribed by the Christian tradition than it did with a decimal delirium indifferent to creed. What was celebrated at 00hrs 01/01/00 was the instant when the numbers changed. To quote from *Time Magazine's* "Commemorative Issue":

> Many cultures celebrated despite the fact that most follow completely different calendars, and despite the fact that too many people were pointing out that the millennium doesn't really start until next year and that our system is all messed up anyway, because Jesus was born 2,004 years ago. They celebrated because the most famous odometer mankind has ever created was displaying three zeroes. It's exciting enough when it happens to your own car; when it happens to the world, it makes you downright giddy.[i]

According to Deleuze and Guattari, the plane of consistency has its own particular semiotic. Intensive multiplicities, immanent machines, or singular occurrences are, for them, marked by a very specific use of signs. Two of the most crucial components of this semiotic are the proper name and the date.[173] There is, of course an 'extensive usage' of names which belongs to the plane of organization and development. On this plane, names function as common nouns "ensuring the unification of an aggregate they subsume."[ii] On the plane of consistency, on the other hand, names function intensively. Tagging singularities rather than unifying aggregates or indicating subjects, they "designate something that is of the order of the event, of becoming or of the haecceity."[174/iii]

173: The other components are the indefinite article and the infinitive verb. The date is particularly relevant because, as Deleuze and Guattari write, it "expresses the floating, nonpulsed time proper to Aeon, in other words the time of the pure event or becoming, which articulates relative speeds and slownesses independently of the chronometric or chronological values that time assumes in the other modes" (*A Thousand Plateaus*, 263).
174: "It is the military men and meteorologists," write Deleuze and Guattari, "who hold the secret of proper names, when they give them to a strategic operation or a

Dates too are sometimes used as if they mark points in an extensive temporality. Yet, as we have seen, this is only when they have already been captured by Chronic time. In relation to Aeon, on the other hand, dates are the intensive markers for threshold events or singular becomings, and thus do not indicate a moment in time, but index instead a plateau or continuum of intensity.[175]

Y2K as a sign is a remarkable condensation of this semiotic. With just two letters and a numeral, it operates intensively to produce an 'asignifying semiotic'[176] that is at once both a proper name and a date. What this sign designates is an event that is neither technical nor cultural,[177] but rather machinic. Singular and immanent, virtual but not at all vague, "[a]bstract, singular, and creative, here and now, real yet nonconcrete, actual yet noneffectuated," Y2K, as a date and a name, is the index of an abstract machine.[178/iv]

According to Deleuze and Guattari, abstract machines cut across Chronos—the time in which experience is caught—as a "leap in place, an incorporeal transformation occurring at a zero hour."[v] Instantaneous and immediate, they interrupt the development of history with transformations that are recognizable by "the simultaneity of the statement expressing the transformation and the effect the transformation produces; that is why [these machines] are precisely dated, to the hour, minute, and second and take effect the moment they are dated."[vi] "The abstract machine does not function to represent, even something real, but rather constructs a real that is yet to come, a new type of reality. Thus, when it constitutes points of creation or potentiality it does not stand outside

hurricane. The proper name is not the subject of a tense but the agent of an infinitive" (*A Thousand Plateaus*, 264).

175: In this way, they act as nomad numbers which populate a smooth space without dividing or segmenting it.

176: In the plateau "587 B.C.-A.D. 70: On Several Regime of Signs," Deleuze and Guattari speak of the coutersignifying semiotic which "proceeds by arithmetic and numeration" as the semiotic system of the nomad war machine (*A Thousand Plateaus*, 111–148: 118).

177: Y2K has both a technical and cultural dimension in the sense that, on the one hand, it concerned the incompatibility of calendric systems (a purely cultural concern) and, on the other, a technical glitch in computing code. It is for this reason that Y2K should be considered as a machinic syndrome, a term which is precisely meant to avoid the segmentation between technical and cultural systems.

178: "Abstract, singular, and creative, here and now, real yet nonconcrete, actual yet noneffectuated—that is why abstract machines are dated and named (the Einstein abstract machine, the Webern abstract machine, but also the Galileo, the Bach, or the Beethoven, etc.). Not that they refer to people or to effectuating moments; on the contrary, it is the names and dates that refer to the singularities of the machines and to what they effectuate" (*A Thousand Plateaus*, 511).

history but is instead always 'prior to' history."[vii] This is why, as Deleuze and Guattari write, "[h]istory will never be rid of dates."[viii]

As an abstract machine, Y2K puts a (virtual) end to the arbitrariness of signs. For though it is entirely semiotic, it has direct and instantaneous effects. Occurring at a zero hour, it 'takes effect the moment it is dated,' mobilizing the worldwide economy in an event that is no different from its date.[179] Y2K thus brings an end to the assumption that the

179: It can be argued that the importance of Y2K stems from the fact that it indexes the 'year zero' of cyberspace time (a claim whose legitimacy can only be tested in the future). It seems plausible, however, that Y2K will be remembered as a time-marking index of this kind, both because in the years leading up to the millennium—when Y2K hype was at its strongest—there was a huge expansion in the worldwide use of the Internet, and also because Y2K was directly responsible for ensuring that billions of dollars were spent in the pre-millennium years to ensure that cyberspace—and in particular cyberspace time—was fully in order for the dawn of the new millennium. The most obvious characteristic of cyberspace time is its speed, or miniaturization. For just as the clock divides the day (the smallest unit of calendric time) into hours, minutes, and seconds, so the computer divides the second (the smallest unit measured by the clock) into a series of gradations (the nano-second, the pico-second, etc.) that are—at least potentially—infinitely subdivisible. Yet, just as it would be a mistake to reduce the distinction between calendric time and clock time to a difference in scale, so too would it be inaccurate to presume that cyberspace time is no different from clock time with the exception of being more finely articulated. For, as we have seen, on the intensive plane where time is produced, changes in size do not occur without simultaneous changes in nature. It thus becomes possible to say that Y2K inaugurated—something yet to be seen—a fundamentally new regime in the production of time. However, as Foucault maintains, radical discontinuities are necessarily accompanied by a certain degree of blindness, for there is an inevitable failure to see that which is conditioning one's own experience of the world. For this reason, it is unavoidable that there is a degree of uncertainty surrounding questions of what cyberspace time is and what it will eventually become. Any outline of the contours of this new 'postmodern' time, however, must take into account following characteristics:
First, cyberspace time can no longer be considered in any way human. For not only does it follow the clock in ceasing to measure 'natural' rhythms of organisms, but it also operates with speeds that are below the level of human perception. It is for this reason that cyberspace time appears instantaneous.
Second, cyberspace time has less to do with a clockwork universe and more to do with machines of simulation. It is because of its power to simulate other devices that Turing called the computer the 'universal machine.' This link between simulation and time has already led to some surprising experimentation. For example, in the summer of 1999, a group of international financial institutions simulated time-travel—a practice that until then existed only in the realm of science fiction—in order to arrive in the future and ensure that their systems were millennium compliant.
Third, since cyberspace is non-localizable, cyberspace time must be considered as transglobal or postglobal, rather than as operating with a globalized standard which co-ordinates various localities in space.
Fourth, cyberspace time constitutes an immanent machinic culture in which time measures nothing outside its own inner workings. Crucial to this is the correspondence

numbers which mark the time are nothing but an empty representation. A statement no different from its effect, Y2K marks a singular occurrence which operates on an immanent plane in which the distinction between the formal expression of time and the events which happen to fill it, has been dissolved. No longer an expression independent of its content, Y2K operates on a plane of exteriority which eradicates the difference between quantity and quality, content and expression, constant and variable. On this exterior plane, the plane of consistency, body without organs, or Aeon, the transcendental nature of time can no longer be separated from the empirical nature of change.

---

between processing speeds—measured in Hertz or cycles per second—and the ever-increasing subdivisions of the second. This machinic immanence is evidenced by syndromes such as Y2K which, as we have seen, are in themselves neither technical nor cultural, and which constitute events that are flat with the production of time.

5 — Conclusion

In the most general terms, this thesis aims to connect abstract philosophical thought to concrete material practices. It does so by concentrating on the convergence between, on the one hand, one of the most abstruse areas of philosophy—that is, the transcendental analysis of time—and, on the other, the actual or concrete changes in the technology of timekeeping systems (and the socio-cultural and economic transformations that necessarily accompany these shifts). However, despite obvious isomorphies and interlinkages between these two 'spheres,' the topics are rendered irreconcilable by a process of reciprocal interiorization that opposes the nature of time—conceived of as an epistemological subjectivity—with the innovations or changes which occur within history—understood as a narrative unity.

Thus, connecting the transcendental philosophy of time with the socio-technics of time-marking processes requires the disorganization of both terms on to a plane of exteriority—or absolute immanence—where change occurs not in time, but to time. This involves the reanimation of a systematic philosophy of abstraction which is drawn primarily from the work of Deleuze and Guattari. This systematic abstraction is a materialist philosophy, not in the sense that it is a theory about matter, but rather due to its practical or pragmatic orientation which treats concrete material events as the instantiation of abstract machines which are themselves 'philosophical' in nature.

The thesis begins by outlining the discussion of time found in Immanuel Kant's *Critique of Pure Reason*, while then seeking to show how, through the discovery of the transcendental, Kant constructs an account of the abstract production of time which is freed from its ties to variation and movement. Time thus becomes a formal structure which is constant and exists in an exterior relationship to the changes which occur inside it.

In the second chapter, this notion of transcendental time is linked to the temporal transformations which have occurred under capitalism by way of the invention of the mechanical clock. It does this by mapping the Kantian notion of formal time on to the quantitative and homogeneous time of the clock, a time which is characterized by its autonomy from the calendar, its standardization across the globe, and its rigorous identification with money.

Yet despite obvious parallels, the socio-history of capitalist time and Kant's critical philosophy remain separate and opposed. This separation corresponds to the fundamental distinction—which both sides insist upon—between historical change and the epistemological structure of time, an opposition which results in each side seeking to envelop the other by way of its own superior unity (which, on one side, is constituted by the transcendental unity of the subject and, on the other, the unity of the historical process).[180] Linking them together thus always seems to occur at the expense of one side or the other, whether this be through the subordination of the nature of time to historical variation, or vice versa.

Nonetheless, both Kantian thought and the production of capitalist time involve—perhaps despite themselves—the dissolution of this distinction (or relation of mutual transcendence) for both are aspects of a singular event, or revolution, which occurs not in time but to time. Thus, though they appear as revolutions in history, they are not in themselves historical. For in altering time itself, both have accessed an abstract realm which conditions experience and which impacts the smooth succession of history only from the outside. Thus, the Kantian and capitalist revolution introduce a mutation or radical discontinuity in both the thought and the material practices of time.

In the classical Western tradition, the only thing capable of changing the very nature of time was the exterior and transcendent power of the eternal. Since it is eternity which is ultimately responsible for the production of time, changes in the nature of time—if they were ever possible—could only be transcendently produced. Restricted to initiations and terminations, these changes were a matter of faith, not reason, for they occurred only as the apocalyptic or miraculous events which accompany divine revelation.[181]

Both critique and capitalism, however, are intrinsically opposed to transcendent impositions. Though they push aside any explicit engagement with the question of eternity, they nevertheless reject this classical conception of the exteriority. Operating with consistent circuits of abstract and effective production, they tend toward the construction of immanent systems which obsolesce structures of faith, essentialized authority, and arbitrary and supplementary dimensions.[182] Dedicated in

---

180: For Marx, this unity culminates in the universality of Proletarian class consciousness.

181: In Christianity, the intrusion of the eternal in history is ultimately realized through the incarnation of Jesus, or the idea of the Word made flesh.

182: Capitalism's tendency to monetarize power differentiates it from other social systems in which power is based primarily on coded and territorial structures of organization. According to Deleuze and Guattari, capitalism is defined by these processes of decoding and deterritorialization, and it is this which is responsible for its great affinity with immanence.

their principles to an immanence of criteria, both imply—however implicitly—the necessity for an immanent production of time to replace the faith in transcendent creation.

However, due to the stratified distinction[183] in both between, on the one side, an idealist structure of time—whether that be the logic of historical development or the universality of *a priori* synthesis—and on the other, the variations which occur in time, neither Kant nor the social history of capitalist time can provide the conceptual immanence which their principles require. In retaining the notion that the interiority of temporal variation is constituted by the intrinsic unity of a higher and more primary structure, they dismantle the traditional faith in eternity but nevertheless leave a quasi-transcendence in place. Incapable of conceiving of a variation that is flat with the construction of time, and abstract syntheses consistent with the multiplicity and becomings of material innovation, they deny the very possibility of time mutation. Blind to the implications of their own respective revolutions, they thus conceal the intensive plane on which time is immanently produced.

In order to uncover this plane, the thesis turns to the writings of Deleuze and Guattari, whose *Capitalism and Schizophrenia* calls for a materialist revolution in the name of transcendental thought. Pushing the Kantian system further in the direction of immanent critique, Deleuze and Guattari manage to dismantle the distinction between conceptual abstraction and material innovations. Though they retain the exteriority of transcendental synthesis, they cease to locate this synthesis inside the mind of the knowing subject, seeing it instead as an operation of abstract machines. Deleuze and Guattari thus discover a plane of consistency on which the nature of time is flat with the variations and mutations that are intrinsic to its own production.

A philosophy based on the immanent production of time requires, as we have seen, not only a reformulation of the nature of time, but also of the relation between time and eternity. To reach the plane of consistency, the implicit faith in transcendent exteriority must be replaced with the participation of an immanent outside. Deleuze and Guattari thus substitute the division between time and eternity with the difference between two modes of temporality: the extensive time of Chronos and the intensive time of Aeon. While Chronos corresponds to the stratified nature of time (with its division between structure and change), the temporality of Aeon is constituted by becomings, intensive

---

183: As has already been noted, stratification acts as double pincer, operates through double articulation, and constitutes the world through binary distinction; see Deleuze and Guattari, *A Thousand Plateaus*, 40.

variations, machinic multiplicities, and singular events which do not differentiate between the abstract production of time and material innovation (which is generally considered to occur in time).

Composed on the plane of consistency, or immanence, Aeon does not transcend, interrupt, or break into time in the same way that eternity does. Rather, as we have seen, it constitutes the virtual field upon which Chronos is continuously being constructed. Functioning in this way, Aeon is not to be understood as an eternal or abstract generality. Instead, the virtuality or abstraction of Aeon can only be accessed through the singular events out of which it is composed. The final chapter of this thesis thus explores the concept of Aeon by focusing on one such singular event, the dawn of the third millennium, a fundamental juncture in the passage of time and in timekeeping's socio-technical apparatus. This event has come to be known by the sign 'Y2K.'

Post-millennium cynicism is such that it seems absurd to even mention Y2K, never mind speak of it as an event of fundamental philosophical importance. For it is now generally agreed that, though it was hyped to apocalyptic proportions, Y2K was—if anything—a non-event. Though glitches were reported—even in such crucial areas as stock exchanges, transportation networks, emergency services, and credit card companies—they were easily dealt with on an individual basis and did not seem to add up to anything significant (certainly, it was nothing like the global catastrophe that was predicted). As an event, Y2K was so diffuse, so quiet, so inconsequential that its very existence has been retrospectively called into question. After all, despite months, and even years, of anticipation, January 1st, 2000 seems to have been just another day.

The real nature of Y2K still remains a puzzle. No one is sure whether the hundreds of billions of dollars spent were wasted, or whether they were crucial in the prevention of a catastrophe. While some maintain that the risk was wildly exaggerated, the few 'glitches' that did occur are sufficient to give evidence that there was indeed a problem. Yet, the fact that countries which appeared to do little to fight the bug (i.e., Russia and China) encountered no more disturbances than countries like United States and Britain which reacted early and poured huge resources into ensuring 'millennium compliance' makes the conclusion that the problem was fixed highly improbable. The alternative, however, that Y2K was a vast conspiracy by the computer industry is even more preposterous.

The confusion which—even now—surrounds Y2K is a result of the fact that—though entirely real—it was an event that never seemed to actualize. Y2K was, and always will be, a virtual catastrophe, a pure potentiality, a non-event. The final chapter of this thesis argues that the virtual nature of Y2K—a nature which allowed it to be entirely affective (as a potentiality) and yet never empirically manifest—suggests that it cannot be understood through the successive temporality of Chronos. Rather, Y2K is a sign—which operates as both a name and a date—for an event composed on the intensive plane of Aeon. This, as we have seen is evidenced by its efficient non-signifying (numerical) semiotic, its resilient virtuality, its disorganization of linear succession, and its dissolution of such stratified distinctions as content and expression, quantity and quality, constant and variable, and technics and culture.

It is as an Aeonic event that Y2K makes the connection between the transcendental philosophy of time and the socio-economics of capitalist timekeeping practices. Flat with an exterior plane of machinic abstraction, it dissolves the distinction between time and the materiality of timekeeping systems. For this reason, Y2K has been used as an exemplary event in addressing the central problematic of this thesis.

There is no question that despite the pervasive sense of anticlimax, Y2K was a crucial event in the history of capitalist time, for though it acted only as a potentiality, it had concrete material consequences whose effects can be measured in billions of dollars. As a technological 'glitch' in cyberspace time, Y2K mobilized the global economy in an unprecedented fashion. Operating within the context of an ever-increasing convergence of time and money, it turned the date that marked the end of the second millennium into the most expensive accident the world has ever experienced.

What makes Y2K crucial to the philosophy of time, however, is that it is also a near perfect example of systematic abstraction. The word abstraction means to extract, remove, or withdraw from any particular concrete instantiation. It thus involves a process through which a particular dimension or aspect of any given context is subtracted and made autonomous. To quote Deleuze:

> The way people talk about abstraction is absolutely amazing, they have absolutely no idea what it is. Philosophy has a kind of technique or terminology like mathematics. Generally the word abstract is used for things in which there is no abstraction. The problem of abstraction is how can I make two things out of what only exists as one in my representations. It's not difficult to make a thing into two when I have two representations, but when I say the back of the piece of paper, I am not abstracting at all since the back is given to me in a representation which itself exists. When I say a length without thickness, there I am

abstracting because I am separating two things which are necessarily given in each other in my representation.[i]

Y2K functions as a model of abstraction in that it subtracts the first two digits from the date. Through this subtraction, it serves to extract the decade, making it autonomous from the interiority of the century. It thus separates out two things from what, until then, had appeared only as one, rupturing the apparent unity of historical time. Y2K, like every abstraction, is a schism. By fracturing the semiotic expression of dated time, it abstracts a scale of time from the history within which it was previously embedded (the year 00, for instance, could belong to any century whatsoever). The anticlimactic character of Y2K only confirms its nature as an abstract event through which time has escaped from the concrete interiority of history.

As this thesis has argued, the tendency of capitalist chronometrics—from inception—has been affined with the transcendental in its trend towards the ambiguous 'liberation' of time from the measurement of change (thus establishing the autonomy of the clock in relation to the calendar). In this respect, Y2K figures as a culmination—although a paradoxical one—since it machinically extracts an abstract temporality from dates themselves. With Y2K, dates cease to function solely as the expressions of celestial cyclicity and implicit historical unity. Instead, they are activated as numerical indices for pure—or Aeonic—events, marking absolute historical schisms which correspond to thresholds of innovation in the abstract production of time.

Lecturing on the *Critique of Pure Reason*, Deleuze maintains that fundamental to Kant's discovery of the immanent plane of the transcendental is that "[t]rue lived experience is an absolutely abstract thing [...] once you have reached lived experience, you reach the most fully living core of the abstract." "Nobody," Deleuze continues, "has ever lived anything but the abstract."[ii]

This thesis has focused on transcendental philosophy in order to investigate the abstract nature of time. What it has discovered is that this most obscure and seemingly distant topic is encountered in the technology or socio-economic practices of contemporary life. For the nature of time is not some eternal given that has descended from above but is rather a process that is itself continuously under production. It is a process under production not, as Kant believed, in the interiority of thought, but rather on the exteriority of an unconscious, immanent, and material plane of machinic transformation.

6 — Notes

Foreword

i.   Ireland, Twitter Post, 2018.
ii.   See CCRU, "Who's Pulling Your Strings?"
iii. Deleuze and Guattari, *A Thousand Plateaus*, 262.
iv.   Ibid.
v.   Ibid.
vi.   Greenspan, "Interview," 70.
vii. Davis, *TechGnosis*, 302.
viii. Hryniuk, "Ouroboros Chronos provides the first high-resilience, cryptographic time source based on blockchain technology," web.
ix.   Nascent, "Distributed Temporal Mutations," 88.
x.   Greenspan, "Interview," 77.
xi.   Ibid., 70.
xii. Ibid., 72.
xiii. Nakamoto, "Bitcoin," 1.
xiv. Alsindi, "Bitcontingency," web.

0: Introduction

i.   Plato, "Timaeus," 1167 [37d].
ii. Plotinus, "Time and Eternity," 226.
iii. Kant, *Critique of Pure Reason*, 76 [A32/B48].
iv. Deleuze, *Kant's Critical Philosophy*, vii.

1.0: Introduction

i.   Kant, *Critique of Pure Reason*, 55 [B19].
ii.   Ibid., 41 [B1].
iii. Ibid., 43 [A1/B2].
iv.   Ibid., 44 [B4].
v.   Ibid., 48 [A6/B10].
vi.   Ibid., 48 [A7/B11].
vii. Ibid., 49 [A7/B12].
viii. Ferrarin, "Construction and Mathematical Schematism," 147–148.
ix.   Kant, *Critique of Pure Reason*, 53 [B16].
x.   Deleuze, "Kant: Synthesis and Time," 11.
xi.   Kant, *Critique of Pure Reason*, 112 [A78/B103].
xii. Ibid., 47 [A6/B9].

xiii. Ibid., 51 [A10/B14].
xiv. Deleuze, *Kant's Critical Philosophy*, 14.
xv. Ibid.
xvi. Heine, *Religion and Philosophy in Germany*, 114.
xvii. Kant, *Critique of Pure Reason*, 22 [Bxvii].
xviii. Ibid., 22 [Bxvi].
xix. Deleuze, "Kant: Synthesis and Time," 5.
xx. Ibid., 6.
xxi. Ibid., 5.
xxii. Ibid., 5–6.
xxiii. Ibid., 2.
xxiv. Deleuze, *Difference and Repetition*, 135.
xxv. Deleuze, "Kant: Synthesis and Time," 1.

1.1: Transcendental Aesthetic

i. Kant, *Critique of Pure Reason*, 92 [A50/B74].
ii. Ibid., 77 [A33/B50].
iii. Ibid., 66 [A21/B35].
iv. Ibid., 67 [A22/B37].
v. Ibid., 68 [A23/B38].
vi. Ibid., 77 [A33/B50].
vii. Ibid., 67–68 [A12/B37].
viii. Deleuze, "Kant: Synthesis and Time," 1.
ix. Plato, "Timaeus," 1167 [37d].
x. Ibid., 1167 [38c].
xi. Deleuze, "Kant: Synthesis and Time," 20.
xii. Kant, *Critique of Pure Reason*, 82 [A41/B58].
xiii. Ibid.
xiv. Ibid., 76 [A32/B49].
xv. Deleuze, *Kant's Critical Philosophy*, vii.
xvi. Deleuze, "Kant: Synthesis and Time," 16.
xvii. Kant, *Critique of Pure Reason*, 74 [A31/B46].
xviii. Aristotle, "Physics," 371 [219a].
xix. Ibid., 372 [219b].
xx. Ibid., 372 [219b3].
xxi. Ibid., 372 [219b4–5].
xxii. Ibid., 373 [220b8–9].
xxiii. Ibid., 372 [219b5–8].
xxiv. Ibid., 375 [221b10–222a9].
xxv. Kant, *Critique of Pure Reason*, 77 [A33/B50].
xxvi. Ibid.

xxvii. Deleuze, "Kant: Synthesis and Time," 16.

xxviii. Deleuze, *Difference and Repetition*, 88.

xxix. Deleuze, "Kant: Synthesis and Time," 19.

xxx. Kant, *Critique of Pure Reason*, 75 [A31/B47].

xxxi. Ibid., 77 [A43/B51].

xxxii. Deleuze, "Kant: Synthesis and Time," 28.

xxxiii. Deleuze, *Difference and Repetition*, 87.

1.2: Transcendental Deduction

i.   Descartes, *Meditations*, 97.

ii.   Deleuze, "Kant: Synthesis and Time," 35.

iii. Schopenhauer, *The World as Will and Representation*, 4.

iv. Kant, *Critique of Pure Reason*, 381 [B428].

v.   Ibid., 136 [A107].

vi. Deleuze, "On Four Formulas," 29.

vii. Kant, *Critique of Pure Reason*, 166 [B153].

viii. Deleuze, *Kant's Critical Philosophy*, 15.

ix. Kant, *Critique of Pure Reason*, 131 [A99].

x.   Ibid., 131 [A98–99].

xi. Deleuze, *Kant's Critical Philosophy*, 15.

xii. Ibid.

xiii. Kant, *Critique of Pure Reason*, 132 [A101].

xiv. Deleuze, *Kant's Critical Philosophy*, 15.

xv. Kant, *Critique of Pure Reason*, 136 [A107].

xvi. Ibid.

xvii. Ibid.

xviii. Deleuze, *Kant's Critical Philosophy*, viii.

xix. Ibid.

xx. Ibid., ix.

xxi. Heine, *Religion and Philosophy in Germany*, 120.

xxii. Ibid., 107.

xxiii. Deleuze, "Kant: Synthesis and Time," 1.

xxiv. Ibid., 28.

xxv. Deleuze, "On Four Formulas," 31.

1.3: The Schematism

i.   Foucault, "Theatrum Philosophicum," 166.

ii.   Deleuze, *Kant's Critical Philosophy*, 15.

iii. Ibid., 8.

iv. Kant, *Critique of Pure Reason*, 93 [A51/B75].

v.   Ibid., 181 [A139/B178].
vi.   Ibid., 180 [A138/B177].
vii. Ibid., 181 [A138/177].
viii. Ibid., 182 [A140/B179].
ix.   Ibid.
x.   Ibid.; Ibid., 146 [A124].
xi.   Ibid., 183 [A141/B181].
xii. Ibid., 7 [Aviii]; Heine, *Religion and Philosophy in Germany*, 107.
xiii. Welchman, "'Wild above rule or art,'" 46.

2.0: Introduction

i.   Mumford, *Technics and Civilization*, 14.
ii.   Deleuze, "Kant: Synthesis and Time," 19.
iii. Foucault, *Power/Knowledge*, 112.

2.1: Clock Time

i.   Mumford, *Technics and Civilization*, 14.
ii.   Ibid., 15.
iii. Crump, *The Anthropology of Numbers*, 85.
iv.   Zerubavel, *Hidden Rhythms*, 73.
v.   Ibid., 81.
vi.   Landes, *Revolution in Time*, 6.
vii. Deleuze, "On Philosophy," 137.
viii. De Quincey, "The Last Days of Immanuel Kant," 341.
ix.   Ibid.
x.   Schopenhauer, *The World as Will and Representation*, 448.
xi.   De Quincey, "The Last Days of Immanuel Kant," 341.
xii. Heine, *Religion and Philosophy in Germany*, 79.
xiii. Zerubavel, "The Standardization of Time," 5.
xiv. Landes, *Revolution in Time*, 89.

2.2: Time Synthetic Culture of Clock Time

i.   Conrad, *The Secret Agent*, 60.
ii.   Ibid., 58.
iii. Ibid., 61.
iv.   Ibid.
v.   Ibid., 63.

vi. Sobel, *Longitude*, 4.
vii. Ibid., 8.
viii. Ibid., 106.
ix. Ibid., 168.
x. Ibid.
xi. Foucault, *Discipline and Punish*, 150.
xii. Mumford, *Technics and Civilization*, 14.
xiii. Ibid., 13.
xiv. Dorhn-van Rossum, *History of the Hour*, 35.
xv. Kardong, *Benedict's Rule*, 382.
xvi. Le Goff, *Time, Work and Culture in the Middle Ages*, 29.
xvii. Mumford, *Technics and Civilization*, 14.
xviii. Le Goff, *Time, Work and Culture in the Middle Ages*, 48.
xix. Mumford, *Technics and Civilization*, 14.
xx. Ibid., 13.
xxi. Weber, *The Protestant Ethic and the Spirit of Capitalism*, 14.
xxii. Weber, *From Max Weber*, 350.
xxiii. Ibid., 148.
xxiv. Weber, *From Max Weber*, 267–301; Weber, *The Protestant Ethic and the Spirit of Capitalism*, 68.
xxv. Weber, *From Max Weber*, 291, 290.
xxvi. Weber, *The Protestant Ethic and the Spirit of Capitalism*, 104.
xxvii. Ibid.
xxviii. Ibid.
xxix. Ibid.
xxx. Schumpeter, *Ten Great Economists*, 151.
xxxi. Marx, *Capital*, 125.
xxxii. Ibid., 126.
xxxiii. Ibid., 127.
xxxiv. Ibid.
xxxv. Ibid., 128.
xxxvi. Ibid., 129; Marx, *The Poverty of Philosophy*, 43.
xxxvii. Marx, *Capital*, 130.
xxxviii. Böhm-Bawerk, *Karl Marx and the Close of His System*, 16.
xxxix. Marx, *Capital*, 300.
xl. Böhm-Bawerk, *Karl Marx and the Close of His System*, 15.
xli. Schumpeter, *Ten Great Economists*, 156.
xlii. Böhm-Bawerk, *Karl Marx and the Close of His System*, ix.
xliii. Schumpeter, *Ten Great Economists*, 165.
xliv. Böhm-Bawerk, *The Positive Theory of Capital*, 17.
xlv. Ibid., 82.
xlvi. Ibid., 83.

xlvii. Schumpeter, *Ten Great Economists*, 163.
xlviii. Ibid., 167.
xlix. Ibid., 174.
l. Ibid., 175.
li. Castells, *The Information Age*, 463.
lii. Postone, *Time, Labor, and Social Domination*, 202.
liii. Mumford, *Technics and Civilization*, 17.

2.3: History and the Transcendental

i. Marx, *Grundrisse*, 83.
ii. Ibid.
iii. Ibid.
iv. Marx and Engels, *The Communist Manifesto*, 60.
v. Schumpeter, *Ten Great Economists*, 13.
vi. Marx, *A Contribution to the Critique of Political Economy*, 12.
vii. Kant, *Critique of Pure Reason*, 653 [A832/B860].
viii. Ibid., 654 [A834/B862].
ix. Ibid., 653 [A832/B860].
x. Ibid., 656 [A836/B864].
xi. Ibid., 657 [A837/B865].
xii. Ibid., 658 [A840/B868].
xiii. Foucault, *Discipline and Punish*, 26.
xiv. Ibid.
xv. Foucault, *The Foucault Reader*, 266.
xvi. Foucault, *Discipline and Punish*, 150.
xvii. Ibid., 154.
xviii. Ibid., 152.
xix. Ibid.
xx. Ibid.
xxi. Ibid., 154.
xxii. Ibid., 157.
xxiii. Ibid.
xxiv. Ibid., 7.
xxv. Foucault, *Power/Knowledge*, 113.
xxvi. Foucault, *The Foucault Reader*, 54.
xxvii. Deleuze, *Foucault*, 87.
xxviii. Ibid., 86.

3.0: Introduction

i. Kant, *Critique of Pure Reason*, 75 [A31/B46].

ii.   Ibid.
iii. Foucault, *The Order of Things*, xxiv.
iv.   Deleuze, *Foucault*, 85.

3.1: Transcendental Materialism

i.   Deleuze and Guattari, *A Thousand Plateaus*, 265.
ii.   Ibid.
iii. Ibid., 266.
iv.   Ibid.
v.   Ibid., 267.
vi.   Kant, *Critique of Pure Reason*, 60 [B27].
vii. Ibid., 10 [Axiii].
viii. Ibid., 13–14 [Axx].
ix.   Ibid., 653 [A833/B861].
x.   Ibid., 136 [A107].
xi.   Ibid., 147 [A126].
xii. Ibid., 257 [A235/B295].
xiii. Ibid., 29 [Bxxix].
xiv. Ibid., 9 [Axii, fn. A].
xv.   Ibid., 7 [Aviii].
xvi. Ibid., 9 [Axii, fn. A].
xvii. Ibid., 9 [Axi].
xviii. Deleuze and Guattari, *A Thousand Plateaus*, 109.
xix. Ibid., 8.
xx.   Deleuze, *Spinoza*, 19.
xxi. Deleuze and Guattari, *Anti-Oedipus*, 10.
xxii. Deleuze, *Logic of Sense*, 102.
xxiii. Deleuze, *Difference and Repetition*, 135.
xxiv. Deleuze and Guattari, *Anti-Oedipus*, 1.

3.2: From Eternity to Aeon

i.   Deleuze, "Kant: Synthesis and Time," i.
ii.   Kant, *Critique of Pure Reason*, 198 [A162/B204].
iii. Ibid., 199 [A163/B204].
iv.   Ibid., 198 [A163/B203].
v.   Deleuze, *Logic of Sense*, 61.
vi.   Kant, *Critique of Pure Reason*, 201 [A166/B208 and fn. *].
vii. Ibid., 201 [A166/B207].
viii. Deleuze, "Kant: Synthesis and Time," 24.
ix.   Kant, *Critique of Pure Reason*, 203 [A167/B209].

x.   Deleuze, "Kant: Synthesis and Time," 24.
xi. Deleuze and Guattari, *A Thousand Plateaus*, 31.
xii. Ibid., 30–31.
xiii. Kant, *Critique of Pure Reason*, 206 [A173/B214].
xiv. Deleuze, *Logic of Sense*, 77.
xv. Kant, *Critique of Pure Reason*, 207 [A174/B216].
xvi. Ibid., 78 [A35–A36/B52].
xvii. Deleuze, *Kant's Critical Philosophy*, viii.
xviii. Deleuze and Guattari, *A Thousand Plateaus*, 262.
xix. Ibid., 261.
xx. Ibid., 255.
xxi. Ibid., 507.
xxii. Ibid.
xxiii. Ibid., 297.
xxiv. Deleuze, *Logic of Sense*, 162.
xxv. Schopenhauer, *The World as Will and Representation*, 278.
xxvi. Deleuze, *Logic of Sense*, 77.
xxvii. Ibid.
xxviii. Deleuze and Guattari, *A Thousand Plateaus*, 262.
xxix. Schopenhauer, *The World as Will and Representation*, 134.
xxx. Kant, *Critique of Pure Reason*, 202 [A166/B208].
xxxi. Deleuze and Guattari, *A Thousand Plateaus*, 154.
xxxii. Ibid., 153.
xxxiii. Deleuze and Guattari, *Anti-Oedipus*, xiii.
xxxiv. Ibid.
xxxv. Deleuze and Guattari, *A Thousand Plateaus*, 72.

4.0: Introduction

i.   Deleuze and Guattari, *A Thousand Plateaus*, 21.
ii. Ibid., 22.

4.1: Time-Mutations

i.   Deleuze and Guattari, *Anti-Oedipus*, 140.
ii. Braudel, *Civilization and Capitalism (Volume 3)*, 621.
iii. Deleuze and Guattari, *A Thousand Plateaus*, 435; Deleuze and Guattari, *Anti-Oedipus*, 8.
iv. Deleuze and Guattari, *Anti-Oedipus*, 151.
v.   Ibid.
vi. Ibid., 15.
vii. Deleuze and Guattari, *A Thousand Plateaus*, 429.

viii. Deleuze and Guattari, *Anti-Oedipus*, 140.

ix. Deleuze and Guattari, *A Thousand Plateaus*, 431.

x. Deleuze and Guattari, *Anti-Oedipus*, 160.

xi. Deleuze and Guattari, *A Thousand Plateaus*, 430.

xii. Ibid., 162.

xiii. Deleuze and Parnet, "Many Politics," 135–136.

xiv. Nietzsche, *Untimely Meditations*, 64.

xv. Deleuze and Guattari, *A Thousand Plateaus*, 295–296.

xvi. "The World in 1998," 135.

4.2: Dates and the Semiotic of Aeon

i. Stein, "Hey, you in that bunker, you can come out now!" 56.

ii. Deleuze and Guattari, *A Thousand Plateaus*, 27.

iii. Ibid., 264.

iv. Ibid., 511.

v. Ibid., 81.

vi. Ibid.

vii. Ibid., 142.

viii. Ibid., 81.

5.0: Conclusion

i. Deleuze, "Kant: Synthesis and Time," 38.

ii. Ibid., 25.

7 — Bibliography

Aristotle. "Physics." In *Complete Works of Aristotle, Vol. 1: The Revised Oxford Translation.* Edited by Jonathan Barnes. Translated by R. P. Hardie and R. K. Gaye, 315–446. Princeton, NJ: Princeton University Press, 1984.

Artaud, Antonin. "To Have Done with the Judgement of God (1947)." In *Antonin Artaud: Selected Writings.* Translated by Helen Weaver, 555–571. New York, NY: Farrar, Straus and Giroux, Inc., 1976.

Alsindi, Wassim Z. "Bitcointingency: An Economics of Indeterminacy." On *Weird Economies.* Published February 14, 2022. https://weirdeconomies.com/contributions/bitcointingency

Benton, Ted. "Kantianism and Neo-Kantianism." In *A Dictionary of Marxist Thought.* Edited by Tom B. Bottomore, 279–280. Oxford, UK: Blackwell Publishers, 1983.

Böhm-Bawerk, Eugene von. *The Positive Theory of Capital.* Translated by William Smart. New York, NY: G. E. Stechert & Co., 1930.

Böhm-Bawerk, Eugene von and Rudolf Hilferding. *Karl Marx and the Close of His System & Böhm-Bawerk's Criticism of Marx.* Edited by Paul M. Sweezy. New York, NY: Augustus M. Kelley, 1949.

Braudel, Fernand. *Civilization and Capitalism: 15th–18th Century, Volume One: The Structures of Every Life: The Limits of the Possible.* Translated by Siân Reynolds. London, UK: William Collins Sons & Co. Ltd., 1981.

———. *Civilization and Capitalism: 15th–18th Century, Volume Two: The Wheels of Commerce.* Translated by Siân Reynolds. London, UK: Book Club Associates, 1983.

———. *Civilization and Capitalism: 15th–18th Century, Volume Three: The Perspective of the World.* Translated by Siân Reynolds. London, UK: William Collins Sons & Co. Ltd., 1984.

Burroughs, William S. *Ah Pook Is Here: And Other Texts.* London, UK: John Calder, 1979.

CCRU. "Who's Pulling Your Strings?" In *Writings: 1997–2003,* ((::))–:(:) ((:)) [17–30]. Falmouth, UK : Urbanomic, 2017.

Castells, Manuel. *The Information Age: Economy, Society and Culture, Volume One: The Rise of the Network Society.* West Sussex, UK: Wiley-Blackwell, 2010.

Conrad, Joseph. *The Secret Agent.* Edited by Tanya Agathocleous. Peterborough, ON: Broadview Press, 2009.

Crump, Thomas. *The Anthropology of Numbers.* Cambridge, UK: Cambridge University Press, 1990.

Davis, Erik. *TechGnosis: Myth, Magic, and Mysticism in the Age of Information.* London, UK: Serpent's Tail, 2004.

De Quincey, Thomas. "The Last Days of Immanuel Kant." In *The Collected Writings of Thomas De Quincey Vol. IV*, 323–379. London, UK: A&C Black, 1897.

Deleuze, Gilles. "Kant: Synthesis and Time, March–April 1978." In *The Deleuze Seminars.* Translated by Melissa McMahon. https://deleuze.cla.purdue.edu/node/50

———. *Kant's Critical Philosophy: The Doctrine of the Faculties.* Translated by Hugh Tomlinson and Barbara Habberjam. London, UK: Athlone Press, 1984.

———. *Bergsonism.* Translated by Hugh Tomlinson and Barabara Habberjam. New York, NY: Zone Books, 1988.

———. *Spinoza: Practical Philosophy.* Translated by Robert Hurley. San Francisco, CA: City Lights Books, 1988.

———. *Foucault.* Translated and edited by Seán Hand. Minneapolis, MN: University of Minnesota Press, 1988.

———. *The Logic of Sense.* Translated by Mark Lester and Charles Stivale. London, UK: Athlone Press, 1990.

———. *Expressionism in Philosophy: Spinoza.* Translated by Martin Joughin. New York, NY: Zone Books, 1992.

———. *Difference and Repetition.* Translated by Paul Patton. London, UK: Athlone Press, 1994.

———. "On Philosophy." In *Negotiations, 1972–1990.* Translated by Martin Joughin, 135–155. New York, NY: Columbia University Press, 1995.

————. "On Four Poetic Formulas That Might Summarize the Kantian Philosophy." In *Essays Clinical and Critical*. Translated by Daniel W. Smith and Michael A. Greco, 27–35. London, UK: Verso, 1998.

Deleuze, Gilles and Claire Parnet. "On the Superiority of Anglo-American Literature." In *Dialogues*. Translated by Hugh Tomlinson and Barbara Habberjam, 36–76. New York, NY: Columbia University Press, 1987.

————. "Many Politics." In *Dialogues*. Translated by Hugh Tomlinson and Barbara Habberjam, 124–147. New York, NY: Columbia University Press, 1987.

Deleuze, Gilles and Félix Guattari. *Anti-Oedipus: Capitalism and Schizophrenia, Volume 1*. Translated by Robert Hurley, Mark Seem, and Helen R. Lane. Minneapolis, MN: University of Minnesota Press, 1983.

————. *A Thousand Plateaus: Capitalism and Schizophrenia, Volume 2*. Translated by Brian Massumi. Minneapolis, MN: University of Minnesota Press, 1987.

Descartes, René. *Meditations on First Philosophy: A Bilingual Edition*. Edited, translated, and indexed by George Heffernan. London, UK: University of Notre Dame Press, 1990.

Dohrn-van Rossum, Gerhard. *History of the Hour: Clocks and the Modern Temporal Orders*. Translated by Thomas Dunlap. Chicago, IL: University of Chicago Press, 1996.

Duncan, David Ewing. *Calendar*. New York, NY: Avon Books, 1998.

Economist, The. "The Millennium Bug: Please Panic Early." *The Economist*, October 4, 1997 (Vol. 345, No. 8037): 25–28.

Elade, Mircea (ed.). *Encyclopedia of Religion: Volume 5*. New York, NY: Macmillan Publishing, 1987.

Encyclopaedia Britannica. "Gregorian calendar." *Encyclopaedia Britannica*, n.d. https://www.britannica.com/topic/Gregorian-calendar

Ferrarin, Alfredo. "Construction and Mathematical Schematism: Kant on the Exhibition of a Concept in Intuition." *Kant-Studien* Vol. 86, No. 2 (January 1995): 131–174.

Foucault, Michel. "Theatrum Philosophicum." In *Language, Counter-Memory, Practice: Selected Essays and Interviews*. Edited by Donald F.

Bouchard. Translated by Donald F. Bouchard and Sherry Simon, 165–196. Ithaca, NY: Cornell University Press, 1977.

———. *Power/Knowledge: Selected Interviews and Other Writings, 1972–1977*. Edited by Colin Gordon. Translated by Colin Gordon, Leo Marshall, John Mepham, and Kate Soper. New York, NY: Pantheon Books, 1980.

———. *The Foucault Reader*. Edited by Paul Rabinow. New York, NY: Pantheon Books, 1984.

———. *The Order of Things: An Archaeology of the Human Sciences*. Translated by Alan Sheridan. New York, NY: Vintage Books, 1994.

———. *Discipline and Punish: The Birth of the Prison*. Translated by Alan Sheridan. New York, NY: Vintage Books, 1995.

Freud, Sigmund. "The Unconscious." In *The Freud Reader*. Edited by Peter Gay. Translated by James Strachey, 572–584. New York, NY: W. W. Norton & Company, 1995.

Grant, John (ed.). *The Book of Time*. London, UK: Westbridge Books, 1980.

Greenspan, Anna. "Interview." In *Temporal Secessionism Sourcebook*, 65–78. Plaza Protocol, 2021. https://www.plazaprotocol.si/assets/other/Temporal_Secessionism_Sourcebook.pdf

Heine, Heinrich. *Religion and Philosophy in Germany: A Fragment*. Translated by John Snodgrass. Boston, MA: Beacon Press, 1959.

Hryniuk, Olga. "Ouroboros Chronos provides the first high-resilience, cryptographic time source based on blockchain technology." On *Input|Output*. Published October 26, 2021. https://iohk.io/en/blog/posts/2021/10/27/ouroboros-chronos-provides-the-first-high-resilience-cryptographic-time-source-based-on-blockchain/

Ifrah, Georges. *The Universal History of Numbers: From Prehistory to the Invention of the Computer*. Translated by David Bellos, E. F. Harding, Sophie Wood, and Ian Monk. New York, NY: John Wiley & Sons, Inc., 2000.

Ireland, Amy. "Twitter Post." Published May 5, 2018. https://twitter.com/qdnoktsqfr/status/992961115112882176

Irigaray, Luce. *Speculum of the Other Woman*. Translated by Gillian C. Gill. Ithaca, NY: Cornell University Press, 1985.

Kant, Immanuel. *Critique of Pure Reason*. Translated by Norman Kemp Smith. London, UK: Macmillan Press, 1982.

————. *Prolegomena to Any Future Metaphysics That Will Be Able to Come Forward as Science* with Selections from the *Critique of Pure Reason*. Translated by Gary Hatfield. Cambridge, UK: Cambridge University Press, 1997.

Kardong, Terrence G. *Benedict's Rule: A Translation and Commentary*. Collegeville, MN: The Liturgical Press, 1996.

King, Stephen. *The Shining*. New York, NY: Doubleday, 1993.

Land, Nick. "Delighted to Death." *Pli* Vol. 3, No. 2 (1991): 76–88.

————. *The Thirst for Annihilation: Georges Bataille and Virulent Nihilism*. London, UK: Routledge, 1992.

Landes, David. *Revolution in Time: Clocks and the Making of the Modern World*. Cambridge, MA: Harvard University Press, 1983.

Le Goff, Jacques. *Time, Work and Culture in the Middle Ages*. Translated by Arthur Goldhammer. Chicago: University of Chicago Press, 1974.

Lenin, Vladimir Ilyich. *Marx, Engels, Marxism*. Translated by the Institute of Marxism-Leninism of the Central Committee, C.P.S.U. Moscow, RU: Foreign Languages Publishing House, 1970 (1960).

Macey, Samuel. *The Dynamics of Progress: Time, Method and Measure*. Athens, GA: University of Georgia Press, 1989.

Marx, Karl. *A Contribution to the Critique of Political Economy*. Translated by N. I. Stone. Chicago, IL: Charles H. Kerr & Company, 1904.

————. *The Poverty of Philosophy*. New York, NY: International Publishers, 1963.

————. *Karl Marx on Colonialism and Modernization: His Despatches and Other Writings on China, India, Mexico, the Middle East and North Africa*. Edited by Shlomo Avineri. New York, NY: Doubleday, 1968.

————. *Grundrisse: Introduction to the Critique of Political Economy*. Translated by Martin Nicolaus. New York, NY: Vintage Books, 1973.

————. *Capital: A Critique of Political Economy, Volume One*. Translated by Ben Fowkes. London, UK: Penguin Books, 1990.

———. *The German Ideology: Including Theses on Feuerbach and Introduction to the Critique of Political Economy*. Amherst, NY: Prometheus Books, 1998.

Marx, Karl and Friedrich Engels. *The Communist Manifesto*. Translated by Samuel Moore. New York, NY: Pocket Books, 1964.

Massumi, Brian. *A User's Guide to Capitalism and Schizophrenia: Deviations from Deleuze and Guattari*. Cambridge, MA: The MIT Press, 1992.

Mumford, Lewis. *Technics and Civilization*. London, UK: Routledge & Sons, 1934.

Nakamoto, Satoshi. "Bitcoin: A Peer-to-Peer Electronic Cash System." On *Bitcoin*. Published October 28, 2008. https://bitcoin.org/bitcoin.pdf

Nascent. "Distributed Temporal Mutations: Consensus-Systems as Novel Temporal Regimes." In *Temporal Secessionism Sourcebook*, 79–97. Plaza Protocol, 2021. https://www.plazaprotocol.si/assets/other/Temporal_Secessionism_Sourcebook.pdf

Nietzsche, Friedrich. *Untimely Meditations*. Edited by Daniel Breazeale. Translated by R. J. Hollingdale. Cambridge, UK: Cambridge University Press, 1997.

———. *Thus Spoke Zarathustra: A Book for All and None*. Edited by Adrian Del Caro and Robert B. Pippin. Translated by Adrian Del Caro. Cambridge, UK: Cambridge University Press, 2006.

Plato. "Meno." In *Plato: The Collected Dialogues*. Edited by Edith Hamilton and Huntington Cairns, 353–384. Princeton, NJ: Princeton University Press, 1961.

———. "The Republic." In *Plato: The Collected Dialogues*. Edited by Edith Hamilton and Huntington Cairns, 575–844. Princeton, NJ: Princeton University Press, 1961.

———. "Timaeus." In *Plato: The Collected Dialogues*. Edited by Edith Hamilton and Huntington Cairns, 1151–1211. Princeton, NJ: Princeton University Press, 1961.

———. "Definitions." In *Plato: Complete Works*. Edited by John M. Cooper, 1677–1686. Indianapolis, IN: Hackett Publishing Company, 1997.

Plotinus. "Time and Eternity." In *The Enneads*. Translated by Stephen Mackenna, 222–238. London, UK: Faber and Faber Ltd., 1956.

Postone, Moishe. *Time, Labor, and Social Domination: A Reinterpretation of Marx's Critical Theory*. Cambridge, UK: Cambridge University Press, 1993.

Prigogene, Ilya and Isabelle Stengers. *Order out of Chaos*. Boulder, CO: New Science Library, 1984.

Rimbaud, Arthur. "Rimbaud to Georges Izambard – Charleville May 13, 1871." In *Arthur Rimbaud: Complete Works*. Translated by Paul Schmidt, 113–114. New York, NY: Harper Perennial, 2008.

Schopenhauer, Arthur. *The World as Will and Representation: Volume 1*. Translated by E. F. J. Payne. New York, NY: Dover Publications Inc., 1969.

Schumpeter, Joseph A. *Ten Great Economists: From Marx to Keynes*. London, UK: Routledge, 1997.

Scruton, Roger. *Kant*. Oxford, UK: Oxford University Press, 1982.

Shaw, William H. "Historical Materialism." In *A Dictionary of Marxist Thought*. Edited by Tom B. Bottomore, 234–239. Oxford, UK: Blackwell Publishers, 1983.

Sobel, Dava. *Longitude: The True Story of a Lone Genius Who Solved the Greatest Scientific Problem of His Time*. London, UK: Fourth Estate, 1998.

Spinoza, Baruch. *The Ethics and Selected Letters*. Translated by Samuel Shirley. Indianapolis, IN: Hackett Publishing Company, 1982.

Stein, Joel. "Hey, you in that bunker, you can come out now!" *Time Magazine*, Vol. 155, No. 1 (2000): 54–60.

"The World in 1998." *Economist Publications*. London, UK (1998).

Virilio, Paul. *Politics of the Very Worst: An Interview with Philippe Petit*. Translated by Michael Cavaliere. New York, NY: Semiotext(e), 1999.

Walsh, W. H. "Immanuel Kant." In *The Encyclopedia of Philosophy: Volume 4*. Edited by Paul Edwards, 305–324. New York, NY: Macmillan Publishing, 1967.

Weber, Max. *From Max Weber: Essays in Sociology.* Edited and translated by H. H. Gerth and C. Wright Mills. New York, NY: Oxford University Press, 1946.

————. *Economy and Society: An Outline of Interpretive Sociology.* Edited by Guenther Roth and Claus Wittich. Berkeley, CA: University of California Press, 1978.

————. *The Protestant Ethic and the Spirit of Capitalism.* Translated by Talcott Parsons. London, UK: Routledge, 1992.

Welchman, Alistar. "'Wild above rule or art': Creation and Critique." Ph.D. dissertation, Warwick University, 1995.

Whitrow, G. J. *Time in History: Views of Time from Prehistory to the Present Day.* New York, NY: Barnes & Noble Books, 1988.

Zimmer, Heimrich. *Myths and Symbols in Indian Art and Civilization.* New York, NY: Pantheon Books, 1963.

Zerubavel, Eviatar. *Hidden Rhythms: Schedules and Calendars in Social Life.* Los Angeles: University of California Press, 1981

————. "The Standardization of Time: A Sociohistorical Perspective." *American Journal of Sociology*, Vol. 88, No. 1 (July 1982): 1–23.

Žižek, Slavoj. *Tarrying with the Negative: Kant, Hegel and the Critique of Ideology.* Durham, NC: Duke University Press, 1993.

8 — Index of Names

9 — Index of Subjects

Index

Copernican Revolution, xxii, 4, 9, 11–42, 78–79, 88, 93, 113

critical thought, 8, 12, 16, 28, 30–31, 36, 87, 92, 102

cryptocurrency, xix, xxi

cybernetic, v, 46, 50, 96, 117–118

cyberspace, x, xii–xiii, xvii, xx, xxii, 6, 54, 110, 115–116, 120–121, 124, 127, 133

D

day, ix–x, xiii, xxii, 2–4, 9, 11, 16, 18, 28–29, 32, 48–55, 57, 60–63, 65, 69, 71–74, 81, 83, 86, 104, 109, 111–112, 114, 123–124, 127, 132

daylight saving time, viii

deconstruction, 1

dialectic, 45, 79
   dialectical, 7, 45, 47, 85
   dialectically, 40, 47, 78, 89

discontinuity, xxii, 47, 51, 82, 130
   discontinuities, xxii, 47, 79, 81–82, 86, 118, 127

distributed network, x, xii, 116, 121

E

Ego, vi, ix, 29–31, 33–34, 98

empirical, vii, ix, xi, xx, 5, 7, 10, 12, 21–22, 25, 29–34, 42–44, 46–47, 55–56, 75–76, 79, 84–86, 96, 98, 105, 111, 113, 115–117, 128
   empiricism, 47, 107

epistemology, vii, 11, 14, 16, 41, 87, 93, 95
   epistemological, viii, xxii 7–8, 11, 41, 43, 56, 86–87, 92, 96, 101, 106, 129–130
   epistemologist, 12

essence, vi, viii, 3, 11, 16–18, 20, 40, 92, 95, 97, 99, 105, 107

eternal, vii, xi, 2–5, 7–9, 17, 20, 36, 40–41, 47, 75, 77, 86, 88, 96–98, 101–105, 107, 109, 119–120, 123, 130, 132, 134

eternal september, xi

eternity, vii, x, xxii, 1–5, 7–9, 18, 20, 23, 31, 86–88, 96–99, 101–102, 105, 107, 109, 111, 113, 130–132
   "image of," 1, 20, 86

everlasting, 3, 85, 88, 97, 100–101

expression, 5–6, 10, 34, 44, 51, 72, 78, 112, 119, 122, 128, 133–134

extensive, xx, xxii, 9–10, 88, 97–104, 118–119, 125–126, 131
   aggregates, 99–100, 125
   magnitude, 98–100
   temporality, 10, 99, 119, 126
   time, 98, 100–104, 118, 131

exterior, vi–vii, 1, 4–5, 8–9, 17, 25–26, 34, 79, 82, 84, 92, 97–98, 105–107, 112, 128–130, 133
   exteriority, xi, 1–2, 7–8, 10, 17, 24–29, 34–35, 42, 82, 85, 88, 107, 113, 128–131, 134

F

forms, vi, ix–x, 16–17, 19, 37, 76–77, 82, 86, 92, 105–106, 118

French Revolution, 48, 93

G

Genesis, Book of, 3–4, 51

Global Positioning System (GPS), xv

God, xxi, 3–4, 8, 20, 26, 41–42, 48, 61–62, 66–67, 80, 89–90, 92–93, 96, 98, 109, 123

Google, xv

Gothic, 88, 107–108

Greenwich, viii, xiii, 43, 45, 58–60, 74, 115
   Greenwich Mean Time (GMT), viii, 43, 45

Gregorian, —
   calendar, x, xvii, 48–51, 115, 120–125
   reforms, 48
   system, 48

H

H4, 58–59

Hegelian, 79, 85
   Hegelianism, 7

Hertz (cycles per second), 128

hierarchy, xiv, xxiii, 40, 89
   hierarchical, viii, xiv, 83, 93, 102

Hindu, 122, 124
   Hinduism, 1, 3

human, —
   intellect, 11, 15, 27, 43, 94
   reason, 15

CPSIA information can be obtained
at www.ICGtesting.com
Printed in the USA
LVHW021613030323
740867LV00010B/416